Hidden New Brunswick & Prince Edward Island

Scott Osmond

100+ abandoned mills, dams, mines, wreck sites, and other off-the-beaten-path destinations

BOULDER
BOOKS

Library and Archives Canada Cataloguing in Publication

Title: Hidden New Brunswick & Prince Edward Island : 100+ abandoned mills, dams, mines, wreck sites and other off-the-beaten-path destinations / Scott Osmond.

Other titles: Hidden New Brunswick & Prince Edward Island
Names: Osmond, Scott, author
Description: Includes bibliographical references and index.
Identifiers: Canadiana 20240535537 | ISBN 9781989417683 (softcover)
Subjects: LCSH: New Brunswick—Description and travel. | LCSH: Prince Edward Island—Description and travel. | LCSH: New Brunswick—Guidebooks. | LCSH: Prince Edward Island—Guidebooks. | LCSH: Curiosities and wonders—New Brunswick. | LCSH: Curiosities and wonders—Prince Edward Island. | LCGFT: Guidebooks.

Classification: LCC FC2467.6 .O86 2025 | DDC 917.15/105—dc23

Published by Boulder Books
Portugal Cove-St. Philip's, Newfoundland and Labrador
www.boulderbooks.ca

Design and layout: Tanya Montini
Editor: Stephanie Porter
Copy editor: Iona Bulgin

Printed in China

We acknowledge the financial support of the Government of Newfoundland and Labrador through the Department of Tourism, Culture, Arts and Recreation.

Funded by the Government of Canada | Financé par le gouvernement du Canada | Canada

Hidden New Brunswick & Prince Edward Island

100+ abandoned mills, dams, mines, wreck sites, and other off-the-beaten-path destinations

To all the grandparent figures who have been part of my life – whether related through family, bond, or love – it was your unwavering support, encouragement and love that made this possible. In particular, I want to acknowledge the love and relentless support of my nan, Blanche, who sadly was not able to see this book published but whose kindness, wisdom, and unwavering faith in me inspired its completion.

Table of Contents

CN
CN

NORTHWEST NEW BRUNSWICK & THE UPPER ST. JOHN RIVER

1. SAINT-JACQUES SLUICE
2. MARVELS OF THE NATIONAL INTERCONTINENTAL RAILWAY
3. FRASER LUMBER MILL
4. RAPIDE DE FEMME BROOK FISH HATCHERY
5. STICKNEY LUMBER MILL
6. CASTLE BRIDGES OF NEW BRUNSWICK
7. FALL BROOK FALLS
8. NAPADOGAN'S VENEER MILL & CN ROUNDHOUSE
9. CHIMNEY ROCK
10. BALANCING ROCK
11. SPRUCE BUDWORM SPRAY AIRCRAFT AVENGER CRASH SITE

NORTHEAST NEW BRUNSWICK

1. ARCH ROCK
2. MORRISSEY ROCK TUNNEL
3. BUDWORM CITY
4. TETAGOUCHE FALLS HYDROELECTRIC DAM
5. BATHURST POWER AND PAPER MILL
6. POKESHAW PARK & THE COASTAL LANDFORMS OF THE ACADIAN PENINSULA
7. CONVENT OF CARAQUET

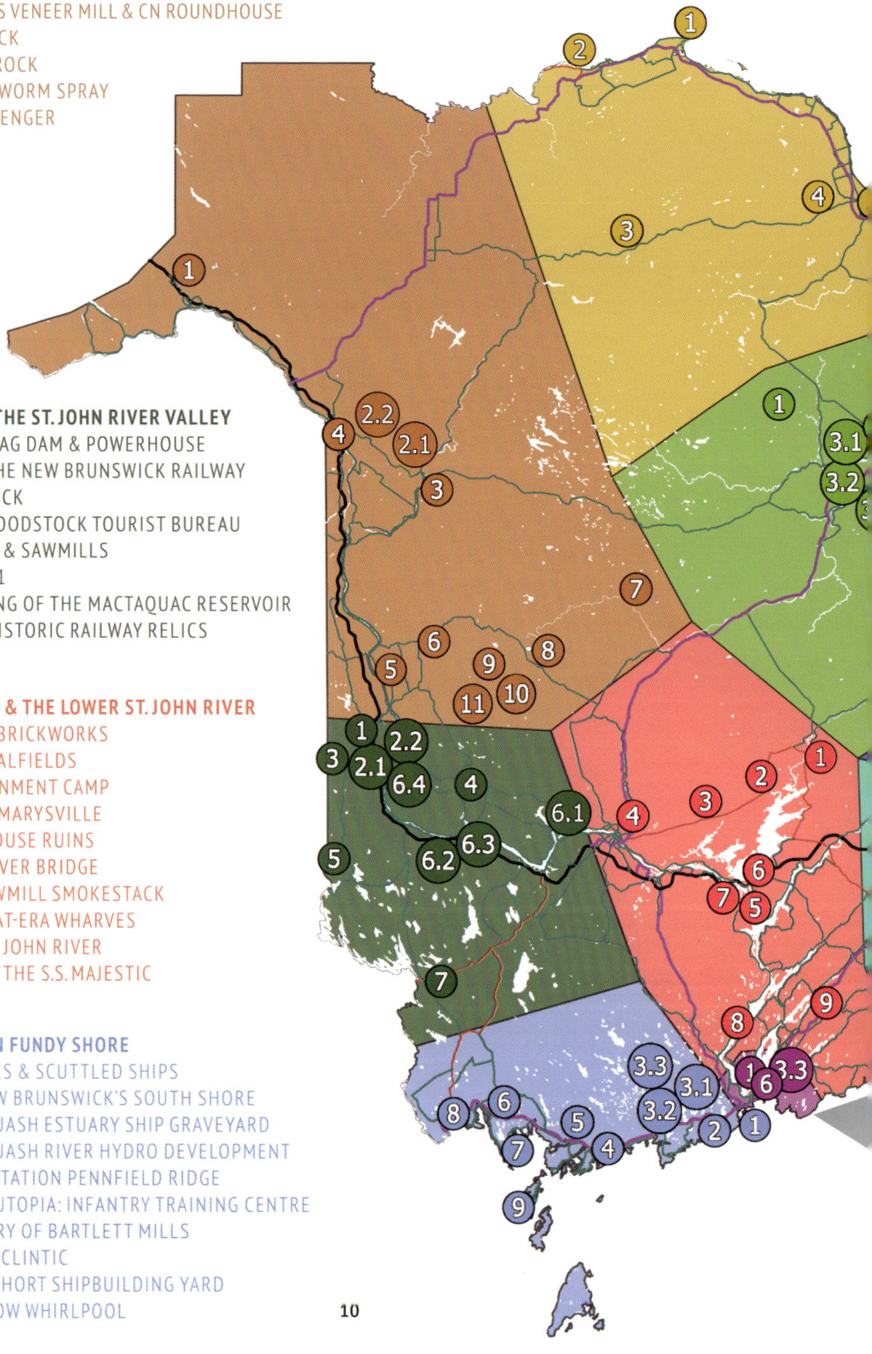

WOODSTOCK & THE ST. JOHN RIVER VALLEY

1. MEDUXNEKEAG DAM & POWERHOUSE
2. RELICS OF THE NEW BRUNSWICK RAILWAY IN WOODSTOCK
3. HOULTON-WOODSTOCK TOURIST BUREAU
4. PINDER DAM & SAWMILLS
5. MONUMENT 1
6. THE FLOODING OF THE MACTAQUAC RESERVOIR
7. MCADAM'S HISTORIC RAILWAY RELICS

FREDERICTON & THE LOWER ST. JOHN RIVER

1. CHIPMAN BRICKWORKS
2. MINTO COALFIELDS
3. B70 INTERNMENT CAMP
4. HISTORIC MARYSVILLE
5. MOUNT HOUSE RUINS
6. JEMSEG RIVER BRIDGE
7. REID'S SAWMILL SMOKESTACK
8. STEAMBOAT-ERA WHARVES OF THE ST. JOHN RIVER
9. WRECK OF THE S.S. MAJESTIC

SOUTHERN FUNDY SHORE

1. WRECKS & SCUTTLED SHIPS OF NEW BRUNSWICK'S SOUTH SHORE
2. MUSQUASH ESTUARY SHIP GRAVEYARD
3. MUSQUASH RIVER HYDRO DEVELOPMENT
4. RCAF STATION PENNFIELD RIDGE
5. CAMP UTOPIA: INFANTRY TRAINING CENTRE
6. HISTORY OF BARTLETT MILLS
7. T. B. MCCLINTIC
8. J. & C. SHORT SHIPBUILDING YARD
9. OLD SOW WHIRLPOOL

MIRAMICHI REGION

1. LITTLE SHEEPHOUSE FALLS
2. MORRISSY BRIDGE
3. REMNANTS OF MIRAMICHI'S HISTORIC FORESTRY INDUSTRY
4. MORRISON COVE PUMPHOUSE & FIREFIGHTER TRAINING CENTRE
5. WOODBURN CONSERVATORY
6. RCAF STATION CHATHAM
7. RCAF STATION ST. MARGARETS
8. KOUCHIBOUGUAC HYDROELECTRIC DAM

UPPER BAY OF FUNDY

1. MARITIME CEMENT'S HAVELOCK PLANT
2. JORDAN MEMORIAL SANITORIUM
3. HILLSBOROUGH GYPSUM MINES & THE KARST LANDSCAPE OF ALBERT COUNTY
4. NEW BRUNSWICK RAILWAY MUSEUM
5. ALBERTITE MINES OF ALBERT COUNTY
6. MARITIME EDUCTION COMPANY
7. THE FORGOTTEN HISTORY OF MARTIN HEAD
8. ANIMALAND & THE FORGOTTEN SCULPTURES OF WINSTON BRONUM

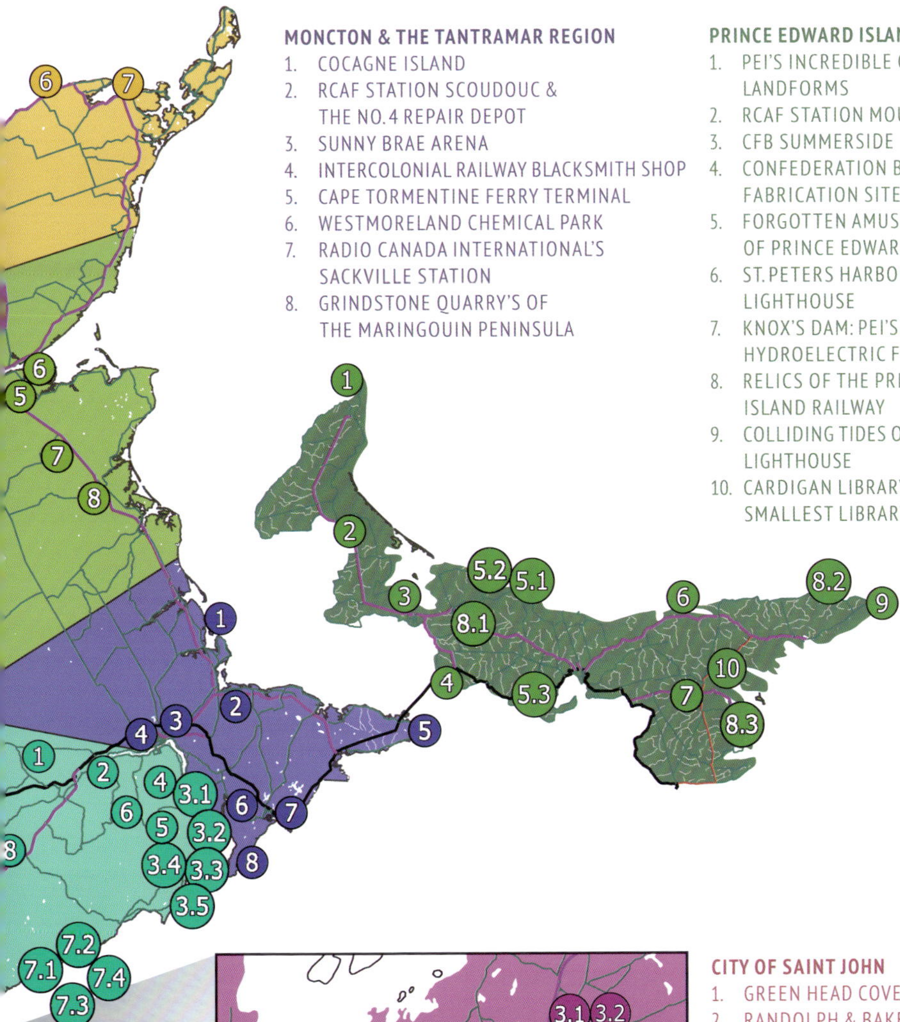

MONCTON & THE TANTRAMAR REGION

1. COCAGNE ISLAND
2. RCAF STATION SCOUDOUC & THE NO. 4 REPAIR DEPOT
3. SUNNY BRAE ARENA
4. INTERCOLONIAL RAILWAY BLACKSMITH SHOP
5. CAPE TORMENTINE FERRY TERMINAL
6. WESTMORELAND CHEMICAL PARK
7. RADIO CANADA INTERNATIONAL'S SACKVILLE STATION
8. GRINDSTONE QUARRY'S OF THE MARINGOUIN PENINSULA

PRINCE EDWARD ISLAND

1. PEI'S INCREDIBLE COASTAL LANDFORMS
2. RCAF STATION MOUNT PLEASANT
3. CFB SUMMERSIDE
4. CONFEDERATION BRIDGE FABRICATION SITE
5. FORGOTTEN AMUSEMENT PARKS OF PRINCE EDWARD ISLAND
6. ST. PETERS HARBOUR LIGHTHOUSE
7. KNOX'S DAM: PEI'S LAST HYDROELECTRIC FACILITY
8. RELICS OF THE PRINCE EDWARD ISLAND RAILWAY
9. COLLIDING TIDES OF EAST POINT LIGHTHOUSE
10. CARDIGAN LIBRARY: CANADA'S SMALLEST LIBRARY

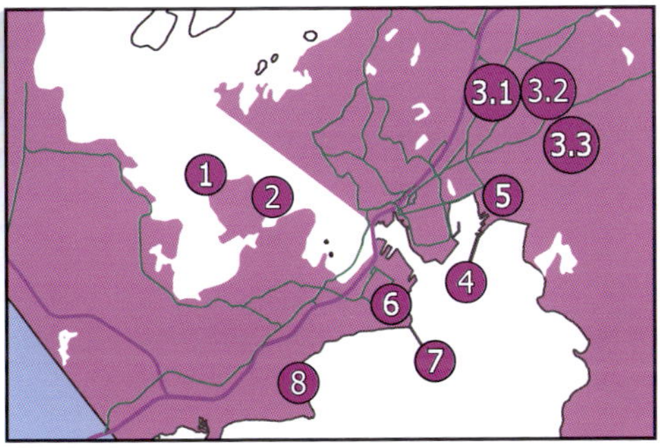

CITY OF SAINT JOHN

1. GREEN HEAD COVE LIME QUARRY
2. RANDOLPH & BAKER MILL
3. THE PECULIAR RELICS AT THE CORNER OF LOCH LOMOND ROAD & MCDONALD STREET
4. COURTNEY BAY BREAKWATER BATTERY
5. SAINT JOHN SHIPBUILDING DRYDOCK
6. FORT DUFFERIN
7. PARTRIDGE ISLAND
8. SAINT JOHN CUSTOMS HOUSE RUINS

Introduction

About This Guide

New Brunswick and Prince Edward Island boast impressive scenery and captivating history. Residents of these two provinces share a profound sense of identity and connection to the land. Farming, fishing, and logging have shaped both provinces—and left hidden histories, geological wonders, and curious structures that tell the story of their development.

NEW BRUNSWICK

New Brunswick's social, political, and cultural heritage has long depended on the province's industries and natural resources: vast forests, fertile farmlands, and dynamic coastlines. Before colonization, the province was home to the Wolastoqiyik, Mi'kmaq, and Peskotomuhkati peoples, who lived in harmony with the land. Beginning in the 16th and 17th centuries, European settlers transformed New Brunswick into a key hub for trade and industry.

Each year, New Brunswick attracts tourists eager to experience its history and natural beauty. From the picturesque Hopewell Rocks along the Bay of Fundy to the bustling streets and industrial history of Saint John, from Mount Carleton—the Maritimes' highest mountain—to the gorgeous Saint John River Valley and the historic fishing and shipbuilding settlements of Passamaquoddy Bay, New Brunswick is home to countless destinations worth exploring.

While New Brunswick's more popular attractions are showcased in tourism brochures and guides, the province's vast backcountry holds hidden and lesser-known natural wonders: waterfalls, coastal landforms, and one-of-a-kind landscapes shaped by geological processes, powerful tides, majestic rivers, and glaciers. In terms of built heritage, evidence of New Brunswick's storied past is found in such relics as lumber and pulp mills, hydroelectric dams, historic railways, mines, and coastal fortifications—remnants of its turbulent history of warfare.

For those who enjoy the outdoors, exploring new landscapes, and experiencing a rich diversity of people, culture, and tradition, New Brunswick does not disappoint.

PRINCE EDWARD ISLAND

Prince Edward Island, though Canada's smallest and least populated province, boasts an incredible history and natural beauty that have long made it a popular tourist and vacation destination. The Mi'kmaq were the first people to inhabit the island; following colonization, European settlers established fishing villages, farms, and logging communities throughout the region. While the island is known for beaches and flat, fertile landscapes, the province's extensive history, dynamic coastlines, and winding roads reveal much more than what is in any promised tourist brochure.

Prince Edward Island's geographic separation from the rest of the Maritime provinces has helped foster its unique culture and identity. It is easy to dismiss the province as having few "hidden gems." But the province's vibrant tourism industry overlooks some of its most fascinating geological and historical destinations. Prince Edward Island's intimate scale and rich heritage make it a treasure trove for anyone willing to look beyond the usual tourist stops.

This guide is for explorers—novice and experienced, local and tourist, off-the-beaten-path hikers and armchair voyagers—who wish to discover more about New Brunswick and Prince Edward Island and experience places that have been lost and forgotten or are yet to be found.

This guide has three main goals:

Introduce new places to visit and explore.

The selection of destinations has not been influenced by ease of access, politics, or economic value. Just because a place does not meet the economic or political viability of many tourist sites does not mean it is not

worth sharing. In many cases, these lesser-known places outshine more popular destinations.

Promote New Brunswick's and Prince Edward Island's incredible built and natural heritage.
Each location represents a piece of New Brunswick's and Prince Edward Island's history and development. My goal is to raise awareness of cultural, historic, and geological preservation while, at the same time, sharing forgotten stories.

Show that exploring is for everyone.
Whether you wish to explore the wonders of New Brunswick and Prince Edward Island by car or are seeking a new hiking destination, this guide is for you. And if you're an armchair explorer, I hope this book brings these places to life and inspires wonder, wherever you are.

USING THIS GUIDE

Assumption of Risk

Many of the places in this guide are abandoned and/or unmarked, and therefore risky to visit. This guide provides general information about

each location, its history, and its approximate whereabouts. Proper caution must be taken at all times.

This guide does not encourage illegal, illicit, or dangerous activities. Those who visit the described locations do so at their own risk, and proper safety precautions must be followed.

To ensure a safe adventure:

- Research and understand potential risks before you go.
- Use caution around cliffs, steep hillsides, and the ocean.
- Never enter an unmaintained or abandoned building/structure. Falling debris, risk of collapse, and other hidden dangers are extremely likely.
- Always obtain permission before entering any structure or property.
- Take out what you take in and leave an area as it was when you arrived.

This guide highlights some of New Brunswick's and Prince Edward Island's obscure attractions and provides general information about the location and condition of each site at the time of writing. However, it is important to note that conditions at these sites can change quickly, and access to certain locations may be restricted or altered without notice. Visitors should be aware that the directions and information provided in this guide may not reflect current field conditions at the time of their

visit. It is the sole responsibility of the explorer to assess whether it is safe and legal to visit any of the listed places and to ensure that all applicable laws, regulations, and safety guidelines are followed.

Land Acknowledgement

We acknowledge that the lands we are exploring and from which we are learning are the traditional, current, and unceded territories of the Mi'kmaq, Wolastoqiyik, and Peskotomuhkati peoples. This territory, which has been inhabited for over 12,000 years, is covered by the "Treaties of Peace and Friendship" which these nations first signed with the British Crown in 1726.

These first peoples have long practiced respectful and sustainable approaches to ensuring that the land and environment remain healthy for future generations and we are grateful for the opportunity to learn from them. In honouring this relationship, we are reminded that it is our shared responsibility to continue this protection and respect for the lands that we occupy.

Storytelling has long been a means of sharing knowledge and wisdom across generations. As we embark on this book, we ask you to reflect on what the land means to you and how we can use stories to build a respectful relationship to those places we visit and the nations who live there.

The Origins of New Brunswick's Lost Wonders

The hidden wonders of New Brunswick fall into several categories. Each site represents a piece of a larger story. Below are the general themes.

FORESTRY AND LOGGING

In Atlantic Canada, New Brunswick has long been synonymous with forestry and logging. The original inhabitants of the land, the Wolastoqiyik, Mi'kmaq, and Peskotomuhkati peoples, held a connection to the province's forest and ecosystem and practiced sustainable management. Following the mass immigration of European settlers, the financial worth of the forest became apparent and soon it was being exploited and developed, with little thought for long-term sustainability.

The forest had been used to construct houses, buildings, and settlements before the 1780s, but following the American Revolutionary War, and with land grants being awarded to Loyalists, logging increased. Small sawmills popped up, each becoming the centre of its community. A shipbuilding industry began to thrive at about the same time; the area's reserves of large white pine were utilized to make large masts and spars.

Larger mills were established by the mid-1800s, driven by new investments, particularly by Great Britan and the United States. The 1854 Reciprocity Treaty between British North America and the United States established new economic alliances. By the end of the century, products from New Brunswick sawmills were being shipped across the country and around the world.

Because there were few roads in the province, logging began close to communities. Logging camps were later built throughout the province; foresters worked year-round to cut logs and transport them to local mills. The province's rivers transported large quantities of logs longer distances (page 84). These log drives, which floated cut timber downstream to mills and collection points, were dangerous for workers and involved the construction of networks of dams, sluices, and log flumes. Railways of

the late 19th century opened up new stretches of forest and a new means of transporting logs to mills and products to markets (page 98).

By the 20th century, entire towns had been built around sawmills and, with this industry booming, many New Brunswickers relied on it for jobs. But as the sawmill industry and forestry lands became monopolized and controlled by fewer sawmill and logging owners (referred to as lumber barons), the industry's volatility increased. In the early 1900s, pulp and paper mills were being established across the country. During World War I, many sawmills experienced financial troubles and market restraints. But after the war, the pulp and paper industry revived (page 66).

One factor that limited the growth of pulp and paper mills was access to electricity; to overcome this, the province provided incentives to establish hydroelectric facilities.

But New Brunswick's forests were vulnerable. For centuries, forest fires wreacked havoc on local forests, often caused by the logging operations themselves. As well, New Brunswick's forests were periodically impacted by outbreaks of spruce budworm. This native insect, which feeds primarily on spruce and fir trees, can destroy large tracts of forest. To control this, huge areas were sprayed yearly (page 116). Even so, between 1970 and 1980, millions of hectares were destroyed by the insect.

Despite this, logging continued at record rates. The 1970s brought new challenges: high inflation, limited timber reserves, and changing markets. In 1974, the Forest Resource Study recommended sustainable management techniques and, in 1982, some of these practices were legislated in the Crown Lands and Forests Act.

Reliance on forestry for lumber, pulp, and paper changed greatly by the year 2000. A decreasing reliance on paper products, increased competition among larger mills, and changing market values led to a sharp decline in the province's forestry industry. Between 2000 and 2008, nearly 15,000 job losses occurred as large mills, once the hub of their home communities, closed. This decline was best exemplified by the rapid closure of multiple mills along the Miramichi River (page 131)

TRANSPORTATION

New Brunswick's transportation networks include railways, roads, rivers, lakes, and coastal waters.

By Water: Coastal and River Navigation

New Brunswick has always relied on transportation by water, whether via the ocean—the province borders on the Gulf of St. Lawrence, Northumberland Strait, and the Bay of Fundy—or its many navigable rivers (the Saint John, Saint Croix, Miramichi, and Restigouche Rivers).

The fishery has long been one of the province's largest industries. From its Indigenous populations to Acadian settlement, thousands have relied on the fishery for food and a means to survive the long winters. Through the early to mid-19th century, an export-oriented fishery flourished. In its early days, the fishery relied heavily on cod, but, over time, herring, lobster, and shellfish became more popular. In the 1970s, salmon aquaculture was introduced. While the 21st-century fishery is only a fraction of what it once was, many coastal communities rely heavily on local fisheries, and the province's interior rivers are popular among recreational fishers.

In the late 18th century, a shipbuilding industry emerged, supported by the province's abundant timber reserves. Large centres such as Saint John, Moncton, Miramichi, and St. Martins owe part of their development to this industry; hundreds of ships ranging from small dories and fishing vessels to oil tankers and modern naval vessels, such as those constructed at the Saint John Shipbuilding yard, were built (page 301). The widespread wooden shipbuilding industry declined during the late 19th century, as larger, steel steamships became a priority. Many of these shipyards have disappeared without a trace, but in some communities the remains of both shipyards and ships are still evident.

The establishment of sawmills, farms, and mines necessitated larger ports and shipping facilities. These were typically focused on larger coastal communities such as Saint John, Miramichi, and Bathurst, but, before long, hundreds of industrial-sized wharves served the province The export of lumber, agricultural products, oil, and minerals continues from select ports such as Saint John, which remains one of the busiest in Canada.

New Brunswick's rivers have played a major role in its development. Specifically, the Wolastoq ("beautiful river") or Saint John River has long been a sacred and valuable waterway. Stretching from Saint John to Fredericton and north to Woodstock, Grand Falls, and Edmundston, the river shaped human settlement in the province. As European settlers and American Loyalists established farms and mills on the upper reaches of the river, reliance on it for transporting people, goods, and services also increased. Beginning in the mid-1800s, a fleet of steamships serviced the communities along the river, long before the existence of a well-defined road network (page 225). The river's industrial and commercial shipping infrastructure has been replaced by recreation boats and summer retreats.

Dotted along the province's rivers and coastline are shipwrecks, the result of both disaster and abandonment. Unforgiving weather and rocky seascapes have long been navigation obstacles, but, additionally, as ships outlived their usefulness, it was common practice to scuttle or abandon them where they would not obstruct marine traffic (page 240). Each of these vessels tells a story about the people who worked on them and the industries they supported.

By Land: Roads, Highways, and Bridges

Throughout the early 18th century, roads helped connect the province's isolated communities, eventually replacing water as the main mode of transport. Bridges of varying types and materials were built—bridges (covered to prolong the life of timber frames), truss, and stone bridges were all popular. To cross the largest rivers, enormous suspension bridges—such as the one across Reversing Falls in 1853 and the Grand Falls gorge in 1961—were built.

In 1924, Premier Peter J. Veniot called for the construction of a new

and upgraded provincial road network to promote new industry and export opportunities across the province. In 1950, the Trans-Canada Highway connected Moncton with Fredericton before following the Saint John River to Edmundston. Around the same time, upgrades to the major highway connecting the United States border crossing at St. Stephen to Saint John and Moncton were made. Both roads dramatically changed the efficiency of travelling in the province.

Over time, these major highways have shifted and realigned to improve their efficiency and, as a result, large, abandoned sections of highway and bridges are evident throughout the province (page 220). The history of this road and bridge network is a fascinating tale of engineering challenges and connecting people and communities.

By Rail: New Brunswick's Historic Railways

Work began in the 1850s on New Brunswick's first major railway line. The European and North American Railway was to connect the border crossing at St. Stephen with Saint John, Moncton, and eventually Quebec. The first train travelled from Shediac to Moncton on August 20, 1857.

Among the first promises of New Brunswick's confederation with Canada was the establishment of a national railway. The result was the Intercolonial Railway (ICR), completed in 1875, connecting Nova Scotia, New Brunswick, and Quebec. By the early 1900s, several independent railways and railway companies operated in the province, with railways heavily influencing the location of mills, mines, and manufacturing plants.

In an effort to strengthen Canada's railway system, in 1918 the federal government nationalized the railway network under the name Canadian National Railway (CN). Rail use declined throughout the rest of the 20th century, largely due to the increasing popularity of road travel. Although most of the province's railway network has closed, freight rail remains an important means of transporting bulk cargo such as lumber, petroleum products, and minerals.

Since their abandonment, many railway lines have been converted into recreation trails, now comprising a large portion of the provincial snowmobile and ATV trail system. Along these public access trails lie railway remains. These may be as unassuming as railway spikes or sections of rails, but in other cases, it includes some of the province's most impressive pieces of built heritage and engineering feats, including tunnels, large bridges, and railyards.

HYDROELECTRICITY

For centuries, the power of flowing water was harnessed by communities and small milling operations across the area that is now the province of New Brunswick. These early applications did not produce electricity but directly powered machinery and equipment.

The first sawmills and gristmills typically consisted of a mill built beside a wooden crib dam. Water was redirected near the mill, where a large wooden wheel rotated with the flowing water. Inside the mill, a system of gears connected directly to the waterwheel transferred the rotation to power saws and grinders. Although highly susceptible to damage from spring floods and ice blockages, this industry was one of

DANGER
DANGER

the first and most widely adopted forms of energy production.

By the mid-19th century, electricity was produced through mechanical motion. By the early 20th century, an early form of a generator, known as a dynamo, was being used by small dams to produce limited electricity, primarily for lighting (page178).

In 1881, the first hydroelectric power was produced at Niagara Falls, New York, to illuminate the falls and provide small quantities of power to the town. The following year, Canada's first hydroelectric power was generated at the 500-horsepower Milltown Generating Station on the St. Croix River. Established by the St. Croix Paper Company, the station provided electricity to homes and businesses in St. Stephen, New Brunswick, and Calais, Maine, and is considered to be the first significant hydroelectric development in North America.

By the early 20th century, more industries relied on electricity than on other means of powering machinery. In 1904, a dam and small hydro plant were built on the Meduxnekeag River to power the Woodstock Iron Works (page168). Similarly, in Bathurst, a dam and power plant were built near Tetagouche Falls to power a large sawmill. For much of New Brunswick, the first electricity to reach communities came from surplus generation at these early facilities. Throughout the first two decades of the 1900s, more hydroelectric plants were constructed, eventually focusing on providing energy primarily for communities rather than solely for industry (page161).

The growing reliance on electricity by communities and industries led to the establishment of the New Brunswick Electric Power Commission. Its purpose was to centralize provincial power generation, harness undeveloped hydro potential, and combat rising electricity costs from private suppliers. The commission aimed to provide affordable power to customers. Its first project, the development of the Musquash River system, marked the beginning of large-scale hydro projects. Private developments, such as the Nepisiguit River Hydroelectric Facility by the Bathurst Power and Paper Mill in 1921 and the Grand Falls Generating Station in 1931, were also critical.

Early hydropower was unreliable and frequently disrupted by flooding and ice jams. Spring floods often breached dams, sometimes causing disastrous downstream impacts. Many early dams, constructed of wooden cribbing, were the first to be destroyed, such as the Meduxnekeag River Dam and Powerhouse in 1923. Early concrete dams were also vulnerable to floods and ice. Some were rebuilt; others, permanently abandoned.

During the 1950s, the demand for electricity surged as more households adopted it for heating and lighting, while industries depended on it almost entirely. This surge resulted in the closure of many smaller power plants and ushered in an era of mega hydroelectric developments. In 1953 and 1955, the Tobique and Beechwood generating stations began operating. In 1968, the Mactaquac Generating Station, capable of generating 672 megawatts of electricity, began operation. The construction of these facilities had environmental and social impacts. For instance, the Mactaquac Dam flooded 84 square kilometres of the Saint John River Valley, submerging roads, railways, houses, bridges, and entire towns. Remnants of the flooded landscape are still visible along the reservoir.

The remains of early dams and hydroelectric plants are still evident throughout the province. While most early wooden crib dams have deteriorated beyond recognition, many concrete structures remain, forming a collection of abandoned and historic sites.

MILITARY

For centuries, wars influenced settlement patterns and population in New Brunswick. The most notable example, the Acadian Expulsion, occurred after the British gained control of Acadia following decades of conflict between Britain and France. Twenty years later, the American Revolutionary War brought new tensions to British-controlled lands, with fears of invasion and further conflict. The end of the war brought many British Loyalists to New Brunswick, fleeing the now-independent United States. Loyalist land grants

helped to establish new settlements and industries in the province's interior—a military tactic to secure the province as part of British North America. St. Stephen, Saint John, Miramichi, and Edmundston became increasingly fortified throughout the 18th century.

The War of 1812 and the Aroostook War of 1838 raised concerns about potential invasion by the United States. These fears were heightened during attempts to establish an official border between the two nations (page182). Border disputes influenced infrastructure decisions, such as rerouting the ICR along the east coast to avoid proximity to American territory. In 1867, New Brunswick joined Confederation with Canada, after which relations with the United States stabilized. However, concerns of potential invasion arose again following the American Civil War.

By the time World War I broke out, Saint John had become an important industrial city and shipping port. Concerned about attacks from German naval vessels, the harbour was fortified with coastal defence batteries. The importance of Saint John's harbour grew after the war, particularly with the establishment of the Saint John shipyard and dry dock, capable of maintaining, refurbishing, and constructing

large steel ships. When World War II began, the harbour was fortified further and coastal defence batteries and anti-aircraft guns were scattered throughout the area to defend against attacks.

Across the province, military bases, airfields, and training centres were established during World War II. Air bases in Chatham, Moncton, and Pennfield Ridge (page 254) became part of the British Commonwealth Air Training Plan, training pilots and air crews for combat and bombing missions.

During the Cold War, bases such as the one at Chatham remained operational, capable of training personnel and responding to potential attacks by the Soviet Union. Radar stations, like the one built at St. Margarets (page 156), were designed to detect threats. In the latter half of the 20th century, advances in technology and shifts in global politics reduced the need for much of the province's military infrastructure; many of these sites were decommissioned during the 1960s and 1970s. However, military operations continue at CFB Gagetown and the Gagetown Range and Training Area. This large plot of land was expropriated in the 1950s, forcing more than 900 families from 19 communities to relocate.

Relics of the province's military past are found in all corners of New Brunswick. As most preserved sites are pre-20th century, many fortifications built during the 20th century have been lost or forgotten. Nonetheless, along the province's east coast, from Chatham to Saint John, remains from this period tell the story of New Brunswickers' fear and uncertainty when the threat of attack or invasion was actual.

MINING

Historically, New Brunswick's mining industry has been overshadowed by its forestry industry, but for more than 250 years, large-scale mining has helped communities thrive. Indigenous populations first used its rocks and minerals to craft tools and shelters. Following colonization, the first mine to operate in New Brunswick was a small coal mine on Grand Lake, with ore being shipped to settlements in the northeastern United States.

As populations and settlements grew throughout the 1700s, new mines were established; one of the more prominent industries was sandstone quarries. Grindstones—large, circular, hand-cut rocks used in mills to grind wood or wheat—were in high demand. In the upper Bay of Fundy, sandstone exposed at low tide became the epicentre of this early industry, establishing communities along the Maringouin Peninsula (PAGE XX GRINDSTONE). Mining expanded dramatically throughout the 19th century. To meet the demand for new buildings in Fredericton and Saint John, limestone was mined and quarried for building stones and processed into lime. In Hillsborough, exposed outcrops of gypsum quickly attracted developers, eventually establishing the area as one of the most industrious in the province (page 331).

Small mines, first established along the Fundy Coast and later inland, exploited small quantities of base metals such as copper, zinc, and manganese (page 360). Historically, mining focused on extracting minerals for tools and building materials. However, by the mid- to late 1800s, the growing popularity of coal and new discoveries of bitumen and oil shales shifted the focus of New Brunswick's mining to fuels (page 206; page 348)).

The mining industry grew as studies revealed additional minerals and improvements in technology allowed for viable mining operations. Base metal mining in the Bathurst-Miramichi region successfully operated for most of the latter half of the 20th century.

Local and global markets, accessibility to the inland of the province, and the establishment of international shipping facilities have long dictated the state and viability of mining in New Brunswick. Mining holds less importance than it once did. What began as one of the province's earliest industries has left a changed landscape. The remains of many former mining ventures and operations still preserve their historical significance to countless communities.

NATURAL WONDERS

The oldest rocks in New Brunswick began forming 1 billion years ago. Contained within them were stromatolite fossils, which, following their discovery in 1890, became one of the oldest pieces of evidence of life on Earth. Over the following 500 to 600 million years, shifting plate tectonics, volcanic activity, and sedimentation moulded much of the current topography. However, it was between 400 and 250 million years ago that most of the rocks making up the province's geologic foundation were produced. Around 370 million years ago, much of the province's rocks were part of Panagea, located in a tropical or

arid climate near the equator. By 340 million years ago, a large inland sea, the Windsor Sea, had formed. As the climate changed, the sea began to dry up, and the evaporation of water left behind dissolved minerals that now constitute the province's important gypsum and limestone reserves. Modern-day erosion of these weak carbonate rocks has created karst landforms and some of the province's most intriguing landscapes.

During the Carboniferous period (359 to 299 million years ago), much of the province was covered in lush swamps, rivers, and wetlands containing vast plant life. When this plant life died, it was preserved as coal, a critical mining resource for the region around modern Grand Lake. Rivers and flood events during this period encouraged the accumulation of sediment, creating much of the province's sedimentary rocks along its east coast and central portions.

At this time, the Appalachian Mountains had reached their peak. Around 200 million years ago, tectonic forces began to pull apart the supercontinent Panagea in a process known as rifting, leading to the early formation of what would become the Atlantic Ocean. This process caused fractures and volcanic intrusions, producing basaltic rocks now found throughout the province, most prominently along the Fundy coastline. As the new ocean opened, the mountains and landscapes weathered and eroded, turning the once-mighty Appalachian peaks into lowlands. Beginning 65 million years ago, another sequence of uplift and tectonic forces, followed by a period of erosion, shaped the foundation of the current landscape.

Beginning 100,000 years ago, the latest period of glaciation affected the province; a 1- to 2-kilometre-thick glacier covered the land, dramatically altering its topography. These moving ice sheets scoured the landscape, voiding it of life and transporting vast quantities of material hundreds of kilometres before depositing it. When the Ice Age ended approximately 10,000 to 12,000 years ago, the melting glaciers reduced the weight exerted on the Earth's crust, causing it to rebound and drastically alter sea levels.

Weather, rivers, and coastal processes continue to erode and shape the landscape. Rivers slowly transform mountains and hills into lowlands, while coastal processes—including wind, ocean currents, waves, and tides—gradually reshape coastlines. Coastal erosion from waves, storms, and surges changes the coastline each year, particularly along the Acadian Peninsula, which has some of the highest erosion rates in the province. Meanwhile, the Bay of Fundy's shape causes tidal heights to change by 6 to 16 metres every 6 hours and 13 minutes. These tides pose dangers to explorers but also create fascinating coastal landforms.

The Origins of Prince Edward Island's Lost Wonders

Like New Brunswick, the hidden wonders of Prince Edward Island fall into several categories, each with its own history and significance in the province's development.

NATURAL WONDERS

Prince Edward Island's natural beauty and scenic landscapes attract thousands each year. Geologic and coastal processes that provided fertile soils for farming and protected harbours for fishing also created some of the island's most incredible hidden wonders. The island's formation began 360 million years ago when ancient rivers deposited sediment eroded from the Appalachian Mountains. Accumulating sediment formed beds of sandstone, siltstone, and mudstone, all of which had a higher-than-normal iron content. Over millions of years, these layers of rocks shifted and twisted, thanks to plate tectonics, eventually orienting them in their current configuration. Once exposed to the air, the rock's iron content oxidizes, creating the red cliffs and beaches for which the island has become known.

Between 75,000 and 10,000 years ago, the Maritime provinces were covered in a 3-kilometre-thick ice sheet. At the end of this period, the island would have been unrecognizable. Lower sea levels around the world meant that the island was connected by land to New Brunswick and Nova Scotia, eventually separating as sea levels rose 5,000 to 6,000 years ago. But as these glaciers moved across the island, they eroded the topography. Deposited soil and till helped create the ideal sandy and clay soils that drive the province's primary industry, agriculture.

One more natural process helped form many of the province's natural wonders: coastal erosion. The red sandstone, siltstone, and mudstone layers that form the bedrock of the island are highly susceptible to erosion. As these rocks are left exposed along the coastline, waves and storm surges relatively quickly break down cliff faces, resulting in such coastal landforms as sea caves, arches, and stacks, as well as the many

sandy beaches that make the island a popular summer destination—even as worsening storms and sea level rise continue to affect the island and its ever-changing coastline.

TOURISM

Every year, around 2 million people visit Prince Edward Island to take advantage of its culture, landscape, and hospitality. The island slowly gained popularity throughout the 1860s and 1870s, fuelled in part by the Charlottetown Conference in 1864, which brought representatives from across Canada to discuss forming a unified federation. But island visitors were limited by a reliance on coastal boats and finite roads throughout the island. This changed in 1875, when the newly opened Prince Edward Island Railway offered an efficient means of travelling

the island. Over the next 50 years, the island became a popular summer getaway (for those who could afford it), with hotels and resorts being constructed throughout it.

In 1917, the MV *Prince Edward Island*, the first reliable year-round ferry service for passengers and railcars, was introduced. In 1931, passenger air travel through the Charlottetown airport opened the island to even more tourists. Six years later, the Prince Edward Island National Park was established. The 20th century's improvements to the province's road network allowed visitors to explore more of the province.

By the 1950s, tourism had expanded again, thanks to the popularity of *Anne of Green Gables*. Released by author Lucy Maud Montgomery in 1908, the novel Anne of Green Gables quickly became a best seller. A new wave of tourists visited the island to see the author's home and the setting that had inspired her first novel. Movie adaptations followed throughout the 1940s, 1950s, and 1960s. Montgomery's Cavendish house remains one of the most visited destinations on the island. This attraction soon inspired others, most notably small amusement parks. The remains of many of these parks still embody the countless stories and joy that they once brought.

In 1997, with the completion of the Confederation Bridge, a new era of tourism began. The island offers countless amusement, cultural, and historical attractions, but the history of the tourism industry is best represented by the many relics that were left behind.

MILITARY

Since the Acadians controlled the island prior to the Expulsion of the Acadians in 1758, Prince Edward Island's history has been heavily influenced by military activity. Following the removal of the Acadian people, new fortifications were built to defend against attacks by American ships during the American Revolutionary War. These defences, and those constructed throughout the 19th century, largely focused on protecting Charlottetown harbour, which had been established as a major hub and industrial centre. One of the only defence batteries preserved from this turbulent time is located in Victoria Park, Prince Edward Battery.

During World War II, multiple locations across the island were transformed into air force training centres by the Royal Canadian Air Force (RCAF) and Royal Air Force (RAF). Between 1940 and 1941, an area northwest of Summerside was selected by the RCAF to host the British Commonwealth Air Training Plan (BCATP), a massive World War II training operation. Before being incorporated into the BCATP, the RAF established its own training ground at the Charlottetown airport. Both centres, along with two relief and reserve airfields, trained flight crews in aerial reconnaissance and intelligence gathering, flight operations and patrols, and even gunnery and bombing operations. While most of the island focused on training, as more ships were sunk by German

U-boats in the Gulf of St. Lawrence, Prince Edward Island's airfields became home to regular patrol and submarine detection operations.

Following World War II, the island's airfields were placed in reserve. The Summerside base was reopened in 1948 and re-established as a training facility, this time under NATO, to train flight crews from around the world in coastal patrol, anti-submarine warfare, and long-range maritime reconnaissance missions. The base hired thousands of workers and became a critical part of the local economy and culture.

TRANSPORTATION

Transportation projects have long been ingrained in the history of development and the people of Prince Edward Island. Because of ice conditions in the Northumberland Strait, early travel to and from the island was confined to the summer months. This was later resolved by the use of iceboats, which transported cargo and mail by traversing the ice-covered strait, but this was limited and often dangerous. Before the

20th century, island travel was limited due to an underdeveloped road network, leading many to rely on boats to travel between communities. Constructed throughout the 1870s, the railway accessed the island's interior and provided industries with a new means of importing and exporting goods—but it came at a hefty cost, becoming a major contributing factor in the government's reversal of its decision to stay out of Confederation and ultimately forcing Prince Edward Island to join Canada in 1873.

The next major project to shape the island was the construction of Confederation Bridge. Since the construction of the Prince Edward Island Railway, a fixed link via bridge, tunnel, or combination of both had been dreamed of, and even designed, at points through history. But it was not until a plebiscite in 1988 that islanders voted for the project to move forward; construction began in 1993. Opened on May 31, 1997, the 12.9-kilometre-long bridge was the longest in Canda and the longest in the world over an ice-covered body of water. The bridge grew Prince Edward Island's industrial, commercial, and tourism sectors and became the primary means of travelling to the island.

OCEAN

Exploring New Brunswick and Prince Edward Island Safely

Exploring comes with risk but, with common sense, proper preparation, and research, these can be minimized.

CLIMATE

New Brunswick is situated farther inland than the other Maritime provinces, giving it a predominantly continental climate with greater temperature variations between summer and winter. The summer months are often warm and humid, particularly in the south and along the Saint John River Valley, making those months ideal for hiking, kayaking, and exploring the province's forests and waterways. Winters are snowy, especially in the northern regions, creating opportunities for snowshoeing, skiing, and snowmobiling, but also increasing the risks associated with cold-weather exposure.

The coast of New Brunswick typically experiences a maritime climate, which is especially true along the Bay of Fundy. Precipitation, fog, and winds can create dangerous conditions for outdoor activities. The interior and northern highlands of New Brunswick often experience strong winds, rainstorms, and sudden temperature shifts, which can pose hazards for those travelling in the region.

Prince Edward Island's coastal regions experience a similar climate to that of parts of New Brunswick along the Gulf of St. Lawrence. These areas are heavily influenced by maritime weather, resulting in fog and frequent and unpredictable weather changes. The island's exposure to the Gulf of St. Lawrence makes it susceptible to strong winds and cool, moist air. This can be dangerous for outdoor activities, especially when spending time on the water. Inland areas, while generally more sheltered, are not immune to sudden shifts in weather, with cooler temperatures and brisk winds often catching visitors off guard, even during the warmer months.

It is essential to be prepared. Checking weather forecasts regularly, dressing in layers, and carrying waterproof gear and navigation tools are crucial for ensuring a safe and enjoyable adventure. This is especially important in remote areas.

ABANDONED BUILDINGS AND DETERIORATED STRUCTURES

Do not enter neglected, deteriorated, or abandoned buildings and structures. In addition to the dangers of falling debris, collapsing structures, and mould or other airborne bacteria or chemicals, many destinations outlined in this book remain under private or government ownership, and exploring them is considered trespassing. Almost all the sites described in this book can and should be experienced from a safe distance. With some preparation and foresight, they can still be exciting and safe places to visit.

Always be respectful of private property. Look for indications of regular use and abide by all posted signs. Check with local landowners and consult online resources to determine site access. Land ownership and land use can change quickly.

ENVIRONMENTAL CONDITIONS

Heights and Loose Rocks

Many hiking trails and lookouts lead to the vicinity of cliffs or other steep slopes. Always wear proper footwear, maintain a safe distance from the edge, and use particular caution when conditions are wet or icy. Avoid going too close to rock cuts and cliffs. Watch for fractured rocks and areas that look prone to collapse.

Ocean Hazards and Tides

Be always mindful of waves, tides, and weather conditions. Slippery rocks and rapidly changing sea conditions pose extreme hazards. Caution should be exercised when exploring the shores and estuaries of the Bay of Fundy, where the world's highest tides can reach up to 15 metres. The powerful tidal currents, particularly around the Fundy Isles and the rivers at the head of the bay, can make access to the shore dangerous, and the tide can come in quickly, trapping visitors. Best practice when hiking along the sea floor during low tide is to plan ahead—keep track of high- and low-tide times—and always have a reliable way off an intertidal zone, such as a clear route to higher ground.

In Prince Edward Island, be mindful of strong rip currents and ocean swell, especially along the North Shore. The island's shifting sands and beaches can hide dangerous drop-offs and create dangerous currents. Approach unfamiliar areas with caution.

Dalhousie
1
2
Campbellton
3
4
5
Bathurst
6
7
Caraquet
Tracadie-Sheila

Northeast New Brunswick

Few places in Atlantic Canada offer the same diversity in scenery, cultures, and languages as the northeast corner of New Brunswick. The Acadian Peninsula stretches 100 kilometres into the Gulf of St. Lawrence and is home to many Acadian families; their culture and language is preserved in each of the peninsula's communities. The low-lying peninsula provides several safe harbours which are surrounded by peat bogs and forests. As a result, the fishing and logging industries were among the first to provide livelihoods to early settlers. Along the north side of the peninsula, coastal terraces and beaches extend along Chaleur Bay to the mighty Restigouche River. At its mouth are Dalhousie and Campbellton, which were among the first locations in the area to be settled by Europeans attracted by sheltered harbours and nearby rivers. The Mi'kmaq people, who first lived here, had long used these rivers to access inland hunting, which became home to the region's first sawmills and gristmills.

By the mid- to late 19th century, ongoing conflicts between the French and English subsided, stabilizing the area. New sawmill and lumber mill operations were established. The construction of the ICR through the area opened up new business and immigration opportunities. The small sawmill and lumber mills scattered across the region were soon overshadowed by large pulp and paper mills, such as those in Bathurst, Dalhousie, and Campbellton. Power generation and mining were introduced; Belledune became a major industrial

centre after a lead and zinc smelter and, later, a coal-fired generating station were constructed there. Despite the environmental impact of these industries, tourism flourished, and the area became a popular destination for anglers, recreational boaters, and hikers. Farther inland, the Appalachian Mountains reach their highest point in the Maritime provinces, with Mount Carleton as both the tallest peak and one of the region's best hiking destinations.

From the south, Highway 11 travels through the Acadian Peninsula to Bathurst before loosely following the coast to Campbellton in the north. At the top of the Acadian Peninsula, many small towns are found among its many harbours and islands, such as Tracadie-Sheila,

Shippagan, and Caraquet. Bypassing the peninsula is Highway 8, which runs between Miramichi and Bathurst. From Bathurst, gravel roads extend into the backcountry, providing access to the upper sections of the Nepisiguit River and the province's remote interior. Travelling east to Saint-Quentin, Highway 180 provides access to Mount Carleton Provincial Park, located at the heart of the province. In the north, Campbellton is the gateway to Quebec and the Gaspé Peninsula, while Highway 17 travels south to meet Highway 180 at Saint-Quentin. The region is filled with the relics of hidden histories, as well as natural wonders yet to be discovered in the province's vast backcountry.

1. Arch Rock

Dalhousie

Unusually shaped rock formations are not uncommon along the coast of New Brunswick, but a small cove near Dalhousie is particularly worth visiting. Resembling an animal—perhaps an elephant or a buffalo—Arch Rock, also known as Bon Ami Rock, is one of the area's best-kept secrets. The coastal landform is technically a sea stack, formed after hundreds of years of erosion separated it from the surrounding rock face. Over time, waves have carved a large arch at its centre, giving it the appearance of having legs.

Arch Rock is composed of extrusive igneous rock formed in ancient volcanoes approximately 400 million years ago. This has given the rock a dark grey appearance, which contrasts with the small shrubs and grass growing atop it. The rock formation is adjacent to Inch Arran Park and Campground, a popular camping, beach, and picnic area.

ARCH ROCK: N 48.057157, W 66.353255

Park at Inch Arran Park (N 48.058752, W 66.352412), walk 150 metres south along the beach to a small rock outcrop. From there a difficult descent over the outcrop is required before tracing the cliff edge to Arch Rock, approximately 50 metres away.

2. Morrissey Rock Tunnel

Tidal Head

Situated 10 kilometres west of Campbellton is Atlantic Canada's last active railway tunnel. The historic landmark, known as Morrissey Rock Tunnel, is located on the CN line between the towns of Tide Head and Flatlands. The tunnel was originally built for the Intercolonial Railway (ICR) between 1871 and 1874. The ICR was one of the first major projects undertaken by the new nation of Canada, intended as a symbol of unity and progress, connecting the Maritime provinces with Quebec and Ontario.

Several routes were surveyed throughout the mid-19th century for the railway line, but ultimately, a route passing through the east coast of the province and along the south shore of Chaleur Bay was selected. The route was recommended by Major William Robinson, who believed that a route passing closer to the United States border could be threatened if another war broke out between the two nations. The route that would become known as the Chaleur Bay Route also allowed for easier construction, with one exception: the route along the south shore of the Restigouche River between Campbellton and Matapédia, Quebec. The rolling hills and steep riverbanks left little room for a track, further complicated by a steep cliff known as Morrissey Rock. With no way to avoid the cliff and possible rockslides if the entire hill were excavated, the decision was made to tunnel through it. Excavated using dynamite and pickaxes, by 1874 a 50-metre-long, 22-metre-wide, and 20-metre-tall tunnel was cut through the cliff face. On July 1, 1876, the first train passed through the tunnel as the ICR officially opened. In 1918, the ICR came under the ownership of CN, which continues to operate the railway in 2025.

Although it is still regarded as an engineering marvel, the tunnel has a history of tragedy. During construction, at least one worker

was killed when the dynamite used to excavate the passage exploded unexpectedly. And on May 11, 1890, a rockslide in the tunnel caused a major derailment that killed a railway worker and severely injured another. Rockslides and derailments plagued ICR's operation, leading some to claim that the tunnel is cursed.

When Restigouche Drive was constructed atop the tunnel, a viewpoint and picnic area were built alongside the road, offering spectacular views of the surrounding mountains and the Restigouche River. Near the edge of the cliff, interpretive signs tell the story and significance of the Morrissey Rock Tunnel, which lies 30 metres below the lookout. The tunnel is one of the few tunnels on the Trans-Canada rail line east of Montreal and the only operating railway tunnel in the Maritime provinces.

MORRISSEY ROCK TUNNEL: N 47.990584, W 66.828185
The Morrissey Tunnel look-off is located 4 kilometres west of the town of Tide Head along Route 11 (Restigouche Drive).

3. Budworm City

Restigouche County

Many species of insects can negatively impact the health of a forest, but few are as damaging as the spruce budworm, a moth whose larvae consume the buds and needles of spruce and fir trees. This native insect has always been present in the forests of New Brunswick, with population outbreaks occurring every 20 to 40 years. This cycle allows forests to rejuvenate and promotes new tree and vegetation growth, but it comes at the cost of the damage or destruction of large areas of trees. For centuries, the forestry industry endured these periodic outbreaks; however, in the 20th century, a more concentrated effort was made to preserve the natural forest.

To mitigate outbreaks of spruce budworm, Forest Protection Ltd., a partnership between the provincial government and local industry, implemented the first large-scale pesticide spraying operation in 1952. For nearly 20 years, the primary insecticide used was dichlorodiphenyltrichloroethane (DDT), which was phased out in Canada and the United States in the 1970s after its negative impact on human health was discovered.

It was a familiar sight for people living in New Brunswick during the 1950s to see small, dual-wing Stearman aircraft flying low over the province's forests. Behind each aircraft was a cloud of mist, coating the forest in a spray of DDT.

The Spruce Budworm Spray Project began in 1952 and continued until 1958. During this time, research camps and dedicated airfields were constructed throughout the wooded backcountry of the province. In a remote area near Mount Carleton, a plot of land was chosen for one of 14 airfields and became known as Budworm City. Construction began on November 24, 1951, with the building of a 760-metre-long runway. Soon after, a second paved runway was constructed, accompanied by a large tarmac area to store and load aircraft with

pesticide. Adjacent to the airfield, a camp capable of accommodating up to 200 people was built to house the many pilots, mechanics, and scientists who called Budworm City home during its years of operation.

The Budworm City airfield housed a fleet of Stearman biplanes. These modified former navy training aircraft and agricultural spraying aircraft had been adapted to carry and spray pesticides. The most notable modification was the removal of the front cockpit to make

room for a 550-litre pesticide storage tank and a larger main engine to accommodate the added weight. Along the lower wing of the small biplanes was a spray system that turned the liquid pesticide into a fine mist, capable of thoroughly covering the forest. Employing many pilots trained during World War II, the spray operation was a dangerous task, requiring pilots to fly as low as 15 metres above the trees at speeds of more than 150 kilometres per hour.

In the few years it operated, Budworm City became a community of scientists, pilots, and others all united in the fight against the spruce budworm. The area was briefly reactivated for spray operations again in the 1990s, but to a much smaller extent. Since then, the area has been largely abandoned and forgotten.

The airfield and the former site of Budworm City are clearly visible near Mount Carleton Provincial Park. Although they are partly overgrown, the former runways can still be delineated as they cut through the forest, and small patches of concrete observed where the Stearman aircraft were stored. The site is occasionally used for temporary storage of herbicides and has also become a popular campsite for hunters.

BUDWORM CITY: N 47.530093, W 66.625047

Drive approximately 75 kilometres west of Bathurst on Route 180, turn onto a gravel logging road named Dalhousie Road (N 47.514695, W 66.596809), drive 2.9 kilometres, and turn left onto the airfield.

4. Tetagouche Falls Hydroelectric Dam

South Tetagouche, Gloucester County

Approximately 10 kilometres west of Bathurst, the Tetagouche River flows through a steep-sided, forested valley before narrowing between two rocky ridges and plunging over a 10-metre drop. In the early 20th century, the falls were problematic for the river's log drives. Logs being floated from the interior to the mills of Bathurst frequently bottlenecked in this area, creating a dam. But it was the power of the river that carried the logs and the narrow gorge where those log jams occurred that caught the eye of local businessman, Bouctouche native John P. Léger.

Léger moved to Bathurst in 1898, where he opened several businesses, including the Gloucester Hotel and Bathurst Opera House. Léger, frustrated with the few street lamps in Bathurst, investigated how he could bring electricity to the area. In 1904, he incorporated the Bathurst Electric and Water Power Company and quickly constructed a wooden dam and sawmill downstream of Tetagouche Falls. The small operation provided power to the adjacent sawmill and delivered the first electric lighting to Bathurst. By 1910, the electricity was supplying power to many of Léger's businesses, and soon the Bathurst Electric and Water Power Company was looking for ways to increase its output.

Tetagouche Falls proved to be an ideal location for a hydroelectric facility. The narrow gorge minimized the size of the dam needed and, below the falls, flat riverbanks provided space for a powerhouse. Work began on the dam and powerhouse in 1911 and the facility officially opened in December 1912.

A 40-metre-wide dam constructed at the top of the falls created a sustainable reservoir where water could be redirected into a 1.5-metre-long iron penstock leading into the powerhouse. The penstock had to be excavated through a large ridge to redirect the water around it and

into the powerhouse. After travelling approximately 20 metres through the hillside, the penstock re-emerged before dropping the remaining distance into the powerhouse and passing through the turbine.

At first, the operation supplied power only at night, but it was not long before the demand for electricity in Bathurst forced the facility to remain open 24 hours a day. The power generated from Tetagouche Falls helped Bathurst expand into an industrial centre. Soon the supply from the Tetagouche River was insufficient.

In 1919, Léger sold his shares in the Bathurst Electric and Water Power Company to the Bathurst Lumber Company. Three years later, the company shut down the operation, deeming it too small to meet the growing demand. After the closure, the power previously supplied by Tetagouche Falls was replaced by a much larger facility constructed at Grand Falls on the nearby Nepisiguit River.

Tetagouche Falls is a local attraction, with many unaware that a dam existed until they see the falls for themselves. Since its closure, a 10-metre-long breach has been made in the dam to allow the water to

flow freely through it and into the gorge below. The concrete dam is partially intact at the top of the falls, but the remains of the penstock are perhaps its most interesting feature. It can still be clearly seen running through the nearby hillside and re-emerging into the turbine house and draft tube, from where the water would have re-entered the river.

The area below the falls is a popular swimming location, though access to it is difficult. Nonetheless, the falls, dam, and penstock can all be viewed from the rim of the gorge, where a small picnic area offers easy access and parking. The site, with the water once again flowing freely over the falls, is a beautiful spot to visit.

TETAGOUCHE FALLS HYDROELECTRIC DAM:
N 47.617270, W 65.825000

From Route 11, take exit 310 toward South Tetagouche. Drive west on Route 180 for 9.8 kilometres and turn right into the Tetagouche Falls Picnic Area. Park and walk the short distance to the fenced-off area overlooking the falls.

5. Bathurst Power and Paper Mill

Bathurst

On the banks of the Nepisiguit River lies the site of the former Smurfit-Stone Container Mill, also referred to as the Consolidated-Bathurst Mill or the Bathurst Power and Paper Mill. The site covers an area of more than 500,000 square metres and contains almost two dozen partially intact structures. While it is considered an eyesore by some, to others it serves as a reminder of the innovation and prosperity that the mill brought to the small town of Bathurst.

HISTORY

By the early 20th century, Bathurst was well known for its shipbuilding industry, which took advantage of the protected harbour tides and nearby forestry resources. Sawmills lined the region's rivers, using the rivers' flow to power machinery to produce masts, spars, and lumber. In 1913, businessman Angus L. McLean established the Bathurst Lumber Company and purchased two large sawmills in Bathurst. Seeing the vast timber resources of interior New Brunswick and the hydropower potential of the Nepisiguit River, McLean announced a plan to build and operate what he hoped would be the largest pulp and paper mill in the country. The New Brunswick government granted McLean a 50-year timber licence for the area, enough to propel the plan forward, despite McLean's requests to be awarded the rights in perpetuity.

In June 1914, construction began on a sulfite pulp mill on the Nepisiguit River banks. The massive undertaking was unlike anything seen before in the region. At its peak, 350 people were employed to work on the mill, which, despite difficulties in securing equipment and machinery due to the outbreak of World War I, opened early the following year. The new Bathurst Pulp and Paper Mill began producing and exporting pulp, with the capacity to produce up to 100 tonnes per day. After the war ended, McLean explored the

possibility of producing paper at the mill. In 1919, the first paper was produced, though it was too thick to be used as newsprint; instead, it was perfect for protecting the mill's pulp shipments as they were transported to market.

Major changes came in 1921, when construction was completed on a hydroelectric dam at the rim of a narrow gorge and waterfall on the Nepisiguit River, approximately 35 kilometres upstream from the mill. Known as the Great Falls Generating Station, the plant consisted of two turbines capable of supplying approximately 3,600 kilowatts of electricity each. The capacity was upgraded in 1929 when a third unit was installed at the facility. This bountiful source of power opened new possibilities for the Bathurst Mill. While the dam was still under construction, McLean announced plans to build a large newsprint mill with a capacity of 50 tonnes of newsprint per day. On August 23, 1923, a local paper, the *Gloucester Northern Light*, was printed for the first time on paper made within the town itself, marking an industrial achievement for the mill and a hopeful future for Bathurst and its residents. It is believed that this was the first newsprint produced in the Maritime provinces.

Over the following decades, the town prospered as the mill produced and shipped pulp and newsprint to markets across North America. The mill's owners purchased land in the town and built more than 100 houses for its workers. Attracted by the booming population, businesses and industries were established, and Bathurst soon grew into more than just a small fishing and shipbuilding village. The mill continued to expand into the mid-20th century as new machines and storage facilities were installed, further increasing the mill's productivity.

By 1960, the mill's primary product was corrugated paperboard, making it the first mill to produce such material in Canada. Additionally, it could produce four types of pulp: groundwood, sulfite, sulfate, and semi-chemical pulp. In the following decade, the mill became the fifth largest of its kind in Canada.

In 1989, the Chicago-based Stone Container Corporation purchased the mill, renaming it the Smurfit-Stone Container Mill. The company expanded production throughout the 1990s; however, as the millennium approached, market demand for its products declined. By the early 2000s, the mill was struggling to make a profit, and in 2005, the company closed the mill, leaving 270 people jobless.

ABOUT THE AREA

In 2010, an Illinois-based company established Bathurst Redevelopment Inc. to decommission and dismantle the mill. While most of the mill's buildings, equipment, and machinery were removed and sold for scrap, the site was far from remediated, with many structures left standing. In 2016, the company was forced to pay $150,000 for failing to clean up the site. Following this, the site was purchased by a local resident who hoped to clean it up and construct condominiums along the riverfront. This concept never materialized, and the mill site has remained abandoned.

As of 2025, the former mill site consists primarily of concrete foundations, which make up most of the northern half of the property. Here, several curious-looking silos stand precariously—the most photographed structures on the site. In the south, several concrete

buildings and support structures protrude from the surrounding forest, and along the water, the remains of the mill's shipping facilities and wharves are visible

The future of this site is not known. With many people calling for the site to be remediated, these last surviving structures—representing the town's historic pulp and paper industry—could soon be gone. In the meantime, the site offers a glimpse into the massive pulp and paper industry that has not only shaped the town but the region itself.

BATHURST POWER AND PAPER MILL: N 47.612639, W 65.643526
The best views of the site are found along Main Street near the intersection with Route 134 in east Bathurst. Many structures can also be found by exploring the shores of the Nepisiguit River.

6. Pokeshaw Park and the Coastal Landforms of the Acadian Peninsula

Pokeshaw

Stretching between Bathurst and Caraquet on the north side of the Acadian Peninsula is one of New Brunswick's most spectacular coastlines. Along the shore, farms, forests, and properties abruptly end at steep coastal cliffs that drop 10 to 15 metres. For most of their length, the cliffs are comprised of 300-million-year-old sandstone, classified by geologists as part of the Clifton Formation. This sandstone's susceptibility to erosion results in dramatic coastal landforms such as sea caves, arches, and stacks. Despite the coastline's collection of natural wonders, much of the shore remains overlooked due to its challenging accessibility. Driving atop the coastal terrace, surrounded by farms and stands of trees, drivers only briefly glimpse the coastline.

Stonehaven, a historic grindstone quarry, now provides access to the water via a local wharf and marina. Another access site is one of the province's most overlooked provincial parks: Pokeshaw Park and Beach. Located in the community of Pokeshaw at the mouth of the Pokeshaw River, the park is nestled in a small cove where a sandy beach has formed at the base of the surrounding cliffs. But it is not the beach that captures attention; rather, it is the towering, vertical sea stacks just metres from the shore. The smaller of the two stacks is pinnacle-shaped and, at low tide, becomes completely exposed and easy to reach. The larger stack is flat-topped and typically located 30 to 60 metres from shore. While it is possible to walk to the sea stack at low tide, it does require wading through the water.

Both sea stacks were once connected to the neighbouring cliffs. Over time, coastal erosion chipped away at the cliff, first forming a narrow headland or peninsula and then creating caves in the side of

the peninsula. After hundreds of years of continuous erosion, the caves collapsed, leaving islands of rock that were once part of the cliffs. At the time of collapse, when the sea stacks separated from the cliffs, they would have hosted the vegetation and plant life found in the surrounding area. As recently as the 1960s, photographs show that the larger of the two sea stacks still supported enough nutrients for a small forest to grow on its top. Grass and small shrubs continue to grow atop the island, but the trees have died, likely due to the double-crested cormorant population that inhabits it. The result is an eerie forest of dead trees, many of which have rotted and collapsed. However, this unique habitat has made the area popular among local birdwatchers.

Since much of the coastline in this area remains inaccessible without a boat, Pokeshaw Park offers the best and most accessible views of what the shoreline has to offer. A small fee is collected during the tourist season upon entering the park to maintain its picnic area, washrooms, and parking lots.

POKESHAW PARK AND THE COASTAL LANDFORMS OF THE ACADIAN PENINSULA: N 47.787852, W 65.254662

Pokeshaw Park is 38 kilometres east of Bathurst, on Highway 11, or 7 kilometres west of the community of Grand-Anse.

7. Caraquet Convent

Caraquet, Gloucester County

The seaside community of Caraquet is known for its Acadian history and traditions. The community's culture has long revolved around the local church and its people. While many tangible pieces of this history can still be found in the community, hidden alongside the beautiful Saint-Pierre-aux-Liens Catholic church is an often-overlooked part of Caraquet's heritage. At first glance, the stone structure that was once the convent of Caraquet may appear like any other building. Upon closer inspection, it becomes evident that it is merely an empty stone shell, but one that serves as a reminder of the community's efforts to build, maintain, and ultimately preserve this former education centre.

HISTORY

In the mid-19th century, the population of Acadians in Gloucester County was steadily increasing. At the time, English was the dominant language in many schools. Recognizing this, bishops from local Catholic parishes turned to the Congrégation de Notre-Dame of Montreal for help. In response, the Sisters of Charity came to the region and established schools to train and educate girls, while upholding Catholic values in a French setting. The schools were built by local parishes in Bathurst, Newcastle, St. Louis-de-Kent, and Caraquet.

In Caraquet, construction began in 1870 on a large stone building alongside the Church of Saint-Pierre-aux-Liens, overseen by Rev. Joseph Pelletier. The school officially opened in 1874, with teachers from Quebec instructing local girls in language, reading, writing, and business skills. The first classes reportedly consisted of 24 students from nearby communities and two boarders who came to the area to further their education.

The Quebec-trained teachers were seen as sophisticated, having come from urban areas surrounding Montreal. This introduced challenges, as the French dialect spoken in Quebec was quite different from that spoken by the Acadians in the region. The school also faced outbreaks of smallpox as well as challenges in recruiting new students. The school and convent relied heavily on financial support from the community to stay open. Since the community was largely dependent on the fishing industry and local merchants for income, many residents found themselves stuck in cycles of debt. Despite this, the residents recognized the importance of the school, and many worked tirelessly to raise funds and support students in need. Nonetheless, the school's numbers continued to decline, prompting the convent to seek new students through boarding programs. This effort was successful, and the student population slowly grew.

By the early 20th century, the convent and school had outgrown their original space and needed to expand. In 1903, the convent hired local architect Nazaire Dugas to design a three-storey stone addition beside the original convent. This section was completed in 1905. The addition allowed the school's attendance to grow to more than 200 students by the mid-1920s.

During its time, the convent provided many new opportunities for girls and women living in the area. Prior to the school's establishment, many had to leave the region to find work, often in other parts of the country or in Maine. The school provided them with an education and the opportunity to gain employment within their community and culture. It also meant that many women stayed in the area to work and raise families.

Between 1950 and 1978, changing social, political, and economic landscapes decreased the demand for the school. After a new public school was built in Caraquet in 1978, the convent was closed. The building was repurposed into an open space for the community. A decade after the convent closed its doors, the former building became home to the newly established newspaper *L'Acadie Nouvelle*, which continues in 2025.

Disaster struck in the early 1990s when a fire inside the convent destroyed everything except the stone walls. Just as the community had

rallied to support the building during its initial struggles, they again came together to salvage what remained. Recognizing the building's cultural significance and impact on the community, efforts were made to clean up and stabilize the structure's stone shell.

ABOUT THE AREA

This restoration was successful. Many of the windows on the outer wall facing the nearby West Saint Peter Boulevard feature beautiful paintings, overlooking a wooden stage built at the base of the refurbished walls. Walking around to the rear of the building reveals that the hollowed shell shelters a small forest. Grass, shrubs, and trees are slowly reclaiming its interior.

The structure has been designated a local heritage site, recognized for its contributions to the community's educational, religious, and cultural history. Commonly used as an event space, the building serves as a community and cultural centre in historic Caraquet.

CARAQUET CONVENT: N 47.789977, W 64.965438

The convent of Caraquet is adjacent to the Church of Saint-Pierre-aux-Liens, located at 213 W St. Peter Blvd. in Caraquet.

HARTLAND
NEW
BRUNSWICK
COME AGAIN
YOU ARE NOW ENTERING THE LONGEST
COVERED BRIDGE IN THE WORLD
1282 FEET
Saint-Quentin
1
Edmundston
2.2
2.1
4
Plaster Rock
3
Perth-Andover
7
Juniper
6
5
8
11
9
Hartland
10

Northwest New Brunswick & the Upper Saint John River

Stretching from the community of Hartland to the province's northern boundary with Quebec, this region encompasses the upper Saint John River Valley and many of its major tributaries, including the Saint Francis and Tobique Rivers. Vast forests and rivers spread out through the hilly landscape, making the area one of the Maritime provinces' best places to explore by snowmobile and ATV. The land was first travelled by the Wolastoqiyik and Mi'kmaq peoples, who continue to have a significant presence in the area. Following the Revolutionary War with the United States, British Loyalists were granted land along the waterways in hopes of securing the former British colony from invasions. The United States border has thus played a critical role in the area; Edmundston and other towns have also played a major role in the defence of the colony. These conflicts eventually ended, and the region's rivers and forests quickly attracted many sawmills and lumber mills.

The Saint John River was the primary means of transportation through the region for centuries, until modern roads and railways were constructed. Sawmills exploited the forests, helping establish the Fraser Lumber Company and other major logging companies. While many smaller mills were conglomerated, some of the first mills are still operational. Improved access to the area also introduced tourism. Many visitors came to angle in the region's rivers; some of the province's first fish population restoration projects occurred here in the late 19th century.

In the 20th century, large hydroelectric dams were built throughout the region, the largest in the town of Grand Falls, where the Saint John River plunges into a spectacular narrow gorge. Farther south through the Saint John River Valley, agriculture flourished in fertile soils.

The main highway through this diverse region is the Trans-Canada Highway, which follows the Saint John River from Hartland

to Edmundston before crossing the border into Quebec. Grand Falls is a connection point for Highway 17, which heads north to the inland town of Saint-Quentin; Highway 385, which leads to Mount Carleton Provincial Park; and Highway 108, which crosses the province's remote interior to Miramichi. The best way to experience region is to travel its secondary highways, such as Highways 103, 105, and 109.

1. Saint-Jacques Sluice

Madawaska River, Saint-Jacques, Edmundston

The Madawaska River winds through 40 kilometres of forest, connecting Lake Témiscouata in Quebec to its confluence with the Saint John River in Edmundston, New Brunswick. For decades, the river was filled with cut logs making their way downstream to the Fraser Companies Ltd. Mill in Edmundston. This natural waterway provided easy access to rich forestry reserves in both provinces, attracting early European settlers, including Acadians fleeing expulsion, and British Loyalists who immigrated following the American Revolutionary War. These settlers established small logging operations and sawmills along the river's banks. In the mid-1800s, the emergence of larger mills drove the demand for timber and marking the beginning of the region's log drives as early as 1850.

At the time, roads were sparse and expensive to construct, making rivers such as the Madawaska an ideal and cost-effective means of transporting logs downstream to mills. Log drives became extensive operations, often employing systems of dams, channels, and sluices to guide the timber. Tugboats aided the process, and teams of workers used specialized tools to keep logs moving smoothly along the river.

In 1917, Fraser Companies Ltd. opened a pulp mill in Edmundston, located at the lower end of the Madawaska River. Although logs were also transported to the mill by horse, truck, and train, they were primarily floated downriver. At the mill, logs were collected at a haul-up station and transported to a woodlot using a conveyor system. The log drives became a massive undertaking, especially during periods of high river flow, when the river was often completely covered with logs, leaving no water visible.

Few remnants of this era remain, except for the foundations of boom piers, where logs accumulated before being pulled into the mill, and the prominent ruins of the historic Saint-Jacques Sluice. Located in the town of Saint-Jacques, the large concrete foundations that resemble giant steps are a relic of the river's logging history. For decades, these foundations

supported a log slide where trucks unloaded cut timber into the river, allowing the logs to float downstream to the mill. Many of these logs came from the Green River and other rivers downstream of the Madawaska.

In 1939, following Fraser's purchase of the Oram Davis sawmill's dam, haul-up, and forestry rights on the Green River, logs floated down the Green River were trucked to the Saint-Jacques Sluice and dumped into the Madawaska. From there, they were again floated to the mill.

Log driving on the Madawaska River continued into the latter half of the 20th century but had ceased entirely by 1970. After the practice ended, Fraser Companies began cleaning up the river in the early 1970s, using cranes and barges to remove logs that had washed ashore or sunk to the riverbed.

Little evidence of this historic industry remains, but the concrete foundations of the Saint-Jacques Sluice on the banks of the Madawaska River offer a glimpse into the region's rich logging heritage.

SAINT-JACQUES SLUICE: N 47.417716, W 68.368147

The concrete foundations are visible on the east side of the Madawaska River. Located on private property, the easiest way to glimpse the site is by paddling the river from Saint-Jacques Park (N 47.426618, W 68.376372) located 2 kilometres upstream, or from Camping Panoramic, a campground located adjacent to the site itself.

2. Marvels of the National Intercontinental Railway

Victoria County

The construction of New Brunswick's extensive railway network has given rise to some of the province's most remarkable engineering feats. These accomplishments often stemmed from the need to overcome challenges posed by the rugged landscape and the logistical hurdles of building railways during times of financial and political turbulence. A prime example is the National Transcontinental Railway (NTR), constructed between 1903 and 1913 to connect Winnipeg to Moncton.

In 1900, the ICR was the only publicly operated railway in eastern Canada. At the time, increased competition among railway companies in western Canada had led to the creation of more than one publicly owned railway. This prompted politicians to explore the feasibility of a second public railway in eastern Canada. In 1903, Liberal prime minister Sir Wilfrid Laurier introduced the Canadian Railway Act, legislation aimed at expanding and regulating new railway development across the country. Under this act, Laurier announced the construction of the NTR, initially planned to run between Winnipeg and Ontario.

However, when the route was extended as far as Quebec, New Brunswick politicians successfully lobbied to extend the railway to Moncton. Unlike the ICR, which followed the province's eastern coastline before entering Quebec through the mountainous Matapédia region, the NTR would take a more direct inland route. This new path passed through Edmundston, Grand Falls, Plaster Rock, Chipman, and ultimately Moncton.

The NTR began operations in 1912 and the final spike was driven on November 17, 1913. The 3,250-kilometre-long line stretched from Moncton to Winnipeg, where it connected to the Grand Trunk Pacific Railway, creating Canada's third transcontinental railway and extending west to Prince Rupert, British Columbia.

The NTR was more expensive than anticipated, with costs reaching

an estimated $160 million. These overruns are widely believed to have been a factor in Laurier's defeat in the 1911 election by Robert Borden's Conservative government. Although Borden's administration completed the railway, the project faced ongoing issues, including low traffic volumes and questions about its necessity.

In 1918, the NTR was transferred to the Canadian Northern Railway, and in 1923 it became part of the newly formed CN. Sections of the NTR remain operational, though with modifications to its original route. Along this historic stretch are two of New Brunswick's most impressive railway engineering marvels: the Blue Bell Tunnel and the Salmon River Trestle.

Blue Bell Tunnel

New Denmark

Construction of the NTR through Victoria County began in 1908. In March of that year, the contract for the 50-kilometre-long stretch of railway between Grand Falls and Plaster Rock was awarded to the Kitchen Construction Company, owned by Willard Kitchen. This section would prove to be one of the most challenging stretches of railway ever built in the province. In addition to the many hills and mountains it had to traverse, the project required the diversion of several rivers, the construction of at least three large steel bridges to span the area's valleys, and the excavation of a 300-metre-long tunnel through a narrow ridge between Jones Brook and Blue Bell Lake.

The company promptly hired workers, which at its peak totalled more than 1,500. They were paid $2 per day, a fair wage at the time, which boosted the local economy. After receiving the contract, the company explored routes around Blue Bell Lake to avoid constructing a tunnel. However, the tunnel ultimately proved to be the most feasible option. Surveying began in 1909, followed by the first blasting in 1910. The tunnel was excavated by steam shovels, drills, and dynamite. The blasted rock was used to fill a portion of nearby Blue Bell Lake, allowing the railway to cross it.

Although the well-paying jobs attracted workers, the construction was dangerous. During the tunnel's excavation, at least one worker was killed in an unexpected explosion. Progress was slow due to the hard rock that made up the ridge, which was difficult to excavate. The tunnel's excavation was completed along with the rest of the railway line in the summer of 1912. That fall, the first train passed through the section, marking its official opening. Once completed, the tunnel was over 300 metres long and 21 metres high, tall enough to accommodate even the largest locomotives.

The tunnel provided safe passage for trains through the ridge for the next 40 years. However, over time, the rock broke apart, and regular maintenance was required to keep the track clear and the tunnel safe. In December 1959, two CN workers were struck on the head by falling

debris during a minor collapse in the tunnel. Both survived, thanks to their hard hats, and were inducted into the company's "Turtle Club," a safety program promoting the importance of wearing protective gear. Although the workers survived, the incident raised concerns about the tunnel's safety and future.

In the following years, a new railway line was surveyed and constructed, bypassing the ridge to the north. When this line opened in 1963, the tunnel tracks were removed and the tunnel abandoned.

The Blue Bell Tunnel remains one of the most impressive engineering feats on this section of railway and is one of only two railway tunnels ever excavated in the province. It is a popular destination for local ATV and snowmobile users. Although both entrances to the tunnel have been partially filled with gravel to prevent vehicle access, much of the structure remains visible to visitors. Although entering the tunnel is ill-advised due to the risk of its collapse, it can still be appreciated and experienced from the safety of nearby trails.

BLUE BELL TUNNEL: N 46.959300, W 67.552115

Drive 5.8 kilometres past the community of New Denmark on Highway 108, and turn onto Deleavey Road (N 46.958431, W 67.541098). Continue to the end of the road. From there it is possible to continue in an ATV or other off-road vehicle; however, you may have to hike the remaining distance. From the end of the road (N 46.959849, W 67.544252), continue 800 metres along the main trail, turn left to arrive at the tunnel.

Salmon River Trestle

New Denmark

When the Kitchen Construction Company was awarded the contract for 50 kilometres of railway line between Grand Falls and Plaster Rock, it was not just the ridges and mountains that posed a challenge. Near the community of Davis Mill, the Salmon River Valley presented the opposite problem. Stretching more than 1 kilometre wide and over 60 metres deep, the valley was too large to bypass without adding more

than 10 kilometres of additional track. The decision was made to construct a bridge to span the valley.

In 1908, the Quebec-based Dominion Bridge Company was awarded the contract to construct the bridge. Construction commenced in 1910 with the pouring of 24 concrete foundations and the bridge abutments. The foundations supported 24 steel towers, with the tallest reaching the height of the bridge deck itself. A crane system carefully lowered the bridge's girders into place. Over 7,000 tonnes of steel were used in the construction. Completed in 1911, the $678,623 bridge spanned almost 1,200 metres and towered 60 metres over the valley below.

The bridge was a remarkable engineering feat. In addition to being the largest structure in New Brunswick, it was also the second-longest viaduct of its kind in Canada, surpassed only by the Lethbridge Viaduct in Alberta.

The enormous structure remains in use and continues to be an eye-catching sight for travellers. At its base, the small community of Davis Mill exists in its shadow.

SALMON RIVER TRESTLE: N 47.029862, W 67.605637

The Salmon River Trestle is 15 kilometres east of Grand Falls in the town of New Denmark.

3. Fraser Lumber Mill

Plaster Rock

The small town of Plaster Rock is located on the Tobique River, east of Grand Falls. Most of the town is situated on the west side of the river, where a grid of early to mid-century houses, schools, businesses, and churches are clustered. Across the river is the town's largest employer, the Plaster Rock Lumber Corporation softwood lumber mill. This mill is the last remaining logging operation at the site. Scattered remnants of former operations are still visible, most notably several large pieces of equipment and a tall brick chimney.

HISTORY

The Tobique River and its surrounding forests fuelled the town's growth. Beginning in the late 19th century, the river was used for log drives. Among the earliest loggers in the area was Donald Fraser Sr., a Scottish immigrant who came from a long line of woodsmen and sawmill operators. In 1896, a small lumber mill operated on the riverbank near the location of the modern mill. This small yet state-of-the-art sawmill was owned and managed by Fred and Archie Hale.

Fraser recognized the sawmill's potential and the region's extensive forestry reserves while working with the Tobique Log Driving Company. Seeking to capitalize on the industry, in 1900 he incorporated the Tobique Manufacturing Company in partnership with his two sons, Archibald and Donald. The following year, the company purchased the sawmill. By 1906, they had expanded the operation to include a dimensional lumber mill and increased storage capacity in the lumberyards. These expansions were successful, and in 1908, the Tobique Manufacturing Company changed its name to Fraser Lumber Company, and the Plaster Rock mill was renamed the Fraser Lumber Company Mill.

This new mill was a wooden structure that stretched along the river. In 1909, the CNR built a railway line to the town with a spur leading to

the mill. Rail travel became the primary means of transporting the mill's lumber to markets. Towering above the mill were several smokestacks used to dry lumber, while boards, bark, and waste were burned to produce energy to run some of the mill's equipment. At the time, most logs delivered to the mill were floated down the Tobique River, where they were collected in a series of booms built upriver. Remnants of these booms can still be seen. From the booms, logs were hauled ashore and placed in a lumberyard adjacent to the mill.

The mill's success impacted the town. As operations grew, so too did Plaster Rock. People from across the region migrated to the town, drawn by employment opportunities in the mill and the nearby forests. In less than 20 years, the once-empty land above the river became home to schools, churches, and all the amenities needed to support the population. In 1928, Plaster Rock was electrified when the Fraser family installed a diesel generator, providing the town with powered streetlights—an early milestone for the area. The Fraser family ran the power plant until 1940, when it was sold to the New Brunswick Power Commission.

In 1917, Donald Jr. took over the mill from his father, while Archibald moved to Edmundston to establish a pulp and paper mill. Building on the profits and reputation of the Plaster Rock mill, the Fraser name became well known across New Brunswick and Maine for its extensive logging operations and sawmills. The Fraser Lumber Company was now part of Fraser Companies Limited, a much larger operation.

Like other logging companies in the province, the Frasers faced challenges. Throughout the 20th century, forest fires periodically disrupted logging, and spruce budworm outbreaks threatened the forests on which the mill relied. Nonetheless, the family successfully ran the operation into the 1990s. In 1994 and 1998, the mill underwent major upgrades, which kept it competitive with neighbouring mills.

However, during the 2000s, the company faced financial difficulties due to a declining demand for paper, which had become its primary source of profits. By 2010, the parent company of the Fraser mills, including the one in Plaster Rock, was Fraser Papers Inc. In April of that year, the company underwent major restructuring after filing for bankruptcy protection. The company's pulp mill in Edmundston, paper mill in Madawaska, and the Plaster Rock lumber mill were consolidated under a new entity, Twin Rivers Paper Company Inc.

Throughout the second half of the 20th century, many original buildings at the Plaster Rock mill site were torn down. As of 2025, a lumber mill continues to operate on the hill above the former mill site, where the Fraser family first made a name for themselves.

ABOUT THE AREA

The most visible of the many relics from the former milling operations is one of the mill's brick chimneys, which stands above the river in a grassy field at the site of the original milling operation. Although it is now on private property, the chimney is visible from anywhere in the town.

Nearby and more accessible is one of the mill's steam engines, which is said to have once powered the mill's planer mill. Other relics are scattered throughout the area and in the town itself, where the influence of the Fraser family is still evident. Nowhere is this influence more exemplified than in the Donald Fraser Memorial School, which continues to honour the legacy of Donald Fraser and his contributions to the town's early development.

STEAM ENGINE AND CHIMNEY VIEWPOINT:

N 46.905730, W 67.392695

To get to the former mill site, follow Highway 108 to the east side of the Tobique River. Take the off-ramp onto Tobique Street and drive north for 850 metres to the site on the left. As the area is still an active logging operation, take precautions when travelling in the area and follow all posted signs and warnings.

4. Rapide de Femme Brook Fish Hatchery

Grand Falls

Among the many tributaries flowing into the Saint John River are several waterfalls that cascade over the valley's hills. One of the most impressive of these is a series of tall cascades on Rapide de Femme Brook, located just south of Grand Falls. Visitors to the area will notice the presence of several vertical concrete walls at the crest of the falls, forming a series of dams and large foundations. These damlike structures might easily be mistaken for remnants of a long-forgotten hydroelectric facility. However, 100 metres closer to the road—and much easier to access—are four linearly aligned, circular concrete pools adjacent to a larger rectangular pool. Best seen from a nearby ATV and snowmobile trail, these peculiar structures are the remnants of one of the province's oldest fish hatcheries.

By the time New Brunswick joined Confederation, its river fish stocks were rapidly declining. Overfishing and the damaging impacts of log drives on many of the province's ecologically sensitive waterways were blamed. In response, the federal government established a network of fish hatcheries across the province to promote and replenish fish populations. Fish born in these hatcheries, such as salmon, had exponentially higher survival rates, giving them a better chance of reaching adulthood before being reintroduced into the surrounding rivers.

The first of these hatcheries opened in the early 1870s, and a hatchery was recorded at Rapide de Femme Brook by 1880. The site was ideal:

the nearby waterfall provided a continuous source of fresh water, and the hatchery's proximity to the recently constructed New Brunswick Railway offered a safer means of transporting fish to surrounding lakes and rivers. This transportation method was much safer than the previous reliance on horse and carriage.

During the 1930s, the provincial government upgraded many existing fish hatcheries and built additional ones. Although specific records are unclear, it is likely that the Rapide de Femme hatchery underwent upgrades at this time, resulting in the site's current layout. A series of dams redirected fresh water from the brook to the base of the hill, where it fed into concrete raceways and holding tanks. Surrounding the tanks were buildings that housed the hatchery's pump, mechanical equipment, and operating staff.

A similarly aged hatchery is operational (as of 2025) in Miramichi, home to Canada's oldest functioning fish hatchery. Like the Miramichi facility, the Rapide de Femme hatchery primarily raised Atlantic salmon, speckled trout, and brown trout.

On September 11, 1954, the hatchery was severely damaged after a major storm caused flooding and overflow of its dams. The destruction of at least one dam and damage to the hatchery's fishways were recorded. While it is unclear if this event directly led to the hatchery's closure, the facility was shut down. Many of the buildings were destroyed or removed, leaving only concrete dams, holding tanks, and a network of pipes.

The area offers insight into the early days of aquaculture in the province. As much of the surrounding land is now private property, be respectful of local property owners and follow any posted signage when exploring the area.

FISH HATCHERY: N 47.007579, W 67.733300

The site is 4.7 kilometres south of the town of Grand Falls. While part of the area is now private property, it can still be viewed from a local ATV trail that passes through the site. Alternatively, visitors can hike from the base of Rapide de Femme Brook (N 47.006780, W 67.731645) and follow the brook upstream to access the falls and view the dams at their crest.

5. Stickney Lumber Mill

Stickney, Carleton County

Nestled at the junction of Stickney Brook and the mighty Saint John River lies the quiet town of Stickney. For thousands of years, this peaceful stretch of the river is believed to have been frequented by the Wolastoqiyik, who used the area as a fishing outpost and camp. The flat, low-lying terraces along the riverbanks and calm fishing waters later attracted a logging operation that would establish the town.

The area's first mill was established in 1823 by John Giberson, who had received land and timber grants in 1809. He constructed a gristmill on Stickney Brook, but the operation was short-lived, as the mill fell into disrepair after his death. In 1839, James Stickney acquired the land and began logging the area for nearby sawmills. Although Stickney established a mill, it was his influence on the small settlement that led the brook and later the town to be named for him.

In 1876, the New Brunswick Railway was built through the region. Despite this, Stickney developed slowly. When the railway arrived, only three families lived in the settlement, and by 1904, there were just eight. This changed when Erlon W. Bell of nearby Bristol purchased the Stickney lands in 1904. Bell and his family moved to the area, where he established a gristmill on Stickney Brook. A small dam was built to redirect water into a sluice, powering a waterwheel that ran the mill's machinery—designed by Bell himself. Though modest, the operation, combined with farming the surrounding lands, provided a stable livelihood.

In 1906, a shift occurred when Dr. Ross, Charlie Smalley, and John Perry founded the Peel Lumber Company. They invested heavily in constructing a large sawmill on flat land adjacent to the Saint John River. The mill's location, near both the railway and the river, allowed logs to be floated downstream for processing. The site featured a steam-powered sawmill, a planing mill, and even a meat skewer

factory that supplied butcheries in England. A company store was also built, sparking a rapid boom in the town. By the time the mill opened, families flocked to Stickney for employment, leading to the establishment of homes, businesses, a post office, and a hotel.

Despite its ideal location and abundant resources, the Peel Lumber Company struggled financially, and ceased operations in 1912. The mill's closure devastated the town, which relied heavily on its success. The site remained dormant for years until the building was dismantled in the 1920s, with the last piece—the boiler—removed later.

Following the Peel mill's failure, Bell expanded his operation, recognizing the region's potential. In partnership with investor F.

Brundage Hay, Bell established a new lumber and shingle mill near the former Peel site. A flood in 1912 destroyed Bell's original dam, prompting him to switch to steam power for his mill, which was operating as Bell & Sons: Long Lumber, Lathe, & Shingles. This provided much-needed jobs and stability to Stickney.

In 1921, a second mill was built on the Peel site by Wilbur Smith. A fire destroyed the mill just a year later, and it was never rebuilt. Meanwhile, Bell's mill continued to thrive. After Erlon Bell's death in 1925, his sons Manderville and Sam took over. In 1927, Sam became the sole owner and upgraded much of the aging equipment, rebranding the operation as S.W. Bell Mill.

The Great Depression brought challenges, but Sam Bell adapted by diversifying production to include barrels for transporting goods, particularly potatoes to the United States. A planer mill was added in 1939, and in 1945, the company officially became S.W. Bell Limited. Despite fierce competition and the decline of small-scale mills in the 1940s, the Stickney operation remained viable until disaster struck again.

On July 21, 1951, a shorted generator sparked a fire that destroyed the mill and several nearby buildings. Undeterred, the town rebuilt the mill, focusing on planed lumber, barrels, crates, and railway ties. Innovations such as a propane bark burner reduced waste and generated energy, allowing the mill to remain profitable for years.

After Sam Bell's death in 1968, his son Malcolm took over, operating the mill through the 1970s. Declining profitability forced its closure in May 1977, marking the end of Stickney's lumber industry. While the loss was a blow to the town's economy, Malcolm Bell's efforts to secure arrangements with nearby businesses, such as the Juniper Mill and McCain Foods in Florenceville, mitigated the impact.

What began as a small family gristmill and farm grew into one of the region's largest employers. Though little remains of the mills, the Bell family's legacy endures, a testament to their resilience and contributions to the town's development.

MILL SITE AND FORMER BURNER

While driving through the beautiful community of Stickney, it is easy to overlook the historic relics that remain from the town's milling past. On both the north and south sides of Stickney Brook, large, flat fields—now dotted with houses—mark the sites of the former mills. A closer inspection near the water reveals remnants of wooden cribbing and pieces of timber jutting out from the riverbanks, indicating the locations of former wharves. At the intersection of Route 105 and Stickney Brook, the former bark burner, installed in the early 1950s, is still visible. Although overgrown with tall trees, this steel pyramid-shaped structure rests on private property. Its impressive size ensures that it can still be clearly seen from the surrounding area.

MILL SITE AND BURNER: N 46.383802, W 67.569665

The former mill sites and bark burner are almost entirely located on private property but can be appreciated from the New Brunswick Railway-turned ATV trail, accessible from nearby Church Road (N 46.384809, W 67.570904).

STICKNEY BROOK DAM

Few remnants remain from the long history of mills and dams along Stickney Brook, with the exception of one. Approximately 500 metres up the river is a large, abandoned concrete dam, along with a short penstock and several foundations, remain. Likely built in the mid-20th century, this dam may have supplied water and possibly electricity to the mill and the town.

DAM: N 46.386397, W 67.565381

From the trailhead (N 46.385946, W 67.566131) located on Lumber Road, walk 80 metres along the unmaintained trail to the river to arrive at the dam.

6. Castle Bridges of New Brunswick

Esdraelon, Carleton County

New Brunswick is famous for its iconic covered bridges, but scattered across the province is another type of bridge that is equally worth seeing. These bridges, commonly referred to as "castle" or "stone" bridges, are built from concrete, stone, and granite and resemble the parapets and towers of a medieval castle. At least ten of these bridges remain, each with its own characteristics, but they share a similar design and origin story.

Two of these bridges cross Cold Stream in the community of Esdraelon, located 15 kilometres north of New Brunswick's most famous covered bridge in Hartland. Spanning each bridge are railings of stone and concrete, designed to resemble the parapets of a castle wall or tower, with alternating crenels and merlons. At the abutments on either side of the bridge, stone towers rise with spiked and arrowhead-shaped rocks, giving the appearance of being prepared for a medieval siege. Like other castle bridges in the province, the design is simple yet striking—stone or moulded concrete creates castlelike walls for railings, with small towerlike structures at each abutment.

The Esdraelon bridges are composed primarily of dark, jagged stones; others, like those that cross the New and Lepreau Rivers south of Saint John, have a smoother appearance with less pronounced features. In contrast, bridges such as the one on Main Street in Sussex feature larger, ornamental towers that rise high above the abutments, complete with working lights, making them impossible to miss.

Despite design differences, most of the province's castle bridges were built in the late 1930s, during the Great Depression. With unemployment rates soaring, the provincial government sought ways to provide meaningful work for the unemployed, leveraging the province's ample supply of granite and skilled local stonemasons. As a result, the government ordered that bridges resemble the stone walls and towers of medieval castles. The promotion and design of these bridges are

often attributed to the province's chief bridge engineer, Charles Andrew MacVey. While some of these bridges may have been built as early as 1910, the majority were completed between 1937 and 1939 as part of a series of make-work projects to bolster the local economy.

Many of New Brunswick's castle bridges are tucked away, but one of its most famous is the Stone Bridge that spans the Nashwaaksis Stream on Sunset Drive in Fredericton. Announced in 1938 and completed the following year, this 40-metre-long bridge was constructed by E.A. Caldwell of Edmundston. Like most castle bridges, the Stone Bridge is a single-arched span.

The largest castle bridge in the province is in the town of Newcastle Bridge, where the bridge on Pleasant Drive (Highway 10) crosses Newcastle Creek. This 88-metre-long bridge features two large arch spans.

ESDRAELON BRIDGES: N 46.436612, W 67.423117
N 46.433907, W 67.430720
NEW RIVER BRIDGE: N 45.137089, W 66.540892
LEPREAU RIVER BRIDGE: N 45.169743, W 66.467727
FREDERICTON (NASHWAAKSIS STREAM): N 45.984295, W 66.664471
NEWCASTLE BRIDGE (NEWCASTLE CREEK): N 46.077720, W 66.050419

7. Fall Brook Falls

Stanley Parish

Nestled within a narrow canyon carved into the steep riverbanks of the Southwest Miramichi River, Fall Brook Falls is a stunning 30-metre-high waterfall, believed to be the largest continuous waterfall in New Brunswick. The falls is located on Fall Brook, a stream that drains the Central Uplands into the Southwest Miramichi River. For most of its course, the river flows gently through the low-lying terrain, before suddenly cascading over an exposed rock outcrop as it makes its final descent into the river valley.

The steep cliffs behind the falls are composed of sedimentary and igneous rocks, indicative of volcanic activity in an ancient deep sea. The dark, Ordovician rocks, approximately 470 million years old, contrast strikingly with the white water that plunges over the edge. After falling 30 metres into a dark pool at the base, the stream continues for 400 metres before emptying into the Southwest Miramichi River. A trail follows this lower section of the stream, leading visitors from a parking lot at the bottom of a steep hill to the falls.

The waterfall is situated on land owned by J.D. Irving, which controls access to the falls. Known as freehold land, the company charges $10 per vehicle to drive the last 13 kilometres of gravel road to the falls, where a narrow path allows vehicles to get closer to the falls—this path can be challenging in heavy rain or two-wheel-drive vehicles. Several parking lots along the route provide safe spots for visitors to park and continue the journey on foot. For those who are comfortable with off-road driving, it is possible to reach the falls at the base of the canyon. From there, a 400-metre-long trail leads the rest of the way to the falls.

FALL BROOK FALLS: N 46.59857, W 66.59015

From the community of Bloomfield, drive 3 kilometres on Holtville Road. Veer left onto a gravel road. Continue for 3.1 kilometres to a check-in station, where a toll must be paid to access the falls. Drive 13 kilometres

and turn left onto a narrow road. From the beginning of this road to the trailhead is 900 metres, with parking lots along the route. The road becomes very steep for the last 100 metres and, depending on the vehicle and weather conditions, it is best to park atop the hill and hike down the incline. From the trailhead, a short but moderately difficult 400-metre-long hike is required.

8. Napadogan's Veneer Mill and Canadian National Roundhouse

Napadogan

In the deep backcountry of New Brunswick's interior is the small town of Napadogan. The area was completely inaccessible until 1911, when the NTR was built through the region, connecting Chipman to Grand Falls. This stretch of railway line was one of the most isolated in New Brunswick, and because of this, railway operators established a maintenance shop and resupply yard at the site. Construction began in mid-1911 on a semicircular brick roundhouse, an adjacent machine shop, a turntable, and a water tank and coal storage building. A large bunkhouse was built to house approximately a dozen workers. In the event that a railcar or locomotive needed maintenance, it would be brought to the roundhouse, where the turntable rotated the vehicle, aligning it with one of 12 service bays. The vehicle would then be backed into the service bay, where inspection pits allowed workers to easily access and service the railcar.

Over the next 40 years, the roundhouse and resupply yard were essential to trains passing through and attracted new industries to the area. Through the 1910s and 1920s, a small sawmill and hardwood mill were established, which slowly attracted more residents. Before long, a small community had been established.

The next boom came in 1960 when Atlantic Veneers Limited purchased the then-defunct roundhouse from CN with the intention of transforming it into a mill to process hardwood into veneer, primarily to produce wooden crates. The mill, which promised to employ as many as 80 people, would be capable of processing up to 10 million board feet annually. Anticipation increased in 1961, when it was announced that the owners had received an order from the Israeli government for 3 million board feet of veneer to manufacture fruit crates.

The mill had only been open for a short time when changes in the company's priorities and management led to the mill being taken over by a new company, Veneer Products Limited. Incorporated in May 1962, this company made its own additions to the former roundhouse and associated structures, and the veneer mill opened in mid-summer of 1963. Similar to its predecessor, the mill imported local hardwoods, such as maple, birch, and beech, which it used to produce thin hardwood sheets. Once processed, the product was sent mainly to Toronto and Montreal for the manufacture of wooden crates to store and ship fruit, fish, poultry, and potatoes. The company soon expanded its market to include manufacturers throughout New England and the rest of the United States and Canada.

By the mid-1970s, the mill was producing hardwood veneer for crutches, skateboards, and furniture. In 1977, Veneer Products determined that, to remain competitive, major repairs were needed. The company turned to the provincial government for financial help but was denied support unless it relocated its manufacturing plant (the largest importer of the mill's products) from Ontario to the province. The company refused, and as a result, shut down operations in 1980.

Ontario businessman Ted Samuel purchased the mill in 1981 and restarted operations. In 1986, a fire destroyed part of the mill, but it was rebuilt. Two years later, road weight restrictions limited the number of logs being imported to the mill, resulting in a temporary closure. Nonetheless, the mill operated smoothly for many years, thanks in part to the mill's long-time general manager, Bruce Dorcas. The mill employed 77 people in 2000 and had by then undergone several large-scale renovations and machinery modernization.

In 2003, the mill was sold to Miramichi businessman Robbie Tozer, head of the Atcon Group. Renamed Atcon Veneer Products Inc., operations continued until the company was forced to shut down due to financial difficulties. The mill, however, was saved when it was purchased by York North Veneer Products. Ownership of the mill changed several more times before coming into the hands of its current

owner (as of 2025), believed to be an American company attempting to refurbish and restart the now 64-year-old mill.

The future of the mill is uncertain, and while it is still privately owned, with periodic work occurring, the building continues to degrade. The rich history of the mill and town is embodied by the conglomeration of different-era buildings, each representing an addition to the mill. The mill helped establish the nearby town of Napadogan, barely a shadow of its former self, with only a small portion of its former population still living there. But the 114-year-old National Transcontinental Railway roundhouse building is a hidden historic gem. This semicircular building now makes up the east side of the mill and is one of the last standing roundhouses in Atlantic Canada.

MILL AND ROUNDHOUSE: N 46.412946, W 66.932816

The mill and railway are still operational and so extra caution should be taken when visiting the area. The town is located along Highway 107, 25 kilometres west of Stanley and 33 kilometres east of Juniper. Its cultural and industrial history is experienced by driving through the town's streets.

9. Chimney Rock

Deersdale

Deep in the forest south of Deersdale, along Highway 107, lies Chimney Rock—a square rocky column that appears to balance on a rocky ledge at the base of a narrow gorge.

Chimney Rock and its surrounding landscape were shaped over thousands of years, with much of the dramatic terrain influenced by the end of the last ice age approximately 12,000 years ago. As massive sheets of ice that once covered the province began to melt, they eroded the land, carving the rugged features we see today. Many of these geological treasures remain concealed within the deep interior of the province, often uncovered and shared by local explorers who venture into these remote areas.

Chimney Rock stands out as one of these landmarks. While frequently visited by locals and ATV enthusiasts, its isolated location makes it a challenging destination for most. Nevertheless, the striking moss-covered rocks and dramatic scenery make it a must-visit spot for hikers, photographers, and anyone seeking to experience the hidden beauty of New Brunswick.

CHIMNEY ROCK: N 46.386853, W 67.185209

10. Balancing Rock

Douglas Parish, York County

The interior of New Brunswick contains countless strange and wondrous natural formations. While some of these features were formed through geological processes over millions of years, much of what is now visible in the landscape formed during the last ice age, when glaciers moved across the landscape. In the backcountry, south of the towns of Juniper and Napadogan, is one of these formations. Here, a large boulder the size of a shed balances precariously atop several smaller boulders.

Appropriately named Balancing Rock, this natural wonder is a glacial deposition landform known as an erratic. During the Wisconsin glaciation, between 20,000 and 10,000 years ago, the province was covered by a large sheet of ice that moved radially outward from its origin in the Appalachian Uplands in northern New Brunswick. Here, freeze-thaw cycles and glacial scouring broke off bits of rock from the underlying landscape. Often, these became embedded within the ice sheet, moving with it. Around 10,000 years ago, when the planet started to warm again, the glaciers melted, depositing the rocks trapped within it.

The feature has become a popular spot for local ATV and snowmobile riders. But while many continue to speculate that aliens or machines placed the rock, it is more likely—and arguably more astonishing—that the rock was placed here by a moving ice sheet.

BALANCING ROCK: N 46.309836, W 67.153938

Approximately 4 kilometres southeast of the town of Millville on Route 104, turn north onto a gravel road (N 46.102357, W 67.166316). Drive 8.4 kilometres and veer left onto a narrow road (N 46.159940, W 67.114433). Drive approximately 20 kilometres, then turn right at the intersection (N 46.303639, W 67.157757). Continue 700 metres, turn left, and continue 350 metres to the trailhead (N 46.309070, W 67.152513). Balancing Rock is at the end of a well-beaten trail.

11. Spruce Budworm Spray Aircraft Avenger Crash Site

Brighton Parish, Carleton County

Outbreaks of spruce budworm occur in New Brunswick every 20 to 40 years, damaging vast areas of trees. To combat these outbreaks, Forest Protection Ltd., a partnership between the provincial government and local industry, began large-scale pesticide spraying in 1952 (page 58).

The first planes to complete these spraying operations were small Stearman biplanes. Given that large tracts of land needed to be sprayed in New Brunswick, in 1958 Forest Protection Ltd. next introduced 12 former torpedo bomber aircraft, Grumman Avengers, for the task. This aircraft was larger than the Stearman, allowing it to carry larger tanks and travel farther distances. In 1958, operations focused on the west side of New Brunswick, in the counties of Carleton, York, and Victoria.

The spraying operations came with risks, as was demonstrated on June 12, 1958, during a routine spray flight from Juniper Airfield. Originally from Stockport, England, pilot Thomas Reginald Marston had learned to fly with the Commonwealth Air Training Program, which trained pilots in Canada during World War II before they were transferred overseas. Marston served as a fighter and glider pilot across Europe and Asia, in Norway, Britain, India, Myanmar (formerly Burma), and elsewhere.

Marston was flying his Avenger aircraft in New Brunswick alongside several others when, while in the process of making a turn, he experienced turbulence from the slipstream of a nearby aircraft. Marston's aircraft suddenly lost airspeed, likely limiting the aircraft's control and causing a stall that forced the plane into the forest below. Marston was killed in the crash, marking the first death of a pilot for Forest Protection Ltd.

The forested backcountry of New Brunswick made accessing the remote crash site difficult, and it took three days for a recovery crew to

finally reach it. The plane's wreckage, which remains scattered across a wetland, is marked by two memorial plaques which honour Marston and his service both overseas and at home.

The site is more accessible in 2025 than it was in 1958, though it is still off the beaten path. Logging roads have since increased access to the province's interior; however, after travelling approximately 36 kilometres on a gravel road, a short but wet hike across a bog is required to reach the site, now popular among ATV enthusiasts. As with most crash sites, the area is considered a historic aviation archaeological site, and therefore the removal or altering of the site is strictly prohibited. Visitors should respectful when at the site.

CRASH SITE: N 46.304930, W 67.248203

Approximately 4 kilometres southeast of the town of Millville on Route 104, turn north onto a gravel road (N 46.102357, W 67.166316). Drive 8.4 kilometres and turn left onto a narrow road (N 46.159940, W 67.114433). Continue along this road for approximately 19.5 kilometres, then turn left (N 46.300219, W 67.158783). Travel 6.5 kilometres, turn right and drive another 650 metres. Turn right again and continue for 800 metres to the trailhead (N 46.303679, W 67.248053) and walk across the wet bog to the crash site. As few signs indicate the site, proper knowledge of the road networks and backcountry is required to safely visit this site.

Burnt Church
Escumin
Wayerton
1
Miramichi
5
2
4
Newcastle
Chatham
3.1
3.4
6
3.2
3.3
7
Quarryville
Kouchibouguac
8
Rogersville

Miramichi Region

Miramichi, the largest town in northern New Brunswick, has long been an important settlement—first by the Mi'kmaq who relied on the majestic Miramichi River for fishing, hunting, and travel, and later by some of New Brunswick's most prominent industries. The Indigenous people living in the area were forced out of their traditional territories by European settlers, who established fishing villages, sawmills, and fortifications. The Miramichi River, which splits at Beaubears Island into its northwest and southwest branches, became lined with small settlements. One of the earliest industries was shipbuilding, best seen at the Beaubears Island Shipbuilding National Historic Site. These industries were also located south of Miramichi in Richibucto and Kouchibouguac, where shipbuilding, lumber mills, and one of the province's earliest hydroelectric facilities were established. The common thread among these industries was the exploitation of the province's vast interior forests. Huge stretches of woodland were logged to provide masts and keels for ships. Over time, as large trees became harder to find, lumber mills, log drives, and new access routes into the interior were developed.

By the late 19th and early 20th centuries, the modern amalgamated City of Miramichi encompasses Northwest Bridge, Newcastle, Nelson, Miramichi, and Chatham, to name a few. The city became the centre of commerce in northern New Brunswick. The outbreak of World War II brought the establishment of a new air force base in Chatham and

a radar station farther south in St. Margarets, both playing a critical role in protecting vessels operating in the Gulf of St. Lawrence. The 2000s brought drastic changes, as many of the region's lumber, pulp, and paper mills shut down.

The region also has a strong Acadian population, with its rich culture and traditions. Along the region's rivers, the Mi'kmaw communities of Esgenoôpetitj (Burnt Church), Natoaganeg (Eel Ground), and Metepenagiag (Red Bank) remain vibrant and resilient.

Miramichi is at the mouth of the Miramichi River along Miramichi Bay. From there, Highway 8 travels north to Bathurst, while Highway

11 follows the north shore of the bay, providing access to the Acadian Peninsula. Roads line both sides of the Miramichi River and its two branches, with only a few bridges providing access to the opposite shore. The region serves as a gateway to the province's interior, with Highway 8 continuing along the river's southwest branch toward Doaktown and Boiestown. Highway 108 cuts directly through the province's empty interior, providing one of the best and most accessible ways to experience New Brunswick's backcountry. To the south, Highway 11 offers a direct route to Moncton, passing through Kouchibouguac National Park and on to historic Richibucto.

1. Little Sheephouse Falls

Northesk Parish

Nestled in the forest northwest of Miramichi lies Little Sheephouse Falls. This picturesque 12-metre-high waterfall cascades through a narrow gorge carved by the Little Sheephouse River. It is one of three stunning waterfalls in the area, each flowing through a scenic river valley. The gorge's walls, composed of sedimentary rocks deposited in a shallow ocean over 470 million years ago, create a striking backdrop for the falls. Over time, tectonic activity has twisted and rotated these rock layers, adding dramatic contrast as the water plunges into the pool below. Surrounding the falls is a diverse forest of hardwood and softwood trees, including white pine, black spruce, birch, trembling aspen, and red maple.

For years, the falls have been a well-kept secret among local adventurers exploring the area on ATVs, snowmobiles, and off-road vehicles. In 1989, the logging company holding forestry rights in the region, Repap New Brunswick (page 134), promoted the site by creating the Little Sheephouse Falls Nature Trail. After the rights were acquired by UPM-Miramichi, the trail system was further developed into a 1-kilometre loop. UPM-Miramichi added informative signs and plaques about the area's ecosystem, geology, and points of interest.

Several lookouts are located along on the trail and a staircase brings visitors from the top of the gorge to the falls. While this location can become busy on a summer's day, it is more often a quiet place to learn about New Brunswick's backcountry and ecology.

LITTLE SHEEPHOUSE FALLS: N 47.095743, W 66.006683
Follow Highway 430 north of Miramichi toward Wayerton. Approximately 3.5 kilometres past the community, turn onto Fraser-Burchill Road. Follow this road for approximately 10 kilometres and turn left. Continue 4.5 kilometres, turn left again and continue 2.5 kilometres. The parking lot and trailhead are located along the road.

2. Morrissy Bridge

Newcastle/Chatham Head

Spanning the communities of Chatham Head and Newcastle, Morrissy Bridge opened on November 12, 1914. The bridge was named for John Morrissy, the minister of public works at the time, who advocated for its construction. Built by the Foundation Company of Canada and Dominion Bridge Company, the opening was celebrated by communities along the Miramichi River for making river crossings more convenient. The approximately 450-metre-long steel truss bridge supported a two-lane road. At the time of its construction, the bridge was not designed to support cars but horse-drawn buggies, the more popular means of travel at the time. When automobiles became common through the 1920s and 1930s, concerns grew over whether the bridge could support the added weight.

The industry along the shores of the Miramichi River meant that ships regularly sailed the river. To accommodate their passage, the bridge was fitted with a swing stage that could rotate 90 degrees, leaving enough room for cargo ships and freighters to pass through. However, the river's currents and tides made this a challenging task even for experienced captains. In 1923, the cargo ship *Woldingham* collided with the bridge's swing stage. The incident led to a court case, with the provincial government arguing that the ship was responsible for the collision and should cover the repair costs. In an interesting twist, lawyers for the ship demonstrated that Morrissy, who oversaw the bridge's construction, had failed to secure the necessary federal approvals. Under the Navigable Waters Protection Act, the ship had struck an "obstruction to navigation," not a "bridge." After losing their appeal, the Department of Public Works was forced to pay for repairs and compensate the company for damages. Following extensive surveys, the federal government eventually recognized the bridge as an obstacle to navigation.

The *Woldingham* was not the last ship to strike the bridge. In 1967,

the tanker *Liquilassie* caused $150,000 in damages, temporarily shutting down this vital transportation route. The hardship endured by locals was memorialized in "The Morrissy Bridge Song," written by Alex Milson and performed at the Miramichi Folk Festival that year. In 1971, the *Grand Valor* struck the bridge's swing stage, closing it for three months. And in 1984, the *John M Hamburg*, a 7,300-tonne freighter, dislodged the bridge's centre span. Several other incidents occurred over the bridge's lifespan, but consistent repairs allowed the route to reopen.

By the mid-20th century, lumber mills on the river's south side relied heavily on logs supplied from the Newcastle (north) side. Logging trucks frequently crossed the bridge to supply sawmills, making it indispensable. In 1961, Member of the Legislative Assembly Clarence S. Menzies remarked, "If anything ever happened to the Morrissy Bridge ... the lumbering industry would be at a standstill in the county."

By 1960, the bridge was showing its age, earning it the nickname "old Morrissy Bridge." After each collision, debates arose over whether constructing a new bridge would be more cost-effective. These plans were often dismissed due to the high expense of spanning the 400-metre-wide river.

In 1995, a new bridge, built 600 metres upstream, became the preferred crossing. Morrissy Bridge remained open, but in 2008, an engineering study revealed catastrophic corrosion in the bridge deck, forcing the provincial government to close it, on September 12, 2008. While demolition was initially planned, the high cost prevented any action. Since then, local advocates have pushed for converting the bridge into a pedestrian walkway, similar to Fredericton's Bill Thorpe Walking Bridge.

As of 2025, the bridge remains closed to the public but stands as a symbol for Newcastle, Chatham Head, and other Miramichi River communities. Once deemed an "obstruction to navigation," it became a vital route for travellers and an essential supply line for the lumber industry. The ghostly structure endures as a local landmark.

MORRISSY BRIDGE: N 46.996894, W 65.562128

The bridge is best viewed from its east and west abutments at the end of Bridge Road in the communities of Newcastle and Chatham Head, both of which are amalgamated into the city of Miramichi.

DOOR
90

3. Remnants of Miramichi's Historic Forestry Industry

INTRODUCTION

For centuries, the Miramichi River has been a centre of industry, particularly forestry and logging. The first European settler in the area was Scottish immigrant William Davidson, who was awarded land and timber rights for the forests surrounding the river. As settlers moved to the area, the logging and shipbuilding industries of Miramichi took shape. Initially, the industry focused on producing masts and even entire ships. However, as wooden shipbuilding declined across the Maritimes, it was replaced by sawmilling, which produced lumber and other building materials.

Sawmilling became the primary source of income for hundreds of people in the area until 1886, when pulp milling—the process of turning wood into pulp for paper production—gained popularity. The first pulp mill was established on the river in 1886 and was followed by two others. These endeavours were relatively short-lived and the last of these pulp mills closed in 1932. Sawmilling once again became the region's dominant industry.

In the ensuing years, the region's forestry industry underwent another transformation. Smaller sawmills either closed or were bought out by larger operations, eventually leaving only a few mass-producing mills. Over time, even these mills were acquired by larger corporations, leaving the region with just a few sawmills, pulp mills, and paper mills.

Despite these changes, the forestry industry brought economic growth to the communities along the Miramichi River in the latter half of the 20th century. In 1995, 11 communities, including five incorporated towns—Newcastle, Chatham, Nelson-Miramichi, Loggieville, and Douglastown—

amalgamated into a single municipality. Each of these towns traced its origins to small 18th- or 19th-century sawmilling operations.

As the demand for high-production, low-cost mills slowly climbed, the number of sawmills, pulp mills, and paper mills in the area steadily declined. By the late 2000s, the Miramichi forestry industry had all but disappeared, leaving hundreds of workers and their families devastated. What had once been the primary source of income and livelihood for generations vanished almost entirely. Many residents were forced to move or relocate to find new sources of income, while the mills that had once fuelled the local economy were either demolished or abandoned.

UPM-Kymmene Kraft Pulp Mill and Paper Mill

Northwest Bridge, Newcastle

Near the confluence of the Northwest Miramichi River and Southwest Miramichi River lies a large fenced-off plot of land that once belonged to the UPM-Kymmene Kraft and Paper Mills. Shrubs and tall grasses grow among the mills' large concrete foundations.

A small sawmill was the first mill built on the site, in 1871. In 1949, a new scale of industry was introduced with the construction of a pulp mill and later a paper mill. For the next 60 years, the site drove the local economy until the mills closed. One of the largest abandoned industrial plots in the region, it symbolizes both the importance of the mills and the tragedy of their closure.

In 1871, Edward Sinclair built and operated a sawmill near this location. The three-storey wooden mill constructed on the riverbanks quickly became successful, attracting many workers to the area. Like most sawmills in the region, the Edward Sinclair Lumber Company used the river to transport logs from inland forests to the mill. From there, cut timber was loaded onto boats and shipped across the region.

The mill and its timber resources were eventually purchased by the Fraser Company in the mid-1920s. At the time, Fraser already operated two large mills in the province and acquired the site primarily for its timber resources, abandoning the mill and temporarily ending 50 years

of logging at the site. However, this hiatus ended in 1946 when the Fraser Company announced plans to construct a new sulfate pulp mill at the location.

While rumours of a pulp mill in 1930 proved false—that project was located in Atholville instead—the 1946 announcement of a pulp mill raised hopes in the community. Groundbreaking began that year, and in 1949, the kraft pulp mill opened. Using a sulfate process to convert wood into pulp, the kraft mill produced 1,250 tonnes of pulp daily and was considered one of the most modern facilities of its time. Subsequent upgrades included a new digester, bleaching plant, and additional pulp machines and dryers, enabling the mill to produce 1,500 tonnes of pulp daily by the 1970s.

On January 22, 1970, the Fraser Company sold the kraft mill to Boise Cascade Canada, which renamed it Miramichi Timber Resources

Limited. In 1978, following the departure of major investors, the company became the sole owner and renamed it the Ontario-Minnesota Pulp and Paper Company. This name was short-lived; soon, it reverted to Boise Cascade Canada Limited: Newcastle Division. To stay competitive, the mill underwent a major upgrade in the late 1970s, including a new bleaching plant, a fourth power boiler, and improvements to its mechanical systems.

In 1985, George Petty of Repap Enterprises purchased the kraft mill and merged it with a groundwood pulp mill acquired in 1974 under Acadia Forest Products. Repap also announced plans for a paper mill adjacent to the kraft mill, which was completed in 1986. Once operational, the paper mill employed 500 workers and became one of the most advanced mills of its kind, producing lightweight coated paper using pulp from the kraft and groundwood mills.

In 2000, UPM-Kymmene purchased the kraft, groundwood, and paper mills, becoming a leader in magazine paper production. The paper machines, with a combined capacity of 450,000 tonnes of coated paper annually, served clients primarily in the US. Global competition and market shifts led to the closure of the kraft mill in 2005, leaving 400 workers unemployed. In 2006, the paper mill faced temporary shutdowns due to financial pressures, foreshadowing its permanent closure in December 2007, which left 600 more workers without jobs.

The closure devastated the community, and while efforts were made to repurpose the site, no new industry has taken its place. Over the years, many buildings were removed or relocated, and the site remains fenced off as cleanup continues. From nearby Highway 8 or Curtis Road, remnants of the vast industrial landscape are still visible.

PULP AND PAPER MILL: N 46.973892, W 65.594725

Due to restricted access to the site, the former mill is best seen from the water. However, remnants of the mill are visible from Curtis Road, approximately 3 kilometres south of Newcastle.

UPM-Kymmene Groundwood Pulp Mill

Nelson-Miramichi

Located across the river from UPM-Kymmene's kraft pulp and paper mills, in the community of Nelson-Miramichi, is the site of the company's former groundwood pulp mill. Logging and sawmills occupied this site for nearly 100 years, but all that remains are scattered overgrown foundations, fragments of equipment, and faint outlines of roads and lumberyards.

The site is adjacent to Flett Cove, where the early-era Flett Sawmill was established. Producing primarily lumber and barrels, the mill operated until 1910, when it could no longer compete with neighbouring operations. In 1914, W.M. Sullivan purchased the mill and reopened it with production focused on cedar shingles. The mill operated successfully for the next 20 years, employing up to 100 workers.

In 1939, local resident and businessman Joseph L. O'Brien purchased the mill and oversaw its operation. Because he was the founder of British-Miramichi Exporters Ltd., O'Brien's connections with mills and buyers in Europe helped the business thrive. Over the next two decades, O'Brien expanded his holdings to include multiple stores, businesses, mills, and timber rights throughout the area. In 1961, he sold his properties in Nelson, including the sawmill, its adjacent lands, and the nearby shipping port, to European investors.

Construction of the groundwood pulp mill began in early 1963 and was completed in October 1964. Operating under the name South Nelson Products Corporation, the mill had a capacity of 250 tonnes of pulp per day, most of which was shipped to European paper mills via a large wharf and loading facility on the south side of the Miramichi River. In 1964, the company also constructed a sawmill adjacent to the groundwood pulp mill, near the site of the former Flett Sawmill. The sawmill, employing 28 people, produced lumber products for markets across the eastern United States and Europe.

In 1967, new owners took control of the mill, renaming it Acadia Pulp and Paper Limited. They invested in upgrades, increasing the mill's production output to 350 tonnes of pulp per day. With international distribution, the mill gained recognition in the papermaking industry as one of the largest producers of dry pulp on the east coast.

Stability arrived in 1974 when George Petty of Repap Enterprises, supported by Canadian investors, purchased the mill under the name Acadia Forest Products. To remain competitive, the mill's equipment was upgraded, with improvements completed by 1980.

In 1985, Repap Enterprises expanded further by acquiring the kraft pulp and paper mills at Northwest Bridge, forming Miramichi Pulp & Paper Inc. While pulp continued to be sold internationally, the company focused on paper production, using both pulp mills to supply its papermaking machines. By this time, Repap managed over 700,000 hectares of timberland, and the mills remained a vital economic driver for the region, providing hundreds of jobs. Major upgrades followed in 1990 and 1995, but by the late 1990s, the industry had begun to decline.

In 2000, Repap sold the mills, including the groundwood pulp mill at Nelson-Miramichi, to UPM-Kymmene. Despite being one of the world's largest magazine paper producers, UPM-Kymmene faced challenges from a declining Canadian dollar and intensifying competition in the pulp and paper industry. In 2007, the company announced the mill's closure, leaving hundreds without jobs and forcing many residents to relocate for new job opportunities.

The site of the groundwood pulp mill is overgrown with shrubs and small trees. The large concrete footprint of the mill is still visible, alongside remnants of machinery, roads, and power lines. By the water, the wharf and loading facility, once used by ocean-going cargo ships, are occasionally used by local boaters and fishers. This land, integral to Miramichi's history and economy for over a century, now stands as a quiet reminder of its industrial past. Despite its historical significance, there is little formal recognition of the site beyond the remnants hidden beneath the overgrowth.

GROUNDWOOD PULP MILL: N 46.973839, W 65.556614

As the site is now private property, follow all posted signs. In the community of Nelson-Miramichi, follow St. Patricks Drive south to its end. From here a narrow trail passes through the site.

Nelson Forest Products Plywood Mill

Nelson

One of the most noticeable abandoned structures along the Miramichi River waterfront is the Nelson Forest Products Ltd. plywood mill. The mill's closure in 2008 marked the end of more than 160 years of lumber milling on the site, including the renowned saw and plywood mills operated by George Burchill and Sons. Since then, the abandoned structure has been fenced off and forgotten.

The flat land along the Miramichi River was ideal for sawmill operations, and the site hosted its first mill shortly after the arrival of European settlers. In 1868, a small sawmill on this site came under the ownership of prominent businessman Charles Sargeant, who operated it for eight years. In 1876, local merchant, shipbuilder, and lumberman George Burchill purchased the steam-powered mill and its surrounding property, continuing its operation. By 1881, he and his two sons established George Burchill and Sons. The business flourished, with its products being sold and shipped across the east coast of Canada. The company also gained a reputation for treating its mill and logging workers well.

George Burchill retired in 1904 and passed the company to his son, John Percival. Over the next six decades, the mill remained a community landmark, growing in size and modernizing its machinery. By the mid-20th century, the facility included an expansive shipping yard, enabling the export of products to various markets. In 1962, the company constructed a plywood mill on the site, diversifying its operations and expanding its export capabilities. The new mill became a major employer, supporting many families in surrounding communities.

In 1967, a fire broke out at the mill, but it was quickly rebuilt. Around the same time, the sawmill was shut down, as the company shifted its focus to plywood production. Over the next decade, upgrades were made, and by 1977 the facility was one of only two plywood mills operating in New Brunswick. Employing approximately 120 workers, the mill produced more than 3.5 million square metres of plywood annually. But growing competition from larger mills worldwide and advances in shipping logistics made it increasingly difficult for the mill to remain competitive.

By the late 1970s, the company faced financial difficulties, leading to the mill's closure in 1981 and ending more than a century of George Burchill and Sons' operations on the site. The provincial government briefly took over the facility but sold it to a private owner from Oromocto in 1984. The new owner reopened the mill for a short time, but it soon closed again, leaving workers struggling to find employment.

In 1991, Robert Tozer of Atco Construction, later part of Atcon Group Inc., purchased the mill. The facility reopened in 1994 as Nelson Forest Products Inc. The mill resumed production and began shipping products globally, though competition in the forestry market again made profitability elusive. In 2001, a fire destroyed the mill, delaying plans for rebuilding until market conditions improved.

In 2004, the community celebrated the announcement of a new $25 million plywood mill, which opened in 2005 with modern equipment and machinery. The company also unveiled plans for a second phase: the establishment of a high-quality veneer mill in Napadogan. Despite the excitement surrounding the reopening, the global forestry market continued to present challenges. The 2008 recession dealt a final blow to the mill, which closed permanently that year.

The closure marked the end of more than 160 years of lumber milling at the site. The empty building remains fenced off, its future uncertain. Despite its current state, nearly every family in the surrounding communities has a connection to the mills that once operated there.

PLYWOOD MILL: N 46.988624, W 65.551454
Although it is fenced off, the mill is visible from nearby St. Patrick Street. However, the best and safest way to view the site is by water, where nearly 100 years of concrete and wharf remains are backdropped by the mill itself.

Lynch's Mill and Fraser's Mill at Chatham Head

Chatham Head

The history of the former Fraser sawmill in Chatham Head remains shrouded in mystery. Situated just south of Morrissy Bridge, the site is now a grassy lot dotted with remnants of its past. Concrete foundations—likely part of the mill's main structure—and towering concrete pillars, thought to be remnants of its loading facility, stand as silent witnesses to its once-thriving operations. Along the waterfront, bricks blanket the shoreline, while thick timbers are all that remain of Fraser's wharf. A short walking trail winds through the area, inviting visitors to explore these intriguing relics. The absence of detailed records adds to the site's mystique, leaving visitors to imagine the stories hidden within the foundations and pillars scattered along the riverside landscape.

The site's industrial history began in the mid-1880s with a small sawmill operated by Timothy Lynch. After Lynch's death in 1908, the mill's manager, William Dolan, took over operations until 1915, when the Fraser Lumber Company purchased the mill and its associated forestry rights. This acquisition was part of Fraser's broader strategy to expand its holdings, beginning with a sawmill in Plaster Rock (page 92). Recognizing the potential of Miramichi's thriving sawmill industry, the company acquired Lynch's sawmill on November 1, 1915, along with 3,600 hectares of grant lands and 350 square kilometres of Crown land rights.

Shortly after the purchase, Fraser replaced the aging mill with a modern facility. The new mill dwarfed its predecessor and was accompanied by additional infrastructure, including storage buildings, warehouses, a large riverfront loading facility, and a lumberyard. To support its employees, the company built a boarding house and cookhouse.

The Fraser sawmill operated until at least 1950, likely shutting down after the company constructed a pulp mill in Nelson (page 132). The sawmill was dismantled and the land left undeveloped.

The site retains many reminders of its industrial legacy. Concrete foundations mark the locations of the mill and surrounding buildings, while two towering concrete pillars likely belonged to the loading facility. Along the beach, bricks, steel fragments, and other artifacts are still being discovered.

CHATHAM HEAD MILLS: N 46.994812, W 65.554570

The trailhead (N 46.997005, W 65.552933) is on Bridge Road in the community of Chatham Head. A short, maintained trail leads to the site, which is located approximately 300 metres away.

4. Morrison Cove Pumphouse and Firefighter Training Centre

Morrison Cove, Chatham

South of Chatham, nestled in the tranquil inlet of Morrison Cove, lies an array of forgotten buildings, remnants of firefighter training facilities, and an abandoned trail network. This site, once home to Chatham's water supply, a firefighter training centre, and a public park, has evolved into a peaceful retreat for hikers and dog walkers.

HISTORY

In the late 19th century, Chatham experienced rapid growth thanks to shipbuilding, fishing, lumber mills, and other industries. Incorporated in 1896, the town's new growth brought challenges, specifically for the supply of water to its residents and industries. The late 1800s in Canada saw the introduction of technologies for municipal water supplies. Prior to this, most people obtained their water from wells, surface water, or springs. As awareness of public health and water sanitation grew, more municipalities established community-operated and -maintained water sources. New technologies, such as the adoption of steel, iron, and lead piping, along with increased access to high-capacity pumps, meant that water supplies no longer needed to be near the populations they served.

With a growing population and increasing demand for water in 1901, Chatham established a new water supply system in Morrison Cove. This system consisted of two dams built on a nearby stream, where water was redirected into a piping system flowing into a newly constructed pumphouse. The pumphouse building, located in the cove, was constructed by local contractor James Mowatt. The 220-square-metre rectangular brick building is recognized for its functional and simple design, a form of utilitarian architecture. The building housed two water pumps, likely driven by a coal- or wood-powered steam engine. On

one side of the building, a tall brick chimney was constructed; it remains the site's most prominent feature.

The pumphouse and its nearby reservoir provided water to the town and continued supplying water for the next 30 to 40 years. By the 1940s and 1950s, increasing demand meant that the pumphouse and reservoirs could no longer fulfill the community's water needs. The pumphouse was shut down and new water sources were developed, including nearby reservoirs and deep groundwater wells around the town.

Following the closure of the pumphouse, the area became a haven for residents wanting to hike and fish. When reservoirs were built on the river, dams and overfishing disrupted fish stocks, particularly in the larger of the two reservoirs, which remains intact. The lake was periodically restocked throughout the second half of the 20th century, becoming a popular ice-fishing location.

In 1981, with financial help from municipal, provincial, and federal governments, the lands were leased to the Miramichi Fire Department. The aging pumphouse and surrounding grounds found new purpose as a firefighter training centre. Work began immediately on the renovation of the old pumphouse, the construction of a new structure to host a firefighting museum, the establishment of a training centre (including a three-storey training tower), and a network of trails and bridges throughout the surrounding valley. After officially opening in October 1983, the centre provided essential training to 16 regional fire departments and hosted sessions for province-wide departments.

Although the training facility proved successful, by the early 2000s the trail system and park had fallen into disrepair and were rarely used. Around this time, a new training centre was established at the New Brunswick Community College campus on O'Keefe Road, which, in 2011, resulted in the closure of the Morrison Cove training facility. The 110-year-old pumphouse building was demolished due to structural problems. The local community council postponed the demolition to the following year but never revisited the issue, miraculously saving the structure, at least temporarily.

In the late 2010s and early 2020s, a project proposed by Kevin Gallant, vice-chair of the Miramichi River Environmental Assessment Committee, aimed to save the site and its history by converting the area into a park, restoring the former trail system, and transforming the pumphouse into an interpretative centre. While nothing has come of the proposal as of 2025, it is hoped that the site's history and natural beauty can be preserved and the historic pumphouse saved.

ABOUT THE AREA

This area has become a popular destination for local hikers, dog walkers, and fishers. The pumphouse is still visible from nearby Water Street, with the words Chatham Fire Centre barely discernible on its prominent chimney. Still used for storage, the pumphouse and its adjacent building are monitored by security cameras. Leaving from the pumphouse parking lot, the trail system established by the Miramichi Fire Department can still be loosely traced. The trail first passes by the remains of the former firefighter training area before leading into the forest and up the river. Once in the valley, the trail continues to the two dams located upstream, passing by the remains of culverts, pipes, and the occasional spring—all relics of the former water supply system. Visitors should exercise extreme caution when exploring the remains of the trail's wooden bridges and boardwalks, as many are in poor condition.

TRAINING CENTRE: N 47.014615, W 65.498774

Turn onto a gravel road, approximately 2 kilometres south of the Highway 8 bridge in Chatham. Park in the designated lot; the trails are on the left side of the building. Be sure to follow all signs on the property.

5. Woodburn Conservatory

Morrison Cove, Chatham

On the outskirts of Chatham, tucked away in the forested hillside above Morrison Cove, are the remains of the historic Woodburn Conservatory. Originally built by a member of the famous Cunard family, the estate later became known as Woodburn Conservatory, gaining a province-wide reputation for its crops, livestock products, and flower gardens. Surrounded by farmland, flower gardens, and a variety of trees, the estate also became a sought-after venue for weddings, parties, and community events. The house and lands were eventually abandoned, leaving only the burned remains of the estate's house and several barns. The area was once a popular destination among the community, and, while it is but a partial reflection of its former self, the beauty and history of the area should not be overlooked.

HISTORY

The story of the estate begins in 1820 when Henry Cunard arrived in Chatham. Partnering with his brother Joseph, the Cunards quickly made a name for themselves in the area by establishing a lumber mill business and a store and by venturing into local politics. The influence and significance of the brothers are sometimes overshadowed by the success of their brother Samuel, who remained in Halifax and established the famous shipping and cruise line company, Cunard Steamship Company. Nonetheless, Henry Cunard played an influential role in the area's school system, politics, and even served as the area's immigration agent before being appointed director of the Northumberland Agricultural Society.

Cunard had a passion for farming and raising livestock, which in 1841 led him to employ Alexander Cormack to construct a large house just outside Chatham. Once completed, the two-storey Georgian-style house boasted decorative trimmings, windows, and doors. Surrounding the house was bountiful farmland, where he eventually constructed

several greenhouses and barns for growing crops and flowers and raising livestock. Throughout his life, Cunard took great pride in his farm, eventually retiring to spend more time following this passion.

When Cunard died in 1885, the farm and house, known as Woodburn Cottage, came into the ownership of George E. Fisher. Fisher moved to the area with his family and capitalized on the farm's potential. Although he focused on producing dairy products, raising livestock, and breeding horses, he also grew vegetables and wheat, which were sold across the province. His products became well known across the country. As for

the house and beautiful gardens, Fisher rented the estate for parties and weddings, making it a popular venue.

On July 12, 1901, a forest fire broke out nearby, destroying many of the farm's crops. Unlike several farms nearby, which were destroyed, some of the estate remained untouched, allowing Fisher to quickly recover. In 1915, he established the area's first commercial nursery, Woodburn Conservatory. It specialized in cultivating a range of fruits and vegetables, supporting the region's agricultural development. Over the next decade, the enterprise flourished, with products being sold at

farmers' markets around the province, and even opening stores in such towns as Moncton.

In November 1926, a second fire broke out in one of the estate's barns, destroying it and a neighbouring greenhouse. The fire also killed some of Fisher's livestock and destroyed part of the following year's crops. Once again, Fisher rebuilt and continued operating the farm for the next several years. In 1932, he sold the farm and moved back to Fredericton with his family, where he died in 1936. Fisher is well remembered and recognized for his influence in the community and the wide reach of his products across the province.

In early 1932, Woodburn Conservatory was purchased by Daniel A. Burns, an English immigrant who moved to the region with his family. Burns died just six months after purchasing the farm, and control was passed to his sons. Referred to as the Burns Brothers, the farm grew fruit and vegetables and raised livestock throughout the summer and sold them to markets by late fall of the same year. In 1941, a third fire broke out in one of the farm's large hay barns, destroying it and two others.

Woodburn Cottage escaped destruction, thanks to the efforts of the Newcastle Fire Department, which had to run hoses from the Chatham Pumping Station located more than 300 metres away.

The family had had enough; in 1943, they sold the house and its farmlands to businessman Benjamin J. Cleland. By this time, the house had begun to fall into a state of disrepair, but appreciating its rich history, Cleland spent enormous sums to restore the house, helping secure its future for the next 60 years. The Cleland family raised livestock and grew crops, which were sold at markets. After Cleland's death in 1964, the farm was passed on to his family, with at least one member remaining there until the early 2000s.

ABOUT THE AREA

Woodburn Cottage and farm are an overlooked piece of Chatham's history. Having been built by the famous Henry Cunard, who took an interest in the property, it was perhaps George E. Fisher who promoted the farm to its province-wide recognition. For more than 160 years, the historic house survived fires, and with each new owner, it was given new life and significance. In 2008, a fire destroyed the house. The property goes unrecognized by most who pass its overgrown entranceway.

Found along Water Street, just east of Morrison Cove, the entrance is marked by two concrete pillars. The driveway brings the visitor to the farm itself, where two towering chimneys, surrounded by debris and a stone foundation, are all that is left of Woodburn Cottage. Nearby, remains of several wooden barns are still visible. As the area is periodically used for farming, when visiting be sure to follow any posted signs and remain respectful of the property.

WOODBURN CONSERVATORY: N 47.014780, W 65.495376

The area is accessed through the former hiking trails in Morrison Cove or nearby Water Street. The entrance (N 47.016589, W 65.495280) is approximately 1.5 kilometres south of Chatham. From there, a short walk along a partially paved road leads to the site.

6. RCAF Station Chatham

Chatham, Northumberland County

From the early 19th century, Chatham was a quiet fishing community built on the banks of the Miramichi River. However, at the outbreak of World War II, Chatham changed forever when a large air force base was constructed to its south. The region was ideal for an airfield. The flat, forested highlands above Chatham allowed for easy construction, it was located alongside a shipping port and railway, and the area was well known for clear skies and good weather. The airfield, completed in 1941, consisted of three 1,500-metre-long runways laid out in the shape of a triangle. At its north end was a large tarmac apron capable of hosting a variety of aircraft, several large hangars, maintenance buildings, and buildings needed to support the personnel stationed at the base. Named RCAF Station Chatham, the field came under the control of Eastern Air Command.

Later that year, the airfield was assigned to become the No. 3 Training Command, a RCAF school and training ground, which was

part of the British Commonwealth Air Training Plan. Their mission was to train pilots and aircrews before they were sent overseas to the war in Europe. Also assigned to the airfield was the No. 21 Elementary Flying Training School, designed to train pilots of small aircraft such as the Fleet Finch Mark II, and the No. 10 Air Observer School, which trained crews to navigate and operate wireless radio transmitters.

Training remained the primary mission of the airfield until 1942, when German U-boats were first spotted in the Gulf of St. Lawrence. Concerned about the risk these could pose to shipping and the ongoing war efforts, the No. 113 (Bomber Reconnaissance) Squadron, equipped with Lockheed Hudson coastal reconnaissance aircraft, temporarily used the base for hunting enemy submarines. By December, the airfield was no longer needed; however, the following year, another squadron, the No. 119 (Bomber Reconnaissance) Squadron once again used the airfield after more U-boats had been spotted in nearby waters.

The end of the war also brought the end of the Commonwealth Air Training Plan, along with the other schools established at RCAF Station Chatham. Following the war, the base was transferred to the War Assets Corporation, where it was placed on standby. This did not last long, and as tensions across Europe and in Asia grew in the following years, it became clear that the airfield's use was critical.

The airfield was reactivated on October 6, 1949, due to increasing tensions between the United States and the Soviet Union. That fall, the No. 421 Fighter Squadron and their de Havilland Vampire Mark III aircraft arrived at the airbase to be used for intercept fighter training in the event an enemy or unidentified aircraft entered Canadian airspace. These aircraft were some of the first jet-powered aircraft to call the airfield home and were joined by a squadron of North American F-86 Sabre jets. The base continued to be used for training; in conjunction with the nearby Pine Tree Line radar site at St. Margarets (page 156), it also remained on alert to intercept potential enemy or Soviet Union aircraft.

While tensions remained high, RCAF Station Chatham was introduced to a new type of fighter jet squadron. To celebrate both the 50th

anniversary of engine-powered flight in Canada and the 35th anniversary of the Royal Canadian Air Force, the RCAF introduced Canada's first aerobatic flying team, the Golden Hawks. Starting in 1959, this national team, made up of F-86 Sabre jet aircraft, called RCAF Station Chatham home for several years before being relocated to Trenton, Ontario. Nonetheless, Chatham remains proud of the claim that it was home to Canada's first aerobatic team, a legacy that helped establish the current aerobatic team well known as the Snowbirds.

At the height of the Cold War, the airfield experienced many changes. In 1962, a new 3,000-metre-long runway was added, and the former triangular airfield layout was abandoned. New facilities were constructed, and the base expanded. Soon after, the No. 416 All Weather (AW) Squadron, flying McDonnell CF-101 Voodoo aircraft, was stationed at the base, acting as a primary intercept squadron in the event of an attack. Additionally, in the fall of 1964, the upgrades allowed the airfield to become home to Detachment 4 of the USAF's 425th Maintenance Squadron. This special squadron oversaw maintenance and storage of the United States' warheads, including its nuclear arsenal. Thus, the airfield was assigned a controlled storage facility for nuclear weapons.

In the late 1960s, RCAF Station Chatham was renamed CFB Chatham. Over the following decade, activity at the airfield continued, but as radar and aircraft technology advanced, the need for many Canadian airfields declined. In 1984, the No. 416 AW Squadron was replaced by the No. 434 Tactical Fighter Squadron, which flew modern CF-5 Freedom Fighter aircraft. However, this change marked the beginning of a slow decline in activity at the base. The last major

change occurred on September 11, 1985, when a modern facility was built to host the Air Defence Artillery School. This school, along with the 119 Air Defence Battery, was established to train crews on ground-to-air weapons. This last endeavour ended in 1996 when the school was relocated to CFB Gagetown, where a large artillery range provided more space for training. This marked the closure of CFB Chatham.

ABOUT THE AREA

Many airfields and military bases were established across Canada at the outbreak of World War II, but few experienced CFB Chatham's level of activity. It played a crucial role in the British Commonwealth Air Training Plan while hosting submarine-hunting aircraft to protect shipping lanes in the Gulf of St. Lawrence. CFB Chatham also worked with the nearby advanced radar networks to seek out and intercept potential Soviet Union aircraft and ward off the risk of nuclear war, becoming, for a short time, a station for the transfer of nuclear weapons overseas. Finally, its legacy as a training facility ended before it closed.

A small portion of the airfield is still used as the Miramichi-Chatham Airport. However, much of the base, including its accompanying buildings, hangars, and large stretches of tarmac, have now been repurposed into industrial lots and housing. At its heart is a mounted CF-101 Voodoo aircraft that signifies just one part of the base's fascinating history.

RCAF STATION CHATHAM: N 47.01669, W 65.44468

The base is located along Route 11, just south of Chatham (now amalgamated into the city of Miramichi).

7. RCAF Station St. Margarets

St. Margarets

In the early 1950s, tensions between the United States and the Soviet Union escalated. As a result, the United States and Canada constructed a series of radar stations concentrated at similar latitudes. Stretching across North America, the northernmost of these was the Distant Early Warning Line. Below this line of advanced radar sites, at approximately 55 degrees latitude, was the Mid-Canada Line. Lastly, located roughly along 50 degrees latitude, was the Pine Tree Line. Operated jointly by the RCAF and the United States Air Force, these sites were the most advanced of their kind and would be the first system to detect Soviet aircraft or missiles threatening the two countries. In 1950, the decision was made to construct a Pine Tree Line radar station in New Brunswick. Looking for a relatively flat, northeastern location, the community of St. Margarets was selected, approximately 25 kilometres south of the World War II air force base in Chatham.

Construction began in 1950 on RCAF Station St. Margarets. Originally staffed by the 21 AC&W Squadron and the 2 Air Defence Control Centre (ADCC), the site eventually came under the control of the No. 2 Aircraft Control & Warning Unit, and in 1958, it changed its name to the 21 Radar Squadron. This Pine Tree Line radar station acted as an early warning station, capable of tracking an aircraft's speed, direction, and altitude. In the event an aircraft did not identify itself and/or posed a threat, the aircraft's data tracked at St. Margarets would be relayed to nearby military aircraft, which could intercept the unidentified aircraft. Three hundred military staff and nearly 100 civilians were employed to run this completely self-sufficient base.

The site was located immediately off Route 11, on what is now Edgar Street. A three-storey control centre oversaw site operations. On each side, large radar domes housed the station's search radar and height-finder radar. Surrounding this complex of buildings were multiple others,

including motor pools, stores, storage facilities, and, beyond that, the housing quarters themselves. In all, the establishment of the military site became a small town.

Innovations in radar and computer technology through the 1950s meant that more systems at the site were becoming automated. Like most Pine Tree Line stations in the early 1960s, the station adopted the Semi-Automatic Ground Environment (SAGE) System in September 1962. This cutting-edge technology allowed the data collected by the site's radars to be transmitted to a centralized operations base instead of being processed on-site. This central operations centre was located at Topsham Air Force Base in Topsham, Maine. However, like any automation system, this also reduced the need for personnel working at RCAF Station St. Margarets, and many people were laid off or deployed to other sites across Canada.

On February 1, 1968, the three branches of the Canadian military were merged, and RCAF Station St. Margarets became the St. Margarets detachment of CFB Chatham. At the time, many Pine Tree Line stations were being downgraded or even decommissioned. This was not the case for the St. Margarets site. In 1969, the St. Margarets Detachment was assigned as a Backup Intercept Control Centre for NORAD, which would become one of the longest lasting in the 22nd NORAD Region, an area that comprised most of northeastern North America. By the 1970s, the number of satellites and spacecraft orbiting the globe was also growing, and the site obtained a new designation in 1974: Satellite Tracking Unit (SITU). The site's role was to monitor and receive data from satellites as they passed overhead.

For a brief period between 1980 and 1984, the site had full control of the 22nd NORAD Region until a large, centralized underground facility could be finished at 22 Wing North Bay. Following this, and with decreasing tensions between the Soviet Union and the United States, the Department of National Defence announced the closure of the Pine Tree Line station. The final day of operations was April 1, 1988. It was not until 1989, when the STU was officially decommissioned, that site activity ceased completely.

The site's equipment, along with many of its buildings, were decommissioned and shipped to other sites around the country or scrapped completely. Since then, the site has been known as James Park, named after Air Vice Marshal Arthur Lorne James, who played an instrumental role in North American air defence during the early years of the Cold War. James Park is now a private subdivision that occupies the former living quarters area of RCAF Station St. Margarets. While some of its houses are relics of the Cold War era, many more are newly constructed. Empty, tree-lined roads, dead ends, and the outline of former building footprints are all that remain of this once crucial chapter in North America's defence history.

RCAF STATION ST. MARGARETS: N 46.909897, W 65.208649
The site of RCAF Station St. Margarets is located approximately 25 kilometres south of Chatham, along Route 11.

8. Kouchibouguac Hydroelectric Dam

Kouchibouguac, Kent County

Located along the Kouchibouguac River, just beyond the boundary of Kouchibouguac National Park, are the concrete remains of a small hydroelectric dam and powerhouse. The dam was one of the first of its kind when it was built in 1917, marking the beginning of a new form of electricity production in the province. But the story of the Kouchibouguac dam goes beyond power production; it is also the story of the O'Leary family, and more specifically, Richard O'Leary, whose vision it was to construct it.

Richard O'Leary was born in 1865 to Henry O'Leary and Mary Ann Brittain. Henry owned many businesses along the east coast of New Brunswick, including shipbuilding facilities, canneries, stores, flour mills, and sawmills. After attending school in Kent, New Brunswick, and Montreal, Richard O'Leary returned to the area in 1881 to manage his family's businesses in Chaleur Bay. In 1892, the businesses O'Leary was overseeing experienced financial trouble and subsequently shut down. O'Leary returned home and, after his father's death in 1897, he became the sole owner of the remaining family businesses.

The mid- to late 19th century brought new technologies capable of producing electricity from flowing water and transmitting that electricity over long distances via transmission lines. Intrigued by these innovations, O'Leary considered how he could implement this technology along the Kouchibouguac River. In 1917, he established the Richibucto & Rexton Power Company.

On the site of an aging flour mill, construction began on a large concrete dam that spanned 60 metres across the river and was more than 8 metres wide at its base. Two spillways at its centre controlled the flow of the river, redirecting the water into a short penstock on the river's north side. The penstock directed the water through the dam into a small powerhouse

adjacent to it. Here, the water flowed through a small turbine, producing electricity that powered houses and stores in Richibucto and Rexton.

The hydroelectric dam, one of the first of its kind in New Brunswick, provided the first power to its neighbouring communities. Despite this remarkable accomplishment, O'Leary became better known for his work establishing Kent County's telephone network, facilitating mergers between communication companies, and serving as a long-serving director of NBTel.

Shortly after the dam was completed, O'Leary passed his businesses to his son. Because he lacked his father's experience, the family's companies slowly encountered financial trouble. As a result, after Richard O'Leary's death in 1932, the family consolidated its assets and downsized. The dam and powerhouse were sold to New Brunswick Power in 1939.

The facility operated until 1953, when it was deemed too expensive to maintain and no longer viable, as larger hydroelectric facilities were being established in other parts of the province. Following its closure, the powerhouse was removed and the dam left to deteriorate.

As of 2025, the dam stands across the river, though a breach in its foundation allows water to flow freely through it. On the dam's north side, the remains of the powerhouse are visible, along with a keyhole-shaped hollow that marks the location of the former penstock.

KOUCHIBOUGUAC DAM: N 46.792767, W 65.057184
The town of Kouchibouguac is approximately 40 kilometres south of Chatham on Route 11. Before crossing the Kouchibouguac River Bridge, turn onto Power House Road. Continue driving for 150 metres to reach the dam.

1
2.2
3
6.4
2.1
Millville
Burtts Corner
4
Nackawic
6.1
Mactaquac
5
6.2
6.3
Canterbury
Graham Corner
Harvey
7
McAdam

Woodstock & the Saint John River Valley

This region follows the Saint John River from Fredericton to Woodstock, from the backcountry wilderness and lakes of southwestern New Brunswick to the rolling hills and farmland north of the Saint John River Valley. The area was first home to the Wolastoqiyik. The Saint John River provided access to the interior, leading to the establishment of sawmills, gristmills, and farms along its fertile banks. The region's proximity to the United States led to turbulence in the wake of American independence. After the Acadian Expulsion in 1755 and the American Revolutionary War, the British sought to solidify their control of the land by granting land rights to Loyalists and, after many years, establishing a clear and defined boundary with the United States.

Despite these efforts, population growth remained slow until new means of transportation in the early 1800s opened the area to industry and trade. Railways transformed the region into an important trade corridor with the United States, while new roads connected settlements and provided access to forests, farmland, and natural resources. In the 1830s, steamships began sailing the Saint John River, linking communities and facilitating commerce and travel. Large sawmills and lumber mills were established, many of which relied on the river's tributaries for power. Waterways such as the Meduxnekeag River, Nackawic Stream, and St. Croix River became some of the first in the colony to produce electricity, spurring new industries—including the ironworks in Woodstock.

The next major transformation occurred in 1967 with the construction of the Mactaquac Dam. This project flooded much of the river valley and displaced entire communities. The flooding had lasting effects on the region's physical and cultural landscape.

The region's natural beauty, cultural diversity, and proximity to the United States have contributed to a modest tourism industry. However, many travellers simply pass through as they follow the Trans-Canada Highway either east to Fredericton or north to Quebec. The Trans-Canada Highway runs along the south and west sides of the Saint John River

between Fredericton and Woodstock. On the north side of the river, a network of roads, including Highways 104 and 105, provides access to rolling hills, farmlands, and logging and recreational trails in the province's interior. South of the river, Highways 3, 640, and 122 access such historic communities as Harvey and McAdam. Near Woodstock, the Houlton border crossing—one of eastern Canada's busiest—marks the beginning of the well-known Interstate 95. Woodstock remains a hub for the region, with cultural landmarks, historic sites, and scenic river views set against the backdrop of the rolling, forested hills of the Saint John River Valley.

1. Meduxnekeag Dam and Powerhouse

Woodstock

Electricity was introduced to Woodstock earlier than to many other Canadian communities. By the 1880s, two electric light companies were operating in the small town, thanks largely to the local ironworks companies operating just north of it, near Lanes Creek. In March 1886, the Woodstock Electric Railway, Light and Power Company was incorporated, and in 1904, it began construction on a large dam and hydroelectric plant on the Meduxnekeag River, approximately 3 kilometres from the town centre. By this time, the Woodstock ironworks had shut down, so the power produced at the plant was used primarily to supply local businesses and houses.

An impressive structure, the dam stretched more than 100 metres across the width of the river. On the north shore, a concrete power plant was constructed to house two small Jenckes Machine turbines, each capable of producing 225 kilowatts of electricity. These turbines supplied electricity to the nearby town and manufacturing plants operating in the area. This required a consistent flow of electricity; to ensure the continuing operation in the event of a problem at the hydro facility, a 225-kilowatt steam-powered backup generator was installed at the power plant to ensure that no disruptions were experienced.

When it was completed in 1906, the $200,000 power plant was commissioned, making it the first hydroelectric facility in New Brunswick. It would be followed by many other facilities, which in 2025 power nearly one-quarter of the province's electricity needs. The power plant supplied power to Woodstock until 1923, when, in the spring, a large storm combined with spring runoff flooded the Meduxnekeag and Saint John Rivers. The floodwaters overwhelmed the dam and led to its collapse and complete destruction. On the north shore, the concrete powerhouse also received heavy damage, and numerous nearby houses and buildings were destroyed. The damage was considered too severe to rebuild, and thus ended the Woodstock Electric Railway, Light and Power Company's efforts to produce electricity.

Two years after the flood, Woodstock purchased the distribution and transmission lines belonging to the Woodstock Electric Railway, Light and Power Company, and these continued to be used to power the town.

Large wooden beams and cribbing are still visible at the dam site. Along the river's north bank, the remains of the concrete powerhouse are visible beneath the Trans-Canada Highway bridge, which crosses the Meduxnekeag River. Inside the structure, conduit and piping are the only remnants of the building's former use. Although many swim and fish in the river nearby, the area has been all but forgotten. The remains of the powerhouse and dam are a lost piece of history.

DAM AND POWERHOUSE: N 46.163316, W 67.608572

The safest way to see the former dam site is to start at the trailhead of the former New Brunswick Railway Trail (N 46.151105, W 67.597704) and walk north for approximately 1.5 kilometres. The ruin is visible across the river at the base of the Trans-Canada Highway bridge. Alternatively, leave the Trans-Canada Highway at Exit 185 and turn west until Scott Street. A trailhead is at the end of Scott Street (N 46.166491, W 67.608605); follow the treeline south to the river. As no official trail exists, knowledge of the area is crucial.

1925

2. Relics of the New Brunswick Railway in Woodstock

Woodstock

In 2021, a granite stone culvert along the historic New Brunswick Railway made news when it collapsed into Shaws Creek. The beautiful culvert, one of the few remnants of the railway, had become a destination for explorers and history enthusiasts. Its loss and replacement by a modern steel culvert was a blow to the area's built heritage. But the culvert is not the only fascinating relic that can still be found along the province's now-defunct historic railways.

The New Brunswick Railway (known as the New Brunswick Land and Railway Company until 1881) was constructed between Fredericton Junction and Edmundston, passing through Millville, Woodstock, Hartland, and other towns. Constructed between 1871 and 1873, the railway was largely supported by businessman Alexander Gibson, who sought new ways to access his large timberland reserves. In 1886, a new section of the New Brunswick Railway connected Woodstock to the main line passing through McAdam and continuing to Maine. These railway lines eventually closed in the mid-20th century due to the growing use of transport trucks and road travel.

Bulls Creek Stone Culvert

Since then, these sections of railway have been converted into recreation trails, popular among ATV users, cyclists, and hikers. Few people are aware of the many historic structures along the former railway track. One of these historic wonders is found on Bulls Creek, west of Woodstock. Similar to the culvert at Shaws Creek, the Bulls Creek culvert would have originally been made of cut granite stone, around 1886. It was repaired in 1926 with the addition of a new concrete wing wall at both its entrance and exit to reduce erosion. The original granite blocks lining the tunnel are still visible. Along the railway, other historic culverts are still found, and while some have been replaced to ensure the safety of trail users, others remain in or near their original condition.

BULLS CREEK CULVERT: N 46.107449, W 67.625616

The culvert is located on the former railbed, now turned into a recreation trail. From the trailhead (N 46.102914, W 67.628782), hike 550 metres; descend a steep embankment to the culvert.

Sharp Island Bridge

One of the more obvious relics of the New Brunswick Railway is the Upper Woodstock Railway Bridge, sometimes referred to as the Sharp Island Bridge. Constructed in the mid-1870s, the bridge, comprised of two sections, provides critical passage over the Saint John River. From the west side of the river, the truss bridge spans 300 metres to Sharps Island, then the railbed continues for 225 metres to a 160-metre-long section of bridge connecting the island to the east side of the river.

The bridge received regular use but, by the 1980s, fewer trains used this section of track. In 1987, high water and ice destroyed two of the bridge's spans on the river's east side. With declining railway use, Canadian Pacific, which had taken over the line in 1890, announced that it would not reconstruct the bridge. Since that time, residents have attempted to pressure the government to rebuild the bridge's missing spans and turn the structure into a pedestrian, ATV, and snowmobile bridge. As of 2025, no work has commenced on the quickly deteriorating bridge.

SHARP ISLAND BRIDGE: N 46.178430, W 67.561223

View the bridge from Highway 105, on the east side of the river. Park along the highway (N 46.178413, W 67.560709) and follow a short path to the bridge.

3. Houlton-Woodstock Tourist Bureau

Richmond Corner

Highway 95 between Woodstock and the Canada-United States border in Houlton, Maine, has long been acclaimed as the busiest border crossing on the east coast of Canada. The American side of the border marks the beginning of the 3,100-kilometre-long Interstate 95, which runs from Maine to Miami, Florida. The border crossing has long served as a major entry point for goods and supplies, as well as for tourists visiting the province. Because of this, the New Brunswick tourism department established a tourist bureau on the highway.

The now abandoned Houlton-Woodstock Tourist Bureau sits atop a grassy hill overlooking the quiet highway, a nod to the important role tourist bureaus and information centres played in developing the province's tourism industry.

A tourist bureau existed in downtown Woodstock at least as early as the 1930s. These bureaus promoted and developed tourism in the province; they were also places to buy local crafts, artwork, and other products. Because the original Woodstock Tourist Bureau was downtown, away from the nearby highway, in the late 1960s local tourism promotion groups pushed for a new location on the Trans-Canada Highway, near its intersection with Highway 5, the main highway between Woodstock and the border crossing at Houlton.

Interstate 95 was completed to Houlton in 1968 and the area experienced a drastic increase in the number of people using the border crossing, soon turning it into the busiest border crossing in eastern Canada. In 1974, the three- and four-lane Highway 95 was opened, replacing the smaller Highway 5.

Construction began in 1975 on a new tourist bureau, 5 kilometres east of the border crossing, one of several tourist bureaus constructed alongside provincial highways, all of which were completed by the summer of 1977. The one-storey structure was supported by steel

and wooden beams and featured a wooden exterior. The building had a grass-covered roof, which improved insulation and absorbed stormwater runoff, and symbolized the province's connection to nature. The building was designed to catch the attention of highway drivers.

The 340-square-metre tourist bureau is situated on 11 hectares of forested land, along with a large playground, a wooden fort replica, and walking trails. Built atop a small hill, the building was surrounded by large, well-maintained lawns, parking lots, and picnic areas. Completed in the spring of 1977, it cost $1 million. While the bureau promoted sites across the province, it was regularly reported that the most frequently asked-about destination was the world's longest covered bridge in the nearby town of Hartland.

The bureau experienced a steady number of visitors in the decade following its opening. Operated by a mix of full-time staff and summer students, it operated exclusively during the tourist season between June and October (eventually reduced to August). By the mid-1980s, it had an average of 12 visitors per day, far less than originally expected. The low number was blamed on poor advertising of the tourist bureau's services and its lack of visibility from the nearby highway. Despite this, it operated for more than 40 years.

By 2010, tourist bureaus across the province struggled to attract visitors, with many tourists using the Internet and social media to plan trips instead of visiting information centres. With dwindling numbers, in 2018 the Department of Tourism and Infrastructure closed the Houlton-Woodstock Tourist Bureau, and the building was declared surplus and put up for sale the following year. In 2022, the building was sold to the Fredericton-based Atlantic Ambika Group for $323,000. Since then, the building and its land have remained vacant, with its future uncertain. Meanwhile, the building overlooks Highway 95, still greeting visitors as they enter the province.

TOURIST BUREAU: N 46.154547, W 67.717146

The land and building are now on private property and its accessibility is subject to change. Abide by any posted signs. To get to the building, travel 15 kilometres west on Highway 95 from the Trans-Canada Highway near Woodstock. Take Exit 7 to Richmond Corner and turn onto Tourist Bureau Road. The building is at the end of the road. It can also be safely viewed from the side of Highway 95, approximately 5 kilometres east of the Houlton-Woodstock border crossing.

4. Pinder Dam and Sawmills

Temperance Vale

Below the former Canadian Pacific Railway (CP) bridge in the community of Pinder is one of the last surviving relics of its sawmills. The first settlers of the area were quick to use the river's fast-moving water to power sawmill and gristmill machinery. It is believed that since at least the mid-19th century, a series of mills have operated on the stream. Local resident Daniel Lucy established the first notable operation in the late 19th century, constructing a dam at the top of a small waterfall where water could be redirected into the mill. This early mill was constructed on the river's north bank and ground locally grown wheat into flour. The operation was relatively small, and the river's potential soon caught the attention of James K. Pinder.

Born in Yorkshire, England, Pinder immigrated to Canada in 1849 and settled in Temperance Vale, where he partnered with Lucy. Lucy retired shortly thereafter, leaving Pinder as the sole owner. On August 2, 1869, the New Brunswick and Nova Scotia Land Company, the British governing corporation for managing land in the two provinces, awarded Pinder the mill and its surrounding lands. Shortly after Pinder's acquiring the mill, a fire in a nearby barn destroyed the mill and surrounding buildings. Determined to restart the mill, Pinder took the mill's machinery to Fredericton to be restored. On his return, he constructed a new mill, this time focusing on lumber instead of flour. The lumber mill employed many more people than its predecessor, both in the mill itself and in logging nearby forests. Alongside the mill and neighbouring storage sheds, Pinder built a boarding house for the mill's seasonal workers.

Logs were floated down the river and accumulated behind the dam. From there, a sluice gate redirected them into the mill, where they were processed before being transported to market. At first, the mill's machinery worked by water flowing through a turbine directly connected to the mill's saws. In the early 20th century, Pinder installed

a dynamo at the mill, which produced electricity from the rotating turbine, similar to a modern generator. The mill was not without its problems, however. Low water levels during the late summer and ice jams during the winter regularly halted production.

The lumber mill was located on the north side of the stream, while, on the south side, a woodworking factory, shingle mill, and lath machine were eventually constructed. The mill produced a variety of products, including long lumber (lumber longer than standard lengths), fence posts, shingles, wooden windows, and crates. By 1910, Pinder, who then operated the mill in partnership with his son, George Thomas Pinder, was praised in the industry for providing jobs and exceptional products, which soon led him to gain the name "King of the Nackawic."

In 1910, Pinder and his son incorporated the Pinder Lumber Company. Looking at ways to expand his operations in Temperance Vale, Pinder petitioned the government to build a railway from Millville to the community. His request was approved, and he received the land grants he needed. Work on the railway began shortly after this. By 1912, the railway had reached the community, providing residents with a new means of travelling to nearby centres, receiving supplies and goods, and, for Pinder, a means of shipping his products to larger markets. The railway line would eventually be purchased and run by CP.

James and George Pinder's mill remained successful throughout the 1920s and 1930s. James represented the county in the Legislative Assembly as both a representative and warden on the county council. In 1929, James Pinder died in his home in Temperance Vale. Just five years later, in 1934, George died. Following his death, the mill was passed on to George's son, Edison Pinder.

On March 16, 1936, a sudden release of water caused by an ice jam on the river destroyed the dam and many structures downstream, including a steel bridge at Cullerton. To restore power to the mill, Edison rebuilt the dam that summer, using steel acquired from the destroyed Cullerton bridge. The mill was operational by the end of the summer.

In 1941, Edison sold the Temperance Vale mill and its lands to Harry

A. Corey, who continued to operate the mill. The mill proved profitable, and after undergoing several upgrades, it continued to operate for the next 20 years. Tragedy struck in the early 1960s when a fire in the mill destroyed it completely. At this time, smaller sawmills were beginning to struggle to compete with larger mills being constructed around the province. Because of this, Corey decided not to rebuild. After more than 100 years, a mill no longer operated at the site. While all the former buildings have been torn down or destroyed, the concrete dam, foundations, and waterfall attract the attention of those passing through the tiny community.

PINDER DAM AND SAWMILLS: N 46.045112, W 67.237911

The best place to view the abandoned structure is from the adjacent ATV/snowmobile trail. Park along the Highway 605 in the community of Pinder (N 46.044375, W 67.237531) and hike 50 metres along the trail to the Nackawic Stream Bridge.

5. Monument One

Monument Brook, Richmond Parish

The international border between the United States and Canada was once one of the most contentious issues facing the two nations—one that almost caused the outbreak of several wars. One tangible reminder of this time is hidden in the backwoods of Richmond Parish. Named Monument One, this large cast-iron marker sits atop a concrete foundation in the middle of a forested bog. The marker, one of the first permanent structures to signify the border's location, symbolizes the turbulent story of how the border, specifically the section between New Brunswick and Maine, came into existence.

The border between the United States and the British colony that would form Canada was established in part following the Revolutionary War between Great Britain and the Thirteen American Colonies. The Treaty of Paris, signed on September 3, 1783, acknowledged the independence of the United States and described the placement of the border separating the two countries. Article II of the treaty stated that the boundary would follow the St. Croix River to its headwaters on a small brook named Monument Brook. There, the boundary would take a sharp turn north and continue straight until it reached the highlands. From there, it would proceed west, following the path of the watershed divide between the the St. Lawrence River and the Atlantic Ocean. Despite much effort in surveying the boundary, the nondescriptive term "highlands" and an unclarified watershed boundary were debated for some time. The British argued that the highlands were the hills northwest of Florenceville-Bristol, where the river would follow the hills into the Aroostook River Valley in what would become the state of Maine. Meanwhile, the United States argued that the highlands were located closer to the St. Lawrence and would follow the hills toward the St. Lawrence. This controversy led to the Aroostook War between 1838 and 1839. Although no actual conflict broke out, the incident led to the signing of the Webster-Ashburton Treaty of 1842 and the Treaty of Washington in 1846, which solidified the modern border.

Before 1843, a simple marker made of iron hoops placed around a yellow birch tree marked the start of the "North Line." In 1843, to secure the border claim, a permanent obelisk was installed at the headwaters of Monument Brook. This square pillar with a triangular top was made of cast iron and was the first permanent monument placed on the border between the two nations. The monument, while off the beaten path, marks the beginning of an almost 125-kilometre-long line north to the Saint John River, northwest of Grand Falls. Monument One represents an often-overlooked turbulent time in Canada's formation, and while it joins many other places along the border that caused conflict and contention, once Monument One was established and the agreements finalized, it represented the first monument on the longest, peaceful, and undefended border in the world.

MONUMENT ONE: N 45.943442, W 67.781234

This location is difficult to access. From Route 540, approximately 2 kilometres south of the community of Kirkland, turn onto Monument Drive. Drive 3.5 kilometres to an unmarked, unmaintained road (N 45.951302, W 67.764439). Follow the road for approximately 1.8 kilometres, making sure to abide by any private property signs. There is no designated trail to the site; leave the road near the trailhead (N 45.942652, W 67.778633) and loosely follow a flagged path through the forest. A difficult trek through wetland and bog is required to reach the site. The border follows the stream through the area and should not be crossed at any point without consulting the United States Customs and Border Protection and the Canada Border Services Agency.

6. The Flooding of the Mactaquac Reservoir

Saint John River—Keswick Ridge to Woodstock

The mighty Mactaquac Dam, located on the Saint John River, is one of the Maritimes' great engineering marvels. Situated 19 kilometres upstream of Fredericton, the dam was built by the New Brunswick Power Commission (now New Brunswick Power) and has six Kaplan turbines, capable of producing 672 megawatts of electricity, or approximately 12 per cent of New Brunswick's power demand. As the Maritime provinces transition to cleaner sources of electricity, the Mactaquac Generating Station has grown in importance, not just for New Brunswick but also for Nova Scotia and Prince Edward Island.

Despite being built to supply New Brunswickers with reliable power, construction of the Mactaquac Dam was controversial, as it required the flooding of extensive areas of land, including the inundation of homes, farms, and entire communities. With the flooding, the area lost countless historic and cultural sites, forever changing both the physical and the social landscape of the valley.

When the demand for energy spiked in the second half of the 20th century, the decision was made to take advantage of the long-recognized hydroelectric potential of the Saint John River. For thousands of years, the Wolastoqiyik people had fished, hunted, and gathered along the river. Following colonization, small settlements were established, but it was not until the British began encouraging large-scale settlement in the area following the American Revolutionary War that the region's population grew. From the late 1700s to the mid-1900s, many settled along the river, establishing farms, sawmills, and gristmills. Prior to the dam's construction, the river meandered through the valley, interspersed with large low-lying islands and surrounded by gently sloping banks, making it ideal for agriculture and navigation. By the time construction began, many small working communities had already been established along the river, and the area even supported a notable tourism industry.

Before construction, a massive expropriation and relocation effort took place. More than 300 buildings and more than twice that number of families living in the flood area were forced to relocate. Many houses and farms were moved to higher elevations nearby, while larger structures and those unable to be safely moved were demolished. The relocation disrupted the lives of thousands of people. Construction of the dam began in 1965 and was completed in 1968. In that year, the dam's gates were shut, impounding the river and allowing for the slow flooding of the upstream reservoir. Over the course of several weeks, the reservoir consumed the low-lying areas of the valleys, including homes, communities, and a network of roads, bridges, and railway lines. The narrow, gently flowing river that at one time barely exceeded 250 metres wide was now a 96-kilometre-long reservoir, which reaches widths of more than 1 kilometre at some sections. Covering approximately 84 square kilometres, the reservoir rose to an elevation approximately 40 metres above the former river surface.

The flooding of the reservoir had far-reaching impacts on people, ecosystems, and the physical landscape of the area. Small streams and tributaries flooded, forming large inlets and bodies of water, such as Longs Creek, Kellys Creek, and Mactaquac Stream, located next to the dam itself. The river's many islands, including Snowshoe Island, Wheelers Island, Long Island, and Great Bear Island, disappeared within a few days. New communities were formed from the relocation of houses and people. The best example of this was the town of Nackawic, which was a planned government town formed following the reservoir flooding to provide a new home to relocated families. A pulp and paper mill constructed in the town became the major employer and one of the highest users of the electricity produced by the hydroelectric facility itself.

Over time, those who were forced to flee their houses and livelihoods found new places to call home; however, the impact of the flooding will not soon be forgotten. Nor will its effects on the landscape, as the banks of the river reveal countless landmarks that once belonged to the communities of the Saint John River Valley: partially submerged bridges and foundations, roads and railway lines that plunge into the reservoir itself, and the concrete remains of industries and buildings along the shores. The Mactaquac Reservoir provides many curious locations to explore, each of which tells a piece of the story and impact of the flooding of the Mactaquac Reservoir.

Submerged Roads and Railways

Before the Mactaquac Reservoir was flooded, a network of roads in the valley provided access to homes, farms, and a route between Fredericton and Woodstock. Because most of the people in the region had settled along the riverbanks, most roads were built parallel to it. In 1968, when the reservoir was flooded, roads that were less than 40 metres in elevation were engulfed.

The Saint John and Quebec Railway line, which connected Saint John with the NTR in Grand Falls, met a similar fate. Built between 1912 and 1914, this line was purchased by CN in 1929. From the time it was finished, the railway became an important connector, transporting supplies and passengers across the region. Passenger service on the line

ceased in 1952, and in 1967, CN closed the line to freight shipments in anticipation of the reservoir's flooding. Similar to the roads in the area, the railway line was built along the river where the flat terrain made for easy construction and avoided steep inclines. Most of the railway line was quickly flooded.

Even though the flooding occurred over 50 years ago, signs of these flooded roads are still visible throughout the region. Jackson Road in Keswick Ridge, Longs Creek Road in Longs Creek, and Upper Pokiok Road in Pokiok now wind through forests and neighbourhoods before disappearing into the reservoir.

JACKSON ROAD, KESWICK RIDGE: N 45.991243, W 66.900494
LONGS CREEK ROAD, LONGS CREEK: N 45.868586, W 66.929077
UPPER POKIOK ROAD, POKIOK: N 45.959818, W 67.249046

Shogomoc Cove Bridge

Shogomoc, York County

Prior to the flooding, larger bridges that spanned the river were demolished. This was the case for Hackshaw Bridge, located south of Nackawic. Nearby, a new cable-stayed suspension bridge was built, which is still in use. Throughout the flooded area, many smaller single-span bridges provided safe passage for residents across the Saint John River and its many tributaries. Deemed too expensive to be removed, many of these bridges still exist beneath the waterline.

Six kilometres west of the community of Pokiok, on the Shogomoc Stream, is one of the reservoir's best-kept secrets. During normal water levels, two set of parallel concrete railings rising from the water mark the location of the Shogomoc Stream Bridge. Just below the surface, the single-span concrete bridge is isolated in the middle of Shogomoc Cove. It is possible to swim to the bridge and walk along the deck; as a result, it has become a popular swimming location and tie-up for recreational boats.

Before it was flooded, the bridge supported one of the main roads

connecting Fredericton and Woodstock. Since then, this road has been replaced by Highway 2, 750 metres to the south. Despite the road's abandonment, the area has slowly gained popularity as a park and picnic spot. The bridge and road are now part of the Trans-Canada Trail. In October 2011, an 80-metre-long suspension bridge was built across the cove, next to the former Shogomoc Stream Bridge, restoring the link across the stream which had been disconnected since 1968. The bridge's visibility depends on the reservoir's water levels, but it can usually be seen from the shore, if not from the adjacent suspension bridge.

SHOGOMOC COVE BRIDGE: N 45.956430, W 67.330101
From the southside of Hawkshaw Bridge in Pokiok, drive 4.6 kilometres west on Pokiok Road. Near the end of the road turn north onto Lower Shogomoc Road, a narrow, forested road. Continue for 2.2 kilometres to the bridge site.

Pokiok Falls and Lodge

Pokiok

Not everything lost during the flooding of the Mactaquac Reservoir was human-made. On Pokiok Stream, parallel to Hackshaw Bridge Road, is the now submerged Pokiok Falls, a 12-metre-high cascade waterfall. For many years, the landmark was widely known by locals and a beloved

tourist destination. The falls were located at the bottom of a narrow slot canyon, just 9 metres wide, with towering 23-metre-high sides. Not only were the falls appreciated by tourists but, for a short time, a mill atop the canyon used the waterfall to power its machinery. Nearby, a bridge was built in the early 1910s to accommodate the crossing of the Saint John and Quebec Railway line. The gorge is still visible, along with the former abutments of the Saint John and Quebec Railway bridge. Although the gorge is not nearly as deep as it once was, it continues to be used as a swimming location, albeit a dangerous one, as strong underwater currents are still said to flow deep beneath the surface.

In 1927, the falls' popularity caught the attention of George T. Pinder and his son Edison of Temperance Vale (page 190), who built a tourist lodge, restaurant, and cabins on the west side of Pokiok Stream. The one-and-a-half-storey wooden building overlooked the river, which visitors could enjoy from a deck wrapped around its front. Surrounding the lodge were small cabins; to ensure that the lodge had a reliable source of water, a large concrete storage tank was placed at its rear. The lodge operated successfully for many years and was a popular stop for travellers between Fredericton and Woodstock. The Pinders eventually sold the lodge, and it had several owners before 1968. Prior to flooding, the lodge was located atop a steep riverbank, high above the flowing river. However, once the reservoir filled, the waters slowly crept to the base of the lodge. The lodge had closed the year before flooding began, and many of the surrounding cabins were dismantled and sold to be used as sheds or personal cabins. Eventually, the lodge itself was torn down, officially marking the end of tourism in Pokiok.

The foundations of Pokiok Lodge are still visible; the paved Upper Pokiok Road juts into the river before disappearing beneath the surface. At the end of the road, trails lead through the woods, bringing visitors to the lodge's foundations. In the surrounding woods are several other artifacts from this time, including the two-storey concrete water tower, on the hill above the lodge. Although they are easy to overlook, the foundations scattered throughout the forest are the last remnants of the region's tourism industry.

The Trans-Canada Highway used to follow Pokiok Road. Above the site of Pokiok Falls and Lodge, the parking lot of an abandoned Irving gas station and nearby motel are still visible, along with remnants of the gas station's sign. If one is travelling west, it is possible to drive a large portion of the original paved highway, which was realigned several hundred metres to the south. The abandoned highway stretches for about 5 kilometres, with other empty lots along the way.

POKIOK GORGE: N 45.959743, W 67.247238
UPPER POKIOK ROAD TERMINUS: N 45.959794, W 67.249085
POKIOK LODGE: N 45.959971, W 67.248068

The Pokiok Lodge and Gorge are visible from the end of Upper Pokiok Road. From Hackshaw Bridge on Highway 102, turn onto Pokiok Road and drive 1.2 kilometres. Turn onto Upper Pokiok Road and drive to its end. Trails through the forest lead to the lodge and gorge, now a popular but dangerous swimming location.

Island Park

Woodstock

Despite being 80 kilometres upstream of the Mactaquac Hydroelectric Dam, the town of Woodstock did not escape the effects of flooding from the dam's construction. Prior to the flooding, buildings, houses, and businesses located along the river were either torn down or moved, and many of the bridges that spanned the Saint John and Meduxnekeag Rivers were either demolished or extended to accommodate for the larger body of water. The most significant loss to the town was Island Park, a 1.7-kilometre-long, 250-metre-wide island once located in the middle of the river.

Island Park had long been used by the Wolastoqiyik, as a summer camp and fishing outpost. After the American Revolutionary War, European settlers arrived in the area, many of whom were awarded land grants in exchange for their war service. One of these was Jacob Smith, who is believed to have been the first settler to take control of the island and surrounding land, in 1784. Aside from its use as a fishing outpost and possibly some farming, little development occurred there. In 1884, a steel bridge was constructed across the Saint John River, spanning King Street in Woodstock to Connell Park, before continuing to the east side of the river in Grafton. As the island gained popularity around the turn of the century, a ramp was built from the bridge to the island.

Around this time, the island was purchased by Allison B. Connell and his family, with the intent to transform the island into a public park. The island, which became known as Connell Park, was frequented by locals and tourists during the summer. As the island's popularity grew, so too did its attractions. By 1910, it hosted a baseball field, several picnic areas, and amusement park rides.

In 1918, the Carleton County Agricultural Society signed a lease

to use the island as the new home of their local exhibition. The society installed a horse racetrack and a 2,500-person grandstand. Nearby, a two-storey, 1,500-square-metre barn was built, with plenty of space for cattle, sheep, and pigs. The racetrack was used primarily for harness racing, where a two-wheeled cart was attached to horses that raced around the oval track. The exhibition grounds brought new life to the island and more attractions. The most popular of these was a miniature railway, installed in the early 1920s, which led around the island and its grounds. Around this time, the island became known as Island Park.

When World War II broke out in 1939, the island was used as a training ground. Even before Canada declared war, the grounds were prepped to become a training ground for soldiers. On September 1, the Carleton York Regiment, a unit of the Third Brigade, First Canadian Division, arrived in Woodstock and began training to head to the war in Europe. The establishment of the training grounds temporarily paused public access to the island.

Island Park reopened in 1946 and provided entertainment and amusement to the residents of New Brunswick until the mid-1960s. With construction of the Mactaquac Dam under way, the island's amusements and buildings were sold, relocated, or demolished. This included the Grafton Bridge, which was removed in 1967. After the reservoir was flooded, the large, forested island, once surrounded by rushing waters, gradually became part of a calm, unobstructed waterway.

In the waters off Woodstock, two small, uninhabited islands are all that remain of Island Park. Each was a high point on the original island: the southern island, the picnic area; and the northern island, the exhibition barn. A line of concrete blocks and partly submerged foundations are the remnants of Island Park still above the waterline.

ISLAND PARK: N 46.144301, W 67.568158

While it is possible to view the islands from the Woodstock walking bridge (N 46.147790, W 67.572313), they are best viewed from a boat; it is 400 metres from Woodstock in the middle of the Saint John River.

7. McAdam's Historic Railway Relics

McAdam

The town of McAdam could be described as being in the middle of nowhere. Situated in the province's forested interior, it is not located on any major highway and or near any major communitities. However, this historic town along Highway 4, between the town of Harvey and the border crossing at St. Croix, played a vital role in the development and operation of the province's earliest railways and trade relations with the United States. The once-thriving railway junction was known as the "Gateway to Atlantic Canada." Its history and story are preserved in the town's architecture and several relics that remain in the railyard, including the majestic McAdam Railway Station.

Until the mid-1800s, the area was uninhabited, except for several logging camps. McAdam can trace its origins to this period, when it was first referred to as City Camp. The area was opened up with the construction of the St. Andrews and Quebec Railway around 1869, followed by the CP line in 1871. Five years later, the junction's name was officially changed to McAdam Junction. It was the first and last settlement encountered by trains entering and leaving Canada, and a large railyard equipped with maintenance shops, fuel storage, and a train station was soon built. McAdam Junction was a stop for up to 16 trains a day, boasting a population of 400, all of whom relied on the railway as a source of income.

Between 1900 and 1901, the McAdam Railway Station was constructed. Designed by Edward Maxwell and W.S. Painter, the three-storey granite châteauesque building became an icon in the growing town. Throughout McAdam, many architecturally designed buildings showcased the town's wealth and class. Throughout the early 20th century, the railyard and its repair facilities were upgraded.

But by 1950, the popularization of diesel locomotives, more reliable railcars, and modern railway construction practices meant

that the town's significance to the railway industry had declined. By 1960, most of the railway infrastructure in the town had been abandoned, and while the railway remained in use, most trains now passed through the town instead of stopping.

The historic character of the town, however, remained largely untouched. While the population has steadily declined since 1950, the town boats a collection of historic buildings, the largest of which is the McAdam Railway Station. Although no longer used as a passenger station, it was named a national historic site in 1990 and has since been maintained and preserved as a museum and event space. For many years, the train station (which once served as a hotel) claimed to have the best Boston cream pies in Canada. The museum serves pies

(including Boston cream pies) on select days throughout the summer. From beautiful architecture to abandoned railway lines and even a pedestrian tunnel under the active railway line, McAdam, a hidden gem in New Brunswick, is home to a fascinating collection of historic infrastructure from its once-thriving railway era.

MCADAM'S RAILWAY RELICS: N 45.590061, W 67.329130

McAdam lies south of the communities of Longs Creek and Harvey. From Harvey, drive 32 kilometres south on Highway 4 to reach McAdam. The best time to visit McAdam is during the tourist season, while the McAdam Railway Station is operating.

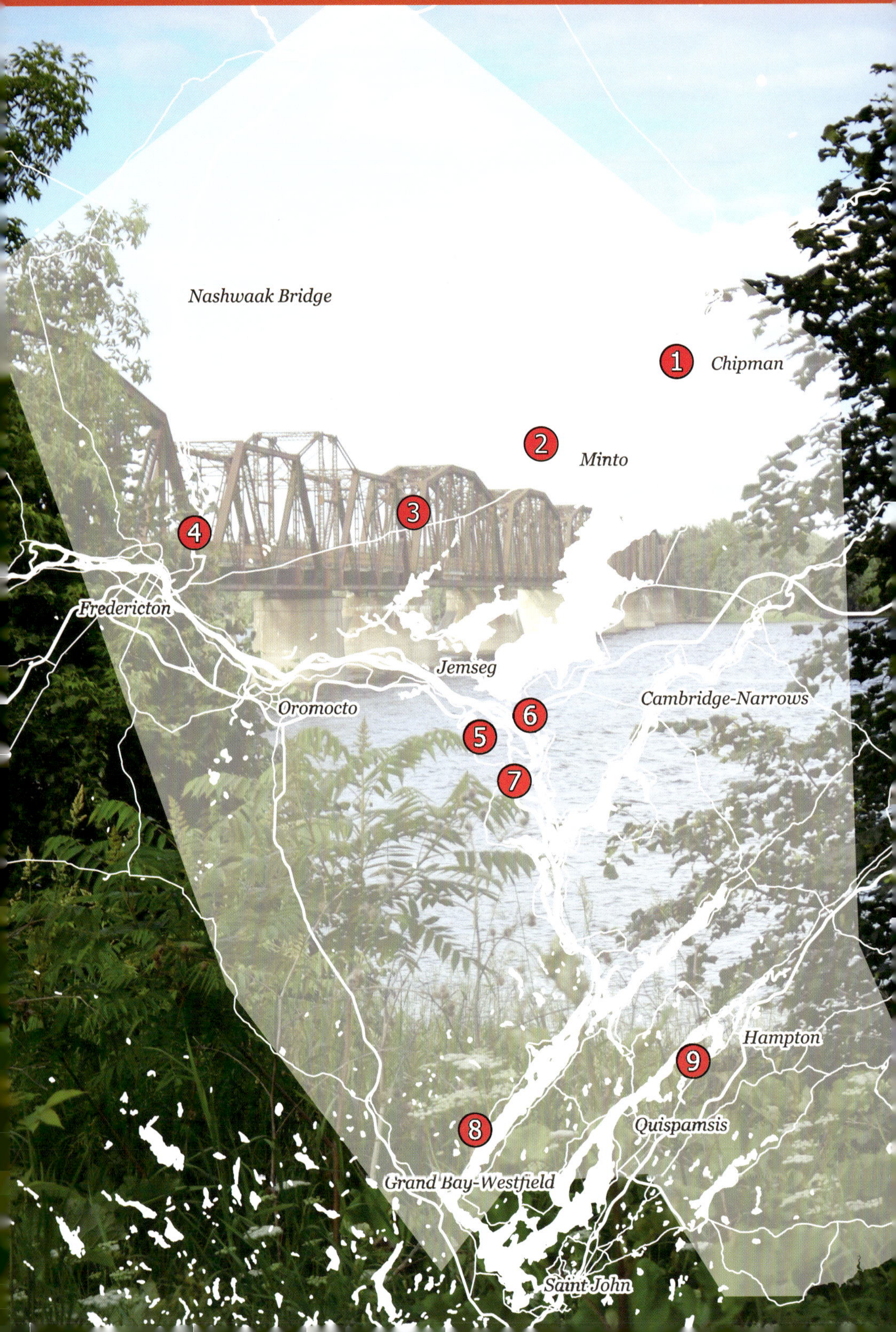
Nashwaak Bridge
1
Chipman
2
Minto
3
4
Fredericton
Jemseg
Cambridge-Narrows
Oromocto
6
5
7
Hampton
9
8
Quispamsis
Grand Bay-Westfield
Saint John

Fredericton & the Lower Saint John River

This region stretches from the province's capital city, Fredericton, down the Saint John River, encompassing Grand Lake and the historic towns of Oromocto, Jemseg, Gagetown, and finally Grand Bay-Westfield in the south. The areas surrounding the Saint John River were first home to the Wolastoqiyik. The ability to navigate the river from the ocean at Reversing Falls allowed European settlers to explore the interior. From the mid- to late 1600s, Acadian settlers established communities and fortified settlements along the river, most notably at Fort Nashwaak near modern-day Fredericton. Around this time, coal was discovered on the shore of Grand Lake, and soon shipments were sent to markets in the northeastern United States, marking one of the earliest exportations of the province's minerals.

The region was plagued by war and atrocities during the 1750s as British colonizers laid claim to the land. The subsequent Acadian Expulsion ushered in a new era of settlement, with land grants being awarded to British Loyalists. In 1785, Fredericton was declared the capital of the colony. The first major communities developed along the Saint John River, Grand Lake, and their tributaries. In these settlements, gristmills and sawmills were established; others engaged in agriculture and livestock farming. Unlike the upper reaches, the lower Saint John River is wide and slow-moving. Wetlands and fertile fields, which regularly flooded, created difficult terrain to traverse but provided ideal conditions for a thriving agricultural industry.

As the populations of Fredericton, Saint John, and the communities along the river expanded throughout the 19th century, a steamship service was established. These vessels initially played a crucial role in transporting cargo, goods, and passengers but later evolved to support the region's growing tourism industry. This diversification of industry led to expansions in manufacturing, transportation, and mining. At the beginning of the 20th century, new railway lines facilitated the regular mining of the Grand Lake Coalfields and establishing Chipman as the centre of brickmaking in the province. The region now relies primarily on agriculture and forestry.

Travelling the area today is easier than during the steamship era

of the Saint John River. The Trans-Canada Highway (Highway 2) intersects the region, passing through Jemseg before continuing to Oromocto and Fredericton. Farther north, Highway 10 runs through the interior forest from Fredericton to Chipman, while Highway 8 follows the Nashwaak River north to Boiestown and Doaktown. Along the Saint John River, Highway 102 provides the best views of the lower Saint John River, following it south toward Grand Bay-Westfield and passing through Gagetown, Evansdale, and other towns. On the river's east side, a network of quiet roads winds through isolated farmland and forests before reaching the Kingston Peninsula and the Kennebecasis River in the south.

1. Chipman Brickworks

Chipman

Chipman, located near the mouth of the Salmon River on the north side of Grand Lake, was established because of its location on local waterways and its access to the forests of interior New Brunswick. By the late 19th century, several sawmills provided employment. And even though the forestry industry helped establish the community, its growth was due to nearby coal mining operations (page 206) and its location at the intersection of two railways. These factors helped to establish Chapman's best-known industry: brickmaking.

The story of Chipman's brickmaking industry begins in 1861 when Robert Shaw started a brick plant in Hantsport, Nova Scotia. As populations and communities grew, so too did the demand for building materials such as bricks. Additionally, rebuilding efforts following the Great Fire of Saint John in 1877 and the Great Windsor Fire of 1897 dramatically increased the demand for bricks made at Shaw's brickworks. With the support and knowledge passed down by his father, Shaw's son Lloyd E. Shaw took over another brickyard in Bridgetown, later expanding into Middleton.

Operating under the name L.E. Shaw Limited, the brickyards provided dozens of jobs. Demand for bricks spiked again after the Halifax Explosion in 1917. By 1920, Shaw's operation experienced challenges in finding competitive-quality shale and clay for brick production. Outcompeted by higher-quality products from Ontario and Quebec, Shaw prospected new sources of shale and clay. Chipman quickly proved to be an ideal location because of its proximity to railways and the area's supply of high-quality shale. Strip mining in nearby coal mines had already excavated reserves of shale, which needed to be removed to access the underlying coal beds. Because of this, a substantial amount of rock was readily available.

In fall 1928, construction began on several large beehive kilns,

moulding and shaping buildings, drying sheds, and storage warehouses. The plant, adjacent to local railway lines, was renovated to accommodate the shipping of bricks throughout the Maritimes, New England, and Quebec. The successful operation did experience setbacks, including difficulties processing the high carbon content of the region's shale and a temporary closure during the Great Depression. However, the brickyard continued to expand, with the plant regularly being upgraded to incorporate the newest machinery and equipment. This included switching the kilns from burning coal to Bunker C fuel in 1953, and the installation of six large shuttle kilns in 1980, which increased the plant's efficiency and output.

Despite the company's success, by the 1980s demand for bricks was decreasing, and the plant struggled to compete with larger brickworks in eastern Canada. In 1978, ownership of L.E. Shaw Limited transferred from the Shaw family to the company's nine managers. The Shaw family continued to play a role in the company, now known as Shaw Group Limited, through Allen Shaw, Lloyd E. Shaw's grandson, who later became its president. However, citing challenging market conditions

and an aging plant, on January 9, 1990, the company announced the plant's shutdown the following month. The announcement devastated the community. In 1991, the plant was demolished, leaving only trace remains of the once-prosperous industry.

Scattered along the New Brunswick Central Railway route are pieces of machinery, large concrete foundations, and the partially buried remains of the plant's kilns. The Shaw family's company and brickyards had a lasting influence on neighbouring communities and the built environment of many major towns in Atlantic Canada. The bricks made at Chipman, proudly bearing the words "Chipman, Made in Canada," are found in nearly every town in the Maritimes, from the historic buildings of Halifax to the brick streets of Moncton.

CHIPMAN BRICKWORKS: N 46.171519, W 65.880219

The site of the brickworks is now intersected by multiple recreation and ATV trails. From the end of Shaw Street or across the street from the Chipman Centennial Arena, the site can be accessed by exploring the local ATV trails.

2. Minto Coalfields

Minto, Grand Lake

Coal was reportedly first discovered in the Minto area in the mid-1600s, with the first shipment to colonies in New England soon after that. But it was not until the 1820s that Minto's coal seams were recognized and studied in depth. When coal reserves were confirmed, large-scale mining began, and by the middle of the 19th century, regular shipments of coal were being floated by boat down the Saint John River.

In 1893, a comprehensive survey conducted in the area estimated that it contained 50 million tonnes of ore located within a 15- to 45-metre-thick layer of rock. The survey revealed that the ore lay just 1.5 to 5.5 metres below the surface: it was relatively accessible without necessitating deep and expensive mineshafts. The New Brunswick government funded the expansion of the Central New Brunswick Railway, from its terminus in nearby Chipman, through to Minto and on to Fredericton. The railway, completed to Minto in 1904, opened up the isolated region to new business and facilitated the easier delivery of advanced coal mining machinery.

Large-scale strip mining soon commenced, with mining companies clearing vast stretches of land before using steam-powered excavators to remove the overlying soil and bedrock, reaching the coal layer below. In 1917, draglines, large excavators that used a boom and hoist to excavate massive quantities of gravel with a suspended bucket, were introduced. These machines, which increased the amount of land that could be razed and mined, excavated long trenches of rock, placing the waste rock alongside in narrow, consecutive piles. These piles have become a feature of the area's landscape. Once excavated, the coal was transported to market by railway or by ship on nearby Grand Lake and the Saint John River.

At the turn of the 20th century, the Minto coalfields were producing just over 10,000 tonnes of ore annually, which increased to 98,000

tonnes by 1914. Production peaked during World War I when up to 260,000 tonnes were being produced; following the war, this decreased to approximately 215,000 tonnes, which remained consistent over the next two decades.

As the mine expanded, so too did the population of Minto and the surrounding area. While most people came for employment opportunities, they were often greeted with dangerous working conditions. The use of large mechanical excavators for strip mining and several ongoing underground mining operations were causes for concern. Over time, the Minto coalfields became a centre for worker unionization and a long fight for safer working conditions and fairer pay ensued.

In 1930, New Brunswick Coal was one of the last mining companies operating in the area. It was a subsidiary of the publicly owned New Brunswick Electric Power Commission. Looking to increase electricity production, and having an abundance of coal, the company constructed the province's first coal-fired thermal generating plant nearby on the shores of Grand Lake. The two-unit generator began producing electricity in 1931, which supplied nearby communities with power, thus helping to grow new industries in places such as Fredericton. In the years following, two additional units were added.

Throughout the 1930s, the Minto coalfields experienced more human-intensive, underground mining operations. This helped the area thrive during the Great Depression, with more than 1,200 people employed by the mines just before World War II. As machinery advanced, draglines were reintroduced as the primary source of mining, with modern draglines excavating to the deep coal seams. Large-scale strip mining continued through the 20th century, with coal being used nearby

to produce electricity or being exported for use in railway operations and smaller generating plants around the province.

In 2000, New Brunswick Coal was the coalfields' only customer. As environmental and climate change awareness became more pronounced, the coal being extracted at Minto was found to have a tragic flaw. In addition to the carbon released from burning the coal itself, the coal had high concentrations of sulfur and mercury, which were damaging to the surrounding environment and air quality. The Grand Lake Generating Plant was described for a while as the "dirtiest power plant in Canada." In 2010, the power plant and the coalfields' last customer were shut down. Shortly after that, mining at the Minto coalfields was also halted.

The massive coal-excavating draglines are gone, and most of the area that was previously razed and strip-mined has been reclaimed by nature. Despite this, sequential patterns of long, narrow piles of waste rock and interspersed linear trenches are visible throughout the region. These trenches are the most notable remnants of the former mining operations. Throughout the reclaimed mines are pieces of equipment and steel. Meanwhile, in the town of Minto are many relics of the mining industry, including historic architecture, interpretive signs, and monuments to the mine's impact.

One of the most notable reminders of the mining operations is the colour of the many ponds and water-filled trenches that were created by the mining. Light reflecting off fine sediment suspended in the water give the ponds a bright blue appearance, resembling water in the Caribbean rather than in the interior of New Brunswick.

MINTO MUSEUM AND INFORMATION CENTRE: **N 46.075441, W 66.073585**

FORMER MINE SITE: **N 46.079448, W 66.120602**

The best way to explore the former mining operations is by hiking or cycling the area's mountain biking trail system. A popular trailhead (N 46.075592, W 66.105312) is at the end of New England Road on the west side of Minto.

3. B70 Internment Camp

Ripples, Sunbury County

On the side of the road between Fredericton and Minto on Route 10 lies a strange concrete structure. Exploring further reveals the start of a short trail system that winds through a former World War II internment camp. After Allied governments questioned the loyalty of Jewish refugees fleeing Europe, they were detained in camps throughout Canada, such as this one. This dark period in Canada's history is now preserved by the New Brunswick Internment Camp Museum, where the story of these refugees is remembered.

HISTORY

The history of the site does not begin in World War II. During the Great Depression, unemployment reached new heights, and in a desperate attempt to create make-work projects, the government of Canada established a nationwide network of "relief camps." First conceived in 1932, these camps provided temporary employment, primarily for young men who were desperately looking for work. One camp was established in this location, as it provided easy access to the province's interior forest and a local railway line. Overseen by the Department of National Defense, workers were given housing and food and instructed to clear bush, log forests, plant trees, and build roads. Although the camp provided temporary relief for unemployed workers, it was controversial, and was shut down in 1936. Following its closure, the camp remained dormant.

Three years later, World War II broke out in Europe following Nazi Germany's aggressive expansion into neighbouring countries and the commencement of its genocidal campaign against those it deemed "undesirable," primarily targeting Jewish, Romani, disabled, and other marginalized groups. As the onslaught intensified, many fled to England. British prime minister Winston Churchill, uncertain about the refugees'

loyalty, turned to the Commonwealth countries of Australia and Canada to aid in housing and detaining them temporarily. The two countries reluctantly agreed with Churchill's request, and in 1940 the first wave of refugees arrived in Canada. Upon their arrival, they were sent to 26 internment camps built across Ontario, Quebec, and New Brunswick.

In New Brunswick, the former Depression-era relief camp near Ripples was selected as one of these camps. It occupied 6 hectares and was surrounded by layers of barbed wire fencing. Surrounding the perimeter were six towers, each with machine guns, spotlights, and guards. In total, it is believed that more than 50 buildings were located on the site, with 14 inside the detainment area, used for barracks, living accommodations, a mess hall, library, and recreation area.

On August 13, 1940, 711 Jewish refugees arrived at the camp. Comprised mainly of men and young boys, they were each paid a small wage to cut wood and lumber in the surrounding forest. By the following spring, the refugees were no longer deemed a potential threat. They were given the option to join the war effort or find a sponsor and remain in the country. Many of those detainees were doctors, lawyers, artists, and business owners, and after being released, they contributed to the war effort and/or made Canada their home. This brief period in Canada's history is still considered to be one of its most shameful and dark chapters.

By the end of June 1941, work began on upgrading the vacant camp's security to accept prisoners of war, mainly German and Italian soldiers. After defying the federal government's mandatory military service requirements, Montreal mayor Camillien Houde was confined at the site. In July 1941, the first of these prisoners of war arrived and occupied the site until September 1945.

ABOUT THE AREA

The area has been preserved and is overseen by the New Brunswick Internment Camp Museum, located on Route 10. A short trail and interpretive signs lead visitors along the perimeter of the overgrown

camp. Throughout the area are concrete supports, manholes, culverts, and levelled areas that mark the sites of camp buildings. The most visible remnant is the concrete structure that once housed the camp's water tank.

B70 INTERNMENT CAMP: N 46.008431, W 66.262282

The camp is approximately 33 kilometres northeast of Fredericton, on Route 10. A small parking lot marks the beginning of a short and accessible trail around the site. While it is free to visit, consider donating to the New Brunswick Internment Camp Museum to help maintain and preserve the site and its history.

4. Historic Marysville

Marysville, Fredericton

The historic town of Marysville is north of Fredericton on the Nashwaak River. For centuries, it was home to lumber mills that used the river to transport logs and generate power. A registered National Historic Site, the town features a collection of nearly identical brick buildings surrounding the centrally located 1885 Marysville Cotton Mill. The visionary behind the buildings and mill was Alexander Gibson, known simply as "Boss."

In the mid-19th century, the town was named Rankin's Mill, with the Rankin Lumber Company's lumber mill its primary industry. In 1862, entrepreneur and lumberman Alexander Gibson took over the mill and the company's forestry rights and operated it for the next 20 years. Although profitable, Gibson shifted his focus to textiles. In 1883, he hired B. Mooney & Sons to construct a large brick cotton mill on the east side of the river; it opened in 1885 and became the region's most prominent industry. The mill's size and location reflected the industry's prominence in the area; rising four storeys above the Nashwaak River, it stood out against the surrounding landscape. The mill was constructed primarily from bricks made locally at a small brickyard established by Gibson. It housed the most modern equipment, including electric lighting—making it one of the earliest adopters of this technology.

Gibson managed the business until 1906, when he retired and sold it to the Montreal-based Canadian Cotton Company. The new company successfully operated the mill between 1906 and 1954 and exported products across North America. In 1954, a new owner purchased the mill, but increasing competition and changing market conditions gradually made the historic mill obsolete. The mill closed in 1980 and was sold to the provincial government, which renovated much of it into offices.

COTTON MILL: N 45.978229, W 66.589237

Brick Town

While the cotton mill provided many stable, high-paying jobs and attracted families to the area, its infrastructure could not support the influx of people. During construction of the cotton mill, Gibson built 15 residences for mill workers. By 1891, another 50 brick houses had been constructed. These structures transformed the town into an assortment of brick buildings.

Comprising duplexes and single dwellings, each building was flat-roofed and symmetrical. Boasting an Italianate architectural style, the buildings were designed to be efficient and functional. Within just 20 years, the parcel of empty land on the east bank of the Nashwaak River had become a busy community, with a maze of brick homes, tightly packed together.

BRICK TOWN: N 45.980391, W 66.586702

Marysville Dam

Although the community of Marysville became synonymous with the textile industry, the forestry industry continued to thrive in the area. The nearby Nashwaak River was a source of power and a route for floating logs from the river's remote origins in interior New Brunswick to collection points closer to Fredericton.

In the early 20th century, the Nashwaak Pulp and Paper Company became one of several companies relying on the river for log drives. It also planned to build a new mill at the river's mouth and use the river as a power source. Although this mill was never completed, the company constructed a large concrete dam across the river at Marysville to control water levels for log drives. Completed in 1920, the dam measured 80 metres in length. Water spilled over most of the dam, while upstream booms directed logs to a sluice gate, where they were either collected by trucks or floated farther downstream.

The dam replaced a previous wooden crib dam that washed away during high water and ice conditions in 1912. The river's ice jams and spring runoff frequently damaged the concrete dam. In its first year, high water levels and a log jam caused unexpected erosion of the riverbank, which damaged a nearby railway line and resulted in a train derailment and the deaths of two operators.

By the 1940s, calls to remove the dam grew louder as concerns mounted over its impact on fish populations. Despite ongoing concerns and continued erosion, the dam was not removed until September 1992, when the Department of Natural Resources, which had acquired it in the 1960s, demolished the main structure and spillway. Diamond Construction, the company responsible for the dam's removal, left a small section of the dam and its sluice gate on the river's western bank. A large block of concrete is still visible several metres into the river, and the former sluice gate and channel can be explored along a former rail trail.

MARYSVILLE DAM: **N 45.984706, W 66.591442**
The dam is located along the railbed-turned-recreation-trail. From the Mill Street trailhead (N 45.980706, W 66.592070), walk north 450 metres to the site.

5. Mount House Ruins

Gagetown Island

Across the waters from the town of Gagetown lies Gagetown Island, a 7.63-square-kilometre island that, like the surrounding area, barely rises above the Saint John River. For hundreds of years, the fertile lands of this region have supported agriculture and livestock. At the heart of the island, a peaceful channel provides access to its interior. At its centre, embedded in a small embankment, are the ghostly remains of a large, two-storey stone house. Speculation over its history has included claims that it is the oldest building in New Brunswick, belonging to the area's first settlers. While this is likely untrue, the house remains a relic of the early European settlement in the Saint John River Valley.

One of the first permanent settlers in the area was John Kendrick, who built a house and cleared the island to establish a farm around 1767. In 1783, James Peters arrived, established the town of Gagetown, and eventually purchased Kendrick's land. By the end of the 18th century, the Peters farm was known as "Intervale Farm," an English term referring to a farm on the low-lying banks of a river. When Peters died in 1820, the farm, renamed Mount Ararat Farm, passed to his wife and family. Historians believe that the house on Gagetown Island was built between 1808 and 1811 and occupied by Peters's son

William Tyng Peters. William Tyng served in the local militia and later passed ownership of the land to his brother, Valentine Peters, who, in partnership with Charles Jeffery, continued to operate the farm.

Several years after his father's death, Thomas Horsfield Peters began purchasing the lands divided among his brothers. By 1837, he had acquired the lands allotted to his brothers James and Harry, and with Valentine's death that same year, he secured most of Gagetown Island. William Tyng is believed to have retained ownership of the house and neighbouring buildings until Thomas purchased them in 1853. Thus, the original lands were re-amalgamated, and the farm continued to operate.

After Thomas Horsfield's death in 1880, the farm passed to one of his sons. The house was abandoned sometime in the late 19th or early 20th century, with the family likely relocating to nearby Gagetown. Photographs from the early 1920s show that the house had already fallen into disrepair. In 1923, the Peters family sold the farmland, ending nearly 140 years of occupation. Although the land continued to be used for crops and livestock, it is believed that the new owners did not live on the island permanently.

The once-beautiful house on Gagetown Island has deteriorated further. Constructed from sandstone blocks sourced from nearby quarries, the thick walls and large brick chimney ensured warmth during the harsh winter months, when the island was nearly inaccessible due to river ice. A large barn once accompanied the house, its foundation also made of sandstone, though the wooden structure has long since decayed.

Since the Peters family's departure, the fertile land of Gagetown Island has been used by local farmers, including members of the Moore and Campbell families. The historical significance of the house was first recognized in 1932 by the York-Sunbury Historical Society. The beautiful trees and vibrant wildlife are reason enough to visit Gagetown Island, but the ruins of Mount House add a layer of intrigue and a glimpse into the lives of the region's early European settlers.

MOUNT HOUSE RUINS: N 45.789101, W 66.127964

6. Jemseg River Bridge

Jemseg, Cambridge Parish, Queens County

A national highway to connect the country's major cities was first proposed in 1912; however, it was not until personal vehicles became popular after World War II that the idea became reality, and soon major construction projects were under way across the country. The New Brunswick segment of the new Trans-Canada Highway would run from the town of Edmundston, through Woodstock, Fredericton, and Moncton, crossing many large rivers along the way.

The original route of the highway was to cross the Saint John River in Fredericton before continuing along the north side, following the modern Route 105. From there, the highway would cross the Jemseg River before continuing to Moncton.

At the time, the only way across the wide river was a steel truss swing bridge built in 1919. Like the Saint John River, this waterway was frequented by large ships traversing into New Brunswick's largest lake, Grand Lake. Although the swing bridge could accommodate the passage of ships, it was deemed too small and slow for the increased traffic expected on the Trans-Canada Highway. The solution: build a bridge with enough clearance to allow the passage of ships beneath, while above traffic could flow uninterrupted. Work began on a 24-metre-high, 650-metre-long concrete bridge in the late 1950s; it opened to traffic in 1960.

The bridge remained the primary crossing of the Jemseg River for the next 40 years. As the number of travellers increased, the need for improvements to the size and alignment of the highway through the area became apparent. Because of this, in 2001 the highway was realigned, and a new bridge was constructed 175 metres north of the original. Opened in October 2002, the new bridge drastically decreased the amount of traffic along the old bridge, which remained open as a secondary crossing for Route 105.

Over the next 10 years, the bridge did not receive the maintenance needed to prolong its life. In October 2013, an inspection determined that it should be closed for major rehabilitation work. Despite this report, the provincial government kept the bridge open. One and a half years later, in May 2015, another inspection resulted in its immediate closure due to the public safety risk. Officially closed on May 22, traffic was detoured around the bridge while the government decided if it should spend the estimated $3 million needed for rehabilitation. The price tag proved to be too high. The following year, netting was installed in places at risk of crumbling concrete, and the concrete spans at each end of the bridge were removed to ensure that people could not climb on them.

Since then, the bridge has continued to deteriorate. A close look at the bridge reveals exposed rebar and small pieces of fallen concrete on the ground surrounding the bridge. The large concrete structure is worth visiting, as its crumbling concrete contrasts with the surrounding lush wetlands. In terms of size, the Jemseg Bridge is one of the largest abandoned structures in the province.

JEMSEG RIVER BRIDGE: N 45.827432, W 66.115388
The Jemseg Bridge is best viewed from the eastern banks of the Jemseg River. Exit the Trans-Canada Highway at Exit 339, drive north along Grand Lake Road for approximately 400 metres. Turn left onto Marine Drive and continue for 700 metres, then turn onto a narrow dirt road (N 45.830996, W 66.113157). Continue down the short road to the river and bridge lookout.

7. Reid's Sawmill Smokestack

Gagetown

South of Gagetown, an odd rectangular tower rises above the treetops. This is all that remains of Reid's Mill, a sawmill that once operated on the banks of the Saint John River.

The mill began in the early 20th century when brothers Frank and Richard Reid acquired timber rights for an area west of the community. By

1917, they had constructed a large sawmill at the site, taking advantage of the river as a source of transport for cut logs and the location's proximity to the local "Valley Line" railway, which transported cut logs to markets.

In 1935, a fire in the mill nearly destroyed it. It is said that the only thing still standing was its smokestack. The fire consumed much of the mill's cut lumber. The sawmill was not rebuilt until 1941. In 1948, the mill changed hands, and while members of the Reid family remained involved in its operation, the mill came under the ownership of the recently incorporated Gagetown Lumber Company.

The new company operated the mill for only five years when the Canadian government began considering the region as a potential site for a new military base and training area. The establishment of Camp Gagetown required the expropriation of over 1,100 square kilometres of land, nearly half of which made up the Gagetown Lumber Company's timber resources. Although the company was compensated for its loss, the mill was forced to shut down, as it was no longer deemed economical to run.

ABOUT THE AREA

The square, 27-metre-tall smokestack is all that remains of Reid's Mill. At the base of the 1.8-metre-wide smokestack, the housing of the mill's furnace and boiler are also visible. The concrete chimney is lined with fire-resistant brick believed to have been exported from Scotland.

The smokestack has been recognized for its historic significance to the town of Gagetown. Exterior steel bars have been added to provide reinforcement to the aging concrete, and at its top, mesh screening protects the opening edges of the smokestack. The stack and the land that once belonged to Reid's Mill are now private property.

REID'S SAWMILL SMOKESTACK: N 45.762428, W 66.140796

Drive approximately 2 kilometres south of Gagetown, and turn onto Old Mill Road (N 45.759940, W 66.148916). Continue to the end of the short road to see the smokestack. As the site is located on private property, remain respectful to those living nearby.

GAGETOWN
1928

8. Steamship-era Wharves of the Saint John River

Saint John River

The majestic Wolastoq, more commonly referred to as the Saint John River, has been a vital waterway for travel and navigation through the inland regions of New Brunswick for centuries. It was long home to the Wolastoqiyik, who used the river to provide food and a way to navigate the forested interior. European settlers arriving in New Brunswick throughout the 17th and 18th centuries were drawn to the area for its rich forestry and agricultural lands. Described by settlers as the "Rhine of North America," an influx of immigrants quickly took advantage of the river's navigable waters.

At first, the boats traversing the river would have been not much larger than the birch bark and dugout canoes used by the Wolastoqiyik. But as the population along the river increased, so did the agriculture, logging, and mining industries. In 1816, steamship were introduced; they moved people, supplies, resources, and products to the many communities, farms, and mines along the river.

The first steamship, the *General Smyth,* set sail on May 20, 1816; it began a new era of transportation along the inland waterway. After leaving the city of Saint John, it travelled nearly 300 kilometres of river channels, opening up the interior like never before. The *General Smyth* quickly demonstrated its practicality and efficiency in transporting people and goods along the river, and soon multiple companies constructed their own steamships to sail the river.

This necessitated wharves for loading people and supplies in those communities that lined the river. The wharves, built in the mid- to late 19th century, were made of timber cribbing and filled with rock, both readily available materials.

By the 20th century, upgrades were needed to these wharves. Between 1925 and 1935, approximately 37 wharves were constructed of

reinforced concrete. Each consisted of two wharves—a high- and a low-water wharf—to account for the river's regularly changing water levels. The wharves ranged in size, with most being approximately 20 to 30 metres wide and extending 10 to 30 metres into the river. Bordered by triangular barriers, these concrete platforms frequently featured one or two varying levels, often allowing access to the water through inclined or staircased ramps.

As ice plagued the Saint John River during the winter, steamship service was limited to the ice-free season between mid-spring and late fall. Within this period, dozens of steamship made daily trips up and down the river.

As road and railway networks improved into the mid-20th century, reliance on steamship declined. This, combined with safety concerns, eventually marked the end of the service. The last steamship, the *D.J. Purdy,* made its final trip in 1946.

Following the end of the steamship service, the wharves were taken over by the Canadian government. In 1997, the government forfeited

maintenance and upkeep of the wharves, giving them to local citizens and heritage preservation organizations. The Saint John River Society took ownership of 12 wharves to provide free access to the water and to preserve these reminders of the Saint John River steamship service.

Although no large commercial or passenger ships sail in these rivers, the Saint John River continues to be an important waterway for recreational boaters and outdoor enthusiasts. Driving along this hidden wonder, it is impossible to miss the many concrete wharves still protruding into the waters, frequently visited by fishers and swimmers and by those looking to admire the spectacular views of the historic Wolastoq.

PUBLIC LANDING WHARF: N 45.406798, W 66.194805
CAMBRIDGE-NARROWS WHARF: N 45.829484, W 65.953026
UPPER MAUGERVILLE WHARF: N 45.868589, W 66.448917

While some of the wharves are now private property, many remain abandoned or under the ownership of local historic preservation groups. Check before visiting and follow all signs and warnings.

9. Wreck of the SS *Majestic*

Darling Lake

In 1816, the first steamship, the *General Smyth,* to sail along the Saint John River ushered in a new era of transportation in New Brunswick that would last 126 years. Along the river, many artifacts from this period are still visible; however, none are as significant as the broken and jagged pieces of steel on the shores of Darling Lake. Here lies the wreck of the SS Majestic, one of the river's last steamships.

The *Majestic* began its life on the Richelieu River. Built by Polson Iron Works in Toronto, the ship was launched on December 12, 1899. Owned by the Richelieu River Navigation Company, the 33.5-metre-long, 6.7-metre-wide ship was sailed to Saint-Jean-sur-Richelieu, where it travelled the Richelieu River into Lake Champlain. The ship was specifically designed for northern rivers. Capable of handling 955 passengers, it had a strong steel hull, which, in addition to its powerful coal-burning compound steam engine, meant that it could easily handle the icy conditions often experienced in the colder months. Despite this, the ship's new owners experienced troubles in its first few years of operation and were forced to sell it in 1902 to the Star Line Steamship Company of Saint John.

The *Majestic* arrived on the river in the spring of 1902, where it became the first steel-hulled steamer and the first screw-propelled passenger steamer on the Saint John River. Once in service, the ship made regular trips between Saint John and Fredericton, as well as up the river's many tributaries, transporting passengers and supplies between communities. The ship's time with the company was once again short-lived, and in 1911, the *Majestic* was sold to the Crystal Stream Steamship Company, owned by Jemseg-born Daniel J. Purdy. Operating in tandem with the *Crystal Stream* and *D.J. Purdy,* the ship continued its trips on the Saint John River.

The *Majestic* became known for its reliable and continuous service.

However, it did not escape all troubles. In the winter of 1912, while tied to a wharf in Indiantown, an onboard fire caused extensive damage to its cabin and superstructure. With the summer season drawing closer, the Crystal Stream Steamship Company had the ship rebuilt immediately, restoring it to its original design, with the exception of the ship's wheelhouse, which was rebuilt on the top deck, having previously been located within the superstructure.

Another setback occurred in 1914 when the ship's engine boiler cracked, leading to the installation of a new engine configuration, changing it from a standard compound engine (where steam is expanded twice to power it) to a triple-expansion steam engine, adding additional steam expansion to the process, making the engine more fuel-efficient and increasing its performance.

In the 1920s, distinguished steamship captain and Sheffield native Charles Taylor partnered with businessman Harold B. Gault to purchase controlling shares in many of the river's steamships, hoping to build on the booming industry. In 1923, the two purchased the *Hampton,* followed by the *Premier* in 1925. Finally, in 1927, the duo purchased a 75 per

cent share in the *Majestic* from the Crystal Stream Steamship Company. The ship continued operating along the river as normal. In 1929, Taylor sold the ships to the Eastern Canada Coastal Steamship Company, who continued to operate the original steamship routes along the river. Taylor's son, Donald, sailed on the *Majestic* and other ships now owned by the new company, acting as mate, purser, and spare captain. Donald Taylor eventually wrote many books on the steamships of the Saint John River, helping to preserve the era's history.

Through the 1920s and 1930s, the Saint John Steamship service slowly declined. The construction of roads and the popularization of the automobile meant that steamship service was no longer as important as it once was. The Eastern Canada Coastal Steamship Company struggled to make the service viable. Steamships such as the *Majestic* were relegated to shorter routes. In 1938, the *Majestic* was making one trip per week to Chipman on Grand Lake and two trips to Coles Island. In November 1942, the *Majestic* made its last trip, becoming the last steam-propelled passenger ship on the Saint John River. The diesel-powered *D.J. Purdy I* operated until September 30, 1946, when 130 years of shipping service ended on the Saint John River.

Following its last trip, plans were to turn the *Majestic* into an entertainment and dance hall. However, before modifications could be made, a strong storm blew through the region on September 11, 1948, breaking the ship's moorings, causing it to drift into Darling Lake and run aground. The ship was eventually burned and left to deteriorate on the shores of Darling Lake near the community of Nauwigewauk. However, its shape, including remnants of its engines and hull, are still visible on the shores of the lake.

WRECK OF THE SS *MAJESTIC*: N 45.486097, W 65.882437

As the ship remains surrounded by private property, the easiest way to see it is from the water. By boat, depart from the Darling Island Bridge (N 45.480790, W 65.897719) and travel west for 2 kilometres into Darling Lake. The ship is on the shore, at the south end of the lake.

Lawrence Station
Oak Bay
6
8
St. Stephen
7
St. George
5
4
3.3
3.2
3.1
2
1
Lepreau
Maces Bay
Blacks Harbour
Lords Cove
9
Campobello Island
Grand Manan

Southern Fundy Shore

Stretching from the Musquash Estuary to the rushing tidal waters of Passamaquoddy Bay and the St. Croix River, the southern reaches of the Bay of Fundy, along with its many coves, rivers, and islands, form one of the most scenic coastal landscapes in Atlantic Canada. The region was one of the earliest to be settled, thanks in part to its access to the fishing grounds of the Bay of Fundy and Gulf of Maine, but also because of its location alongside the international border with the United States. As Canada's southern neighbour grew in population, so too did trade between the two countries, helping establish such communities as St. Stephen and St. Andrews. The region's history and culture have long been influenced by fishing and shipbuilding, with settlements established in nearly every little cove and protected harbour. The shoreline is relatively flat and rocky, with forests beginning at the waterline and continuing far inland. Combined with the region's high tides and rivers, which created natural dry docks, few places in Canada are better suited for shipbuilding.

The area's rivers—including the St. Croix, Magaguadavic, Lepreau, and Musquash Rivers—have long been used as sources of power for small mills and, later, for generating electricity for Saint John and elsewhere. The St. Croix was home to one of the first hydroelectric developments in Canada, which helped power large pulp and paper mills along the river. Farther inland, the landscape flattens and provides a habitat for vast forest biomes. Near Lake Utopia, slow-moving inland

waterways have become a haven for cottage owners and recreational boaters, while in Pennfield the flat terrain provided the necessary location for military training facilities. One of these facilities was an airfield established to train pilots heading to Europe during World War II, as the area replicated the foggy coastlines of the British coast.

The Trans-Canada Highway loosely follows the coastline from Saint John to the border crossing at St. Stephen, bypassing many of the smaller coastal roads that wind along the intricate shoreline. Close to St. Stephen, rural communities stretch far inland; this is one of

the few in the province where farming and logging remain dominant. South of the town of St. Stephen is St. Andrews, a popular summer destination for international visitors. Several roads lead north from here, with Highway 3 from St. Stephen and Highway 785 from St. George providing access to areas farther north, such as Fredericton. The mouth of Passamaquoddy Bay is filled with islands; Deer Island, Campobello Island, and the outermost Grand Manan Island are accessed by ferries.

1. Wrecks and Scuttled Ships of New Brunswick's South Shore

Saint John to St. Stephen

New Brunswick is more often associated with forestry products than with its maritime history. But the waters surrounding the province have long been a means of travel, fishing, and economic growth for the many people and communities along its coast. Nowhere in the province demonstrates this more than the jagged stretch of coastline between the city of Saint John and the town of St. Stephen.

The Mi'kmaq and Passamaquoddy peoples have long used the region's rivers and inner coastline for travelling and fishing. Settlers, including the Acadian people, later established settlements along the coast, using its protected harbours and easy access to the bountiful fish stocks of the lower Bay of Fundy.

In the early 19th century, a new industry emerged. The coast offered easy access to the region's plentiful forests, and the Bay of Fundy's extreme tides meant that a natural dry dock was created every 12 hours at low tide. As communities grew, wooden shipbuilding was established in nearly every major settlement. By the mid- to late 19th century, wooden ships were being replaced by larger, steel ocean-going vessels, and the industry slowly declined.

Throughout the 20th century, this region underwent many changes: communities grew and roads were built to connect coastal settlements; fishing remained vital but shipbuilding diminished rapidly. Additionally, the small cargo vessels that had delivered goods and supplies along the coast were slowly made redundant by larger, ocean-going ships that delivered cargo to ports such as Saint John, where it was then distributed by truck.

Relics offering insight into the maritime history of New Brunswick are in nearly every corner of the province, but the many shipwrecks and remains of abandoned vessels along its southeast coast are perhaps the most striking.

One of these relics is found in Lorneville, where, at low tide, the skeleton of a wooden schooner is visible on the north side of the harbour. At its peak, Lorneville harbour would have been filled with fishing vessels, many of which were themselves built there. One of the most prominent boatbuilders was Walter Wilson, who had a boatbuilding workshop near the wreck. Despite the harbour's natural protection, in 1961 a breakwater was constructed on its east side to mitigate against damaging northeast winds. Little is recorded about the schooner, but it is believed that Wilson grounded the ship in the 1940s or 1950s to provide protection for his wharf. Other stories suggest that the ship ran aground during a hurricane.

The keel and ribs of the approximately 40-metre-long schooner stick out of the mud, a ghostly reminder of the historic town of Lorneville.

A similar mystery wreck is found in Maces Bay, where the skeletal remains of a large ship are visible. Located in a quiet inlet within the bay, the wooden ship measures approximately 40 metres long and 9 metres wide. Like the Lorneville wreck, it is likely that the ship was scuttled there after it was no longer useful.

LORNEVILLE WRECK: N 45.189915, W 66.156239
MACES BAY WRECK: N 45.122551, W 66.471851

2. Musquash Estuary Ship Graveyard

Musquash River

Situated 20 kilometres south of the city of Saint John is the Musquash Estuary Nature Reserve. This conservation area was established by the Nature Conservancy of Canada at the mouth of the Musquash River as it enters the Bay of Fundy to protect its sensitive ecosystems and wildlife habitats. Its beautiful and ecologically important tidal flats, salt marshes, wetlands, and stretches of Acadian forest have made it a prime destination for hikers, birdwatchers, and kayakers. At its centre is the Musquash River, a large tide-dominated river that flows through the centre of the reserve before discharging into Musquash harbour and finally into the Bay of Fundy.

The protection and conservation efforts of such groups as the Nature Conservancy of Canada are relatively new. For decades, the harbour and river were the largest of their kind near Saint John harbour and became a dump site for derelict and aging ships. The hulls and remains of more than 10 ships and barges are still visible, making it one of the largest ship graveyards in Atlantic Canada. Thanks to local historians, a few of the ships' stories have come to light.

The stringent rules and environmental regulations surrounding the scrapping and abandonment of ships nearing the end of their lives are now taken for granted. But for hundreds of years, it was common practice that if a ship was not worth scrapping for parts and materials, it would be scuttled—purposely run aground or sunk. Given the condition of the ships in the Musquash Estuary, it is likely that they were discarded around the middle of the 20th century. That time brought a substantial increase in activity in Saint John harbour. The Saint John Harbour Commission and the Canada Shipping Act oversaw regulation and enforcement in the harbour, and prohibited the abandonment of vessels due to their risk to other ships. Shipowners would tow their aging or outdated ships to nearby

harbours, coves, or inlets outside the jurisdictional boundary of local harbour commissions, and abandon them.

This was the case for at least two of the ships abandoned in Musquash River. In the 1940s, one of Saint John's largest tugboat operators was the Saint John Tugboat Company Limited, run by Charles Wilson. In 1945, Wilson purchased controlling interest in the Saint John Dry Dock and Shipbuilding Company, leading to increased operations for his fleet of salvage tugboats and barges. Wilson purchased second-hand and aging ships, which were cheaper than new ships but had shorter service lives. In 1946, to keep up with the work being contracted to the Saint John Tugboat Company Limited, Wilson purchased his sixth tugboat,

the *Rockswift*. Renamed Ocean *Rockswift*, it joined his other tugs with such names as *Ocean Osprey* and *Ocean Hawk*.

After World War II, ships, machinery, and equipment used by the United States and Canada during the conflict were put up for auction. The Canadian government sought to regulate these sales, concerned about potential disruptions to market stability. This did not stop Wilson from purchasing four United States Navy amphibious assault and landing ships at auction in October 1948. The four ships were of the LSM-1-class Landing Ship Medium: *LSM-46, LSM-56, LSM-78,* and *LSM-89*. Wilson converted the vessels into towboats and barges for salvage operations, towing cargo such as pulpwood, and performing odd jobs at the Saint John Dry Dock.

In the estuary, *LSM-46* and *LSM-56* are the most notable shipwrecks. Toward the end of World War II, shortages in assault and landing craft

forced the United States Navy to order the construction of 558 Landing Ship Medium vessels. Constructed between 1944 and 1945, these were built in shipyards across the United States. *LSM-46* and *LSM-56* were both commissioned at Brown Shipbuilding Company in Houston, Texas, and launched in August 1944. Like all the ships in their class, they were approximately 62 metres long and 10 metres wide. They were equipped with two 1040-kilowatt diesel engines, ensuring that the vessels could easily carry a cargo of five medium tanks, three large tanks, six tracked amphibious vehicles (known as Landing Vehicle Tracked), or nine six-wheeled amphibious trucks, depending on the need in battle. To protect their personnel and cargo, the ships were equipped with several machine guns and as many as six anti-aircraft guns mounted on their decks. Once commissioned, both ships were sent to the Western Pacific.

Between February 19 and March 26, 1945, *LSM-46* carried supplies and personnel to and from navy ships at Iwo Jima. Taking heavy fire and losses during the battle, the ship's unit received the prestigious Navy Unit Commendation for its efforts. Its sister ship, *LSM-56,* fought in the battle of Okinawa between April 2 and June 17, 1945.

After Japan's surrender on September 2, 1945, the ships returned to the United States. On March 18, 1946, they were decommissioned at the Norfolk Navy Yard, Portsmouth, Virginia. After Charles Wilson purchased the ships in 1948, he converted them for carrying cargo and pulpwood, likely between Maine and New Brunswick. Information on the ships after this becomes less clear, but it is thought that, in 1960, they were sold for scrap and towed to the Musquash River to await delivery to the scrapyard. The ships were never retrieved but left in their current location, deteriorating with each tide. Two of the landing craft are visible above the water, while it is believed that at least one has sunk to the bottom of the channel. The ship's connection to the Saint John Tugboat Company is apparent through the faint outline of the word *Ocean* on the side of its hull—a nomenclature used exclusively by Charles Wilson when naming his ships.

At high tide, the two ships are almost completely submerged, while at low tide their hulls stand high above the waterline, sometimes 6 metres below the deck. Following the shoreline south, nearly a dozen other ships, barges, and indistinguishable remains are visible. Most of the wooden vessels have deteriorated and assimilated into the neighbouring wetland and salt marshes. Others continue to withstand the powerful currents and tides, standing high above the waterline. In one case, thick wooden columns and crossbeams rise 2 or 3 metres above the water at low tide; others, the imprint of a keel and ribs. A large steel barge denotes one of the few steel vessels in this section of the river, while, at its centre, a large sunken ship, submerged almost entirely even at low tide, can be identified by its steel boiler rising above the water.

Considering the forces of tides exerted on the ships, it is amazing that so much can still be seen. The ship graveyard is shrouded in

mystery and history. While the full story of how each ship arrived there may never be known, the Musquash Estuary shipwrecks reflect New Brunswick's industrial use of ships and its shipbuilding industry. When contrasted with the natural beauty and ecological importance of the estuary, it is one of the province's most incredible places to visit.

***LSM-46* AND *LSM-56*:** N 45.193145, W 66.271605
MUSQUASH SHIP GRAVEYARD: N 45.191221, W 66.267414

The ships are in the Musquash Estuary Nature Reserve and special care must be taken to minimize human impact while visiting.

Hiking: From Highway 1, take Exit 96 and drive south on Highway 790. Follow this road for 1.7 kilometres and turn onto South Musquash Road. Continue to the road's end; park along the road. From here, the road turns into an ATV trail. Hike the trail for 450 metres, turn left and continue another 1.5 kilometres. Continue straight to the ship graveyard or follow an overgrown path on the left to the two land craft.

Paddling: Due to strong tidal and river currents, paddling the river can be extremely dangerous to inexperienced paddlers. Leave from Five Fathom Hole, at the end of Five Fathom Hole Road, launch from the wharf, and paddle north for 1.3 kilometres.

3. Musquash River Hydro Development

Musquash Parish

The Musquash River played a significant role in the development and industrial history of New Brunswick. In the early 20th century, the river and its east and west branches hosted the inaugural project of the newly established Crown corporation, the New Brunswick Electric Power Commission (NBEPC), which later evolved into the modern-day New Brunswick Power. The facility brought power to communities between Saint John and Moncton, helping lower electricity rates for others. Before its closure in 2009, the system consisted of four large concrete dams, more than 12 earthen dams, a 1-kilometre-long tunnel, and two penstocks, which redirected water into a powerhouse built at the mouth of the east branch of Musquash River.

HISTORY

In 1918, 20 suppliers of electricity operated in New Brunswick. These were a variety of public and private organizations, confined mostly to larger urban centres. In Saint John, for example, power had been supplied to residents since its first commercial power plant was installed on Paradise Row in 1884. Elected as premier in 1917, Walter E. Foster understood the importance of electricity in industrializing the province. On April 24, 1920, Foster's government created the NBEPC. The government appointed former premier and politician Clifford W. Robinson as president, who quickly set his sights on developing a hydroelectric system near the city of Saint John to combat rising electricity rates and provide communities in eastern New Brunswick with their first power.

The Lepreau River was the first location investigated for hydro development, but the NBEPC soon turned to the Musquash River system, which was closer to Saint John and had a higher potential for

power generation. Originally granted to Moses Perley in 1838, much of the land around the Musquash River—specifically its east branch—had a history of sawmilling and log drives until 1903, when a forest fire and devastating flood led to the abandonment of the river. In 1920, Inglewood Pulp and Paper Company owned the forest surrounding the river system. The NBEPC took control of the land, compensating the company $59,000. This decision was contested in court by Inglewood; the company lost the case and subsequent appeals.

The soil and bedrock around the Musquash River system allowed for the construction of large concrete dams, with little seepage through the groundwater. The river itself efficiently transferred rainwater and snowmelt into runoff, with minimal water percolating into the ground. Additionally, the river's two branches consisted of multiple tributaries and ponds which could be managed and redirected to supply even more water to a powerhouse. Overseen by chief engineer Charles Foss, work began on two dams—one on each branch of the river—and a single powerhouse at the mouth of the East Branch Musquash River.

Completed in June 1922, dams on the east and west rivers—named East Branch Dam and Scott's Falls Dam, respectively—directed water into an intake structure, where it was funnelled into wooden-stave penstocks. The three turbines of the powerhouse produced a total of 6.96 megawatts of electricity. To deliver this power to customers, a 21-kilometre-long high-voltage transmission line was constructed to connect with local distribution lines near Saint John.

Shortly after construction was complete, disaster struck. At 10 p.m. on April 30, 1923, the earthen sidewalls of the concrete dam on the West Branch Musquash River gave way, sending a flood of water downstream. It destroyed several homes, buildings, and bridges, taking the life of at least one person. As the floodwater entered the Musquash Estuary, it destroyed many of the surviving dykes and farmland originally established by Acadian settlers. The dam was rebuilt and, to slow and control future water surges, a second concrete dam was constructed farther up the system, at Log Falls. The hydroelectric system operated successfully for many years but not without incident, the worst of which was a workplace accident that took the life of employee Robert Roy Daniel on July 16, 1930.

By 1960, new technology and engineering capabilities led to a trend toward constructing large hydroelectric facilities such as the Mactaquac Hydro Development on the Saint John River. Smaller hydroelectric systems received less attention. Around the same time, the city of Saint John faced water supply challenges, and the Musquash System was identified as a possible water source. In 1972, a 14.5-kilometre-long pipeline was constructed from the East Branch Reservoir to the Irving Pulp and Paper Mill in Saint John, nearly doubling the capacity of the Saint John water supply system. That year the Department of Energy and Mines took ownership of the hydroelectric development, with the NBEPC continuing to oversee its operation and maintenance.

This transition of ownership marked the beginning of the end for the Musquash Hydro Development. In the early 1980s, the West Branch Musquash penstock and its surge tank were demolished and the system decommissioned. In 1981, Number 3 turbine was also decommissioned and put up for sale. The dam remained in place, and to accommodate future low water levels or increased water demand by the city of Saint John, a 1-kilometre-long tunnel was excavated between the west and east reservoirs, allowing additional water to enter the system when needed. The powerhouse now operated with two turbines, capable of producing a total of approximately 5 megawatts of electricity.

By the early 2000s, the system continued to draw on both rivers, controlled through four concrete dams and more than 12 earthen dams. The powerhouse still produced a small amount of electricity, but the system's primary purpose had shifted to supplying water to Saint John's industry. Following the forced evacuation of 75 Musquash residents in March 1998 after flash floods threatened one of the system's dams, the provincial government ordered a study on the integrity of the surviving structures. As a result, the government invested $1 million in dam repairs and restoration.

In 2009, New Brunswick Power determined that the system was too small to warrant continued investment in electricity production, and the powerhouse was closed and decommissioned. In 2016, much of its equipment, including its neighbouring substation, was demolished. Since then, there has been interest in redeveloping the Musquash System to produce electricity, but little has been done to date.

Abandoned dams, intake structures, and the powerhouse are significant landmarks of the former site.

Musquash Powerhouse

Only one powerhouse was required to service both branches of the Musquash River. Behind the structure, two large surge tanks prevented damage to the plant from the enormous force of water travelling through the penstocks.

Adjacent to the plant, a large substation was built to transfer power to the nearby transmission lines, which then delivered electricity to Saint John customers. The powerhouse remains a ghostly presence on the side of Stillwater Road. Surrounding it are concrete foundations, penstock remains, and components of its former substation and nearby bridges.

MUSQUASH POWERHOUSE: N 45.196722, W 66.325182
From Highway 1, take Exit 96 and drive north on Musquash Road for 1.4 kilometres. Turn left on Stillwater Road and drive 180 metres to the site.

Scott's Falls Dam and Intake Structure

After a fatal collapse shortly after its construction in 1923, the rebuilt Scott's Falls Dam can be seen from nearby West Branch Road. Its concrete section stretches approximately 125 metres in length, but connected earthen dams extend for more than 1 kilometre beyond this. The dam was decommissioned in the late 1970s, following the decommissioning of the powerhouse's Number 3 turbine and the connection of the east and west reservoirs via a tunnel.

Despite a section at the dam's centre being demolished to allow the free flow of water, the dam remains an imposing structure. Below it are several small waterfalls, which have become a popular, though dangerous, swimming location among locals.

To the east of the concrete dam is the former intake structure. This concrete building once marked the beginning of the 2.2-kilometre-long, 2.4-metre-diameter wooden-stave penstock that delivered water to the Musquash powerhouse. The building is now completely overgrown with vegetation.

DAM AND INTAKE: N 45.186102, W 66.356928

East and West Reservoir Tunnel

The 3-metre-diameter tunnel connecting the west reservoir to the east reservoir remains in use. Submerged in water, this 1-kilometre-long tunnel is a testament to the innovative engineering used to address the Musquash River system's persistent low-water issues. While the tunnel itself is not visible, the intake structure marks its location. Situated far inland, the location offers offers breathtaking views of the surrounding reservoir and the natural beauty of the landscape.

RESERVOIR TUNNEL: N 45.216762, W 66.361333

4. RCAF Station Pennfield Ridge

Pennfield, Charlotte County

To train pilots and aircrews during World War II, dedicated airfields were constructed across Canada, with several locations in New Brunswick. As these aircrews would primarily be based out of England, the air force sought a a location whose conditions would replicate those of the foggy, rugged, English coastline. This location was found on a plot of flat land overlooking the Bay of Fundy, near what is now the town of Pennfield. Known as Pennfield Ridge, the site offered easy access to the Bay of Fundy's coastline and weather, while also being conveniently located alongside the Canadian Pacific Railway line and the busy shipping ports of Saint John and St. Stephen.

Construction of the airfield began in the summer of 1940, with over 200 workers employed on-site. As with many infrastructure projects during World War II, the construction was urgent, and by November the three 1,500-metre-long paved runways were complete. In the ensuing months, hangars, living quarters, and other amenities were built at the south end of the airfield, transforming this once-quiet landscape into a small town. By the end of the war, the base contained more than 40 buildings, including barracks, ammunition storage bunkers, maintenance hangars, shops, restaurants, and even a church. Before construction began, only 188 civilians lived in the area; by 1942, this number had grown to almost 5,000, both military and civilian.

The base housed the No. 2 Air Navigation School, the first unit to occupy the airfield after it officially opened on July 21, 1941. This training program taught pilots and aircrews to fly and navigate at night. The most notable unit to occupy the base was the No. 34 Operational Training Unit, which was transferred to the site on June 1, 1941, from Greenock, Scotland. The unit was part of a joint Commonwealth training program known as the British Commonwealth Air Training Plan, or more simply "The Plan." Administered by the RCAF, the training program at

Pennfield Ridge trained crews for bombing and gunnery missions on the Lockheed Ventura, a small bomber aircraft. Between May 1942 and June 1944, crews participated in live bombing missions over Lake Utopia and along the coastline near the community of Musquash.

While the No. 34 Operational Training Unit was the best-known unit to use the base, many other training programs occurred throughout World War II, including air-to-air combat training, survival skills, and search and rescue operations. In May 1944, this unit ceased operations at the airfield, after which the base shut down. Any remaining aircraft, equipment, and materials were quickly put into storage, and the RCAF began a massive cleanup operation at the site.

Many of the base's buildings were deconstructed or destroyed, while some of the larger structures, such as the hangars, were sold to private owners. Following the cleanup, the land and any remaining structures were sold to the province for $58,000.

The airfield was used for a brief period as a civilian airfield but became redundant when the Saint John Airport opened in early 1952. Subsequently, part of the airfield's former runways was taken over by the New Brunswick Drag Racing Association, which hosted races there until the 1970s.

ABOUT THE AREA

Although the land has been converted into blueberry fields, the three runways are still visible, as are the foundations of the former hangars. Each year, the runways are used to dry seaweed, which is later used in fertilizers.

Most of the land that once housed the airfield's buildings is now overgrown with trees and shrubs, with ATV trails outlining the former roads. The only structure remaining on the plot is a large concrete gunnery backstop, which rises above the trees not far from Route 175.

Four concrete ammunition bunkers are in the northwest corner of the airfield. Conveniently accessible by nearby ATV trails, these ground-covered bunkers once stored the airfield's explosives and ammunition at a safe distance from buildings, people, and equipment.

PENNFIELD AIRFIELD: N 45.122454, W 66.692542
AMMUNITION BUNKERS: N 45.131013, W 66.702968

Travel approximately 54 kilometres south of Saint John on Route 1, take Exit 69 onto Route 175. Continue west on Route 175 for 4.4 kilometres to the former airfield. As the site is periodically used for commercial purposes, abide by all private property and warning signs in the area.

5. Camp Utopia: Infantry Training Centre

Pennfield, Charlotte County

In the first two years of World War II, it was identified that additional training was needed by Canadian soldiers, specifically in advanced combat. New training areas were selected across the country, including a large stretch of land north of RCAF Station Pennfield Ridge. Construction of the A-30 Canadian Infantry Training Centre began in July 1942; until it was completed, the centre temporarily operated out of Camp Aldershot, Nova Scotia.

Construction began with the clearing of large tracts of land and then the establishment of the centre's barracks, supply depots, and drill hall. A hospital, dental clinic, fire station, and other services were established, transforming the site into a small town seemingly overnight. Officially opened on August 1, 1942, the training centre began training soldiers the following year. The centre contained two rifle ranges, a model village replicating a typical European town, two machine gun ranges, and a portable infantry anti-tank firing range. Additional facilities included a grenade range, skeet shooting range, mortar range, and obstacle courses, with simulated minefields and an assault course.

Between 1943 and the end of the war, the centre trained more than 300 officers and 12,000 soldiers, most of whom belonged to the Carleton and York Regiment and the North Shore (New Brunswick) Regiment. The training centre officially closed on April 30, 1946, though the site remained under the ownership of the federal government. In May 1954, it was reactivated when the 4th Field Regiment of the Royal Canadian Horse Artillery took control of the site. This new occupation was short-lived and, in 1955, most of the regiment was relocated to Germany. The only remaining presence at the site was the W Battery

of the Royal Canadian Horse Artillery. The Battery operated the site as the regimental depot for two years before being relocated to Petawawa in 1957. With this move, military activity at the site ceased, and the following year, the land was sold to the province for $90,000.

When the site was built, it was the largest military facility in New Brunswick, thanks to the vast stretches of live-fire ranges. Although no buildings remain on-site, large foundations that once housed the site's ammunition and explosives are still visible. The site is still considered to possibly contain unexploded ordnance (as indicated by signs throughout the area), but this has not stopped the area from being transformed into commercial blueberry fields during the summer.

Easily confused for explosive craters, the now-cleared Camp Utopia site contains dozens of large, circular indentations, some of which are large enough to contain small ponds. These natural landforms are believed to be dissolution sinkholes, a type of sinkhole created by the slow erosion of underlying limestone and gypsum. These holes are another reason to be cautious when visiting the area.

The former Grand Southern Railway, now an ATV/snowmobile trail, provides the safest and easiest access to the site. Do not interfere with blueberry farming activities, but abide by all posted signs and remain on designated trails.

TRAINING CENTRE: N 45.149354, W 66.727096

The area is now intersected by Highway 780 and a local ATV/snowmobile trail. From the town of Utopia, drive 4 kilometres east on Highway 780 to reach the site.

6. History of Bartlett Mills

Bartlett Mills, Charlotte County

Alongside Highway 1, 14 kilometres west of the town of St. Stephen, lie the remains from a long history of milling on Goldsmiths Stream. The first mill was likely constructed in the area in 1789 when Henry Goldsmith established a small gristmill on the river. It operated for only a few years before being destroyed by fire; it was never rebuilt.

After immigrating from the United States, British Loyalist Leonard Bartlett purchased the land at the beginning of the 19th century, and by 1841, with the help of his son John, he had constructed a gristmill and carding and weaving operation at the site. Bartlett constructed a dam on the river atop a series of small waterfalls and redirected the water to paddle a large wheel, producing the necessary power needed for the mill. The mill operated under the ownership of John Bartlett until 1870, when his son, Edward, took over the business.

Recognizing that there was profit to be made in the woodworking industry, Edward installed a box shook sawmill that produced cut lumber used to make wooden crates and boxes. Edward installed a turbine at the base of the dam which could supply more energy to the mill's machinery than the paddlewheel. By 1888, the Bartlett family had built their home on the plot of land adjacent to the mill, turning part of the property into a farm where they grew vegetables and raised livestock. Along the river, the two mills operated beneath the dam, with a large storage warehouse adjacent and piles of cut timber lining the nearby roadway, waiting to be processed.

In 1913, Edward Hollis Bartlett (more commonly referred to as Hollis) took over the mill operation from his father, Edward. Hollis slowed the operation of the gristmill and weaving and carding mill, focusing more on the profitable box shook sawmill. Hollis's sons, Lawrence and Marvin, joined the milling operation in 1934 and 1949, respectively. The mill had operated reliably and profitably for

many years, but its future was jeopardized when a fire broke out there in 1950, destroying the mills and many surrounding buildings. The Bartlett family wasted no time in rebuilding, and a new mill was in operation by the following year. Once rebuilt, the Bartlett family property contained two mills: the box shook sawmill, proudly displaying the company name E. Hollis & Sons Ltd., and a smaller mill operated by Hollis's brother under the name Lewis V. Bartlett & Son. Until then, the box shook mill had relied on hydro power to operate the saws and machinery. While they were rebuilding the mill, the Bartletts installed a diesel generator, which became the primary source of power for the mill's machinery.

By this time, the community of Bartlett Mills was thriving. The area also hosted a convenience store, post office, church, cemetery, and, of course, the Bartlett family farm. In 1963, Hollis passed full ownership to his sons. Just two years later, a lightning strike hit a pile of sawdust, and fire consumed three of the mills operating at the site under the ownership of E. Hollis & Sons Ltd. and Lewis V. Bartlett & Son. Once more, the mills were rebuilt. Lawrence and Marvin took advantage of the tragedy to again upgrade the power supply to the mill, introducing electricity as a source of power for the first time.

Once completed, the mill could process 3,000 cords of wood annually, almost twice the amount it had produced before the fire. The operation continued to produce wooden boxes and crates used to transport vegetables, fish, and lobster, which were shipped to communities across the east coast of Canada and the United States. Lawrence Bartlett designed and manufactured most of the new machinery being used in the mill, now deemed one of the most modern custom sawmilling operations in Canada.

The Bartlett mills operated until the late 20th century. Eventually, the mills, no longer profitable, were torn down, leaving the historic traces of foundations, dam remnants, and land.

Proud of their heritage, members of the Bartlett family donated part of their land to a nature trust, creating the Bartlett Mills Nature Preserve, for the enjoyment of others and preservation of the beautiful landscape.

BARTLETT MILLS : N 45.204572, W 67.125790

Part of the mill site is located on private property; respect all posted signs and notices. From Highway 1, take Exit 25 and turn south onto Highway 127. Drive 450 metres and turn onto Bartletts Mills Road. The site is at the end of this road. Remains of the dam are visible along the river, while parts of the mill can be seen across the river. The buildings are now used for storage by local landowners.

★T.B.Mc CLINTIC★
BATH MAINE

7. *T.B. McClintic*

Chamcook Harbour, Saint Andrews

In Chamcook Harbour, north of the town of Saint Andrews, is the ship *T.B. McClintic,* now resting on the shores of the narrow inlet. It appears to be a retired fishing or tugboat—but in fact, it is a monument to the history of quarantine stations on the east coast of the United States.

Beginning in 1799, the United States implemented a national quarantine system to reduce the spread of smallpox, yellow fever, and cholera. Ships that departed ports known to have cases of such contagious diseases were ordered to anchor outside ports of entry into the United States and await an inspection from a quarantine or medical officer. A network of quarantine stations was built in major harbours along the east coast, and upon receiving an inspection request, an "intercept" ship would sail to the anchored ship and examine all crew and passengers. The quarantine officer would determine if the ship could continue to its destination or if it was to be subjected to further restrictions or quarantine.

In the early 1930s, the Baltimore Quarantine Station needed a new intercept ship, so the United States Public Health Service requested proposals for a new ship. In March 1931, the contract was awarded to the Bath Iron Works shipyard on the Kennebec River in Bath, Maine, for a cost of $29,980. The ship, completed in 1932, was christened *T.B. McClintic* after Thomas B. McClintic, an inspector with the United States Public Health Service who died 1912 after contracting Rocky Mountain spotted fever while on the job. McClintic was 38.

The 18.5-metre-long ship had a breadth of 5 metres and a draft of 2.8 metres, with a displacement of 59 tonnes. A four-cylinder Standard Motor Construction Company diesel engine powered the ship through a single propeller. The hull was constructed of strong riveted steel and supported a small pilothouse to shelter its occupants. Along the hull and pilothouse, the windows were trimmed in mahogany, and its deck was

made of a similar wood. While similar in design to a tugboat, the ship was not fitted with winches, machinery, or the typical reinforcements found on tugboats of a similar size. The *T.B. McClintic* was primarily stationed at the Baltimore Quarantine Station; it also spent time in Boston, Massachusetts, and Norfolk, Virginia. For 29 years, it inspected thousands of vessels entering the harbour, minimizing the spread of diseases.

In 1961, advances in public health and improved port screening and sanitation diminished the need for the quarantine station, and it was shut down on February 16, 1961. Following this, the *T.B. McClintic* was sold to the City of Wilmington, North Carolina, to replace its aging firefighting boat *Atlantic III*. In Wilmington, the ship underwent major upgrades, including the addition of hose platforms, powerful water pumps, and a spray nozzle to battle potential oil fires. In addition to these upgrades, the ship was fitted with a more powerful engine, and large sections of its steel hull were replaced. The hull was painted white, and it was renamed *Atlantic IV*.

The ship operated in Wilmington until 1985, when it was replaced

by a new fireboat. At that time, the historic ship was sold at auction to a private purchaser with the intention of restoring and preserving it. Most of its firefighting additions were removed, and it was re-registered under the name *America*. In 1994, the owner registered the ship under the United States government's National Register of Historic Places, hoping that it would help highlight its significance and further preserve it. Although it was used as a private vessel, it also made occasional appearances at boat shows over the years, helping spread its story.

In 2012, the ship was sold to a private purchaser in New Brunswick, who sailed the former *T.B. McClintic* to Saint Andrews, where it has remained. Although the future of this ship is unclear, it holds historic and cultural significance to the story of the United States Quarantine System.

VIEWPOINT: N 45.130833, W 67.065671

The historic ship still occasionally sails the waters around Saint Andrews; however, it spends much of its time tied up in Chamcook Harbour. It is best viewed from across the harbour at Glebe Road. A reminder: this ship is privately owned, not abandoned.

8. J&C Short Shipbuilding Yard

St. Stephen

Shipbuilding has long been an important industry for the communities established along Passamaquoddy Bay. Throughout the 18th and 19th centuries, hundreds of people found employment in this industry, specifically along the St. Croix River, where shipbuilders took advantage of the tide-influenced river, abundant forests, and trade opportunities with the United States. One such builder was the J&C Shipbuilding Yard, established on the east side of St. Stephen.

The shipyard was founded by Charles and John Short, Irish settlers who learned their trade from shipbuilders in Passamaquoddy Bay and throughout Maine. Charles began his career working with shipbuilders in Digdeguash, Chamcook, and Saint Andrews to build schooners, brigs, and barques, three- or four-masted ships used for carrying cargo. In 1861, after years of working for other firms, Charles partnered with his brother John to form the J&C Shipbuilding Firm. The brothers purchased a plot of land east of the town of St. Stephen and constructed a shipyard, wharf, and several shops and buildings.

Between 1861 and 1878, the firm constructed 20 ships, mostly for clients in London and Liverpool, England. In their first few years of operation, their endeavours were successful, and soon the firm had opened or purchased several other shipyards throughout New Brunswick, including those in Brandy Cove, Saint Andrews, Digdeguash, and Oak Bay. A large shipyard was also established in Calais, Maine, where the firm constructed 16 ships during the same time period.

The shipbuilding industry on the St. Croix River, and across Atlantic Canada, declined in the latter half of the 19th century. This was due partly to the rising popularity of ships being built with steel instead of wood and the invention of steam-powered ships. Changing global economic conditions also favoured larger ships capable of carrying more goods and supplies. The aging brothers launched their last ship from the site on

October 1, 1878: *The Rocklands*, built for Zachariah Chipman, partial owner of the well-known St. Croix Cotton Manufacturing Company.

Charles Short retired to British Columbia, John Short moved to central Canada and settled in Kenora, Ontario, and the St. Stephen shipyard was claimed by nature. As for the company's other shipyards, some continued operating, such as the one in Calais, which continued to build and repair small ships.

Little remains of the shipbuilding industry in the region. However, by venturing into this overgrown field east of St. Stephen, it is possible to glimpse the scale of these former shipyards. Concrete walls line the site, paralleled with railway tracks that once launched ships. Along the water's edge are the remains of the wharf, along with scattered pieces of steel and equipment.

SHIPBUILDING YARD: N 45.189973, W 67.262262

Drive east on Prince William Street, turn onto a gravel road (N 45.191949, W 67.261279), and continue driving to its end. Several trails lead around the former shipyard.

9. Old Sow Whirlpool

Deer Island and Campobello Island

The Bay of Fundy tides are an incredible natural phenomenon. Twice a day, an estimated 100 billion tonnes of water rush into the bay; six hours later, it empties. This tidal power has shaped the coastline for millions of years, causing the tidal bore in the Petitcodiac River and the switching of current directions at Reversing Falls. But one of the bay's most awe-inspiring events is the Old Sow Whirlpool, which occurs in Passamaquoddy Bay.

Originally believed to be named for the whirlpool's piglike noise, it is more likely that the name comes from the term *sough*, which describes a moaning or rushing sound made by water, but also a type of drain. The whirlpool, one of five significant whirlpools in the world, is the largest in the western hemisphere. Its formation is due to the unique bathymetry and topography of the entrance to Passamaquoddy Bay. The dangerous 75- to 100-metre diameter whirlpool forms with each incoming and outgoing tide.

The Old Sow forms from a combination of fast-moving currents, confined and directed by deep underground trenches. Passamaquoddy Bay has two primary channels through which the tide enters the bay. A small but deep channel is located on the north side of Deer Island, where water depths drop to more than 35 metres in 500-metre-wide channels. The islands along the north side of Deer Island prohibit much of the water from entering. Instead, most of the 1.1 billion cubic metres of water that flow into the bay does so through the bay's south entrance. Here, at the south end of Deer Island, and between Campobello Island and Moose Island in the United States, a deep trench has been carved over hundreds of thousands of years, reaching depths of over 125 metres in channels as narrow as 750 metres.

As the 7.9-metre tide leaves Passamaquoddy Bay twice a day, most of the water is forced south. This water comes not only from the

bay's tides but is also fed by additional currents from the St. Croix and Magaguadavic Rivers. The water is funnelled through the western passage between Deer Island and mainland United States. As it reaches the south end of Deer and Moose Islands, the water is forced northward, redirected by a sudden and dramatic increase in water depth between Moose and Campobello Islands. This sudden turn north, combined with the currents' interaction with the edges of the trench and nearby islands, creates the rotation and turbulence needed to form the massive

whirlpool. The water then continues moving north until discharging into the Bay of Fundy near Head Harbour Lighthouse. In the waters surrounding the lighthouse, deep water and dramatic underwater landscapes add to the dangerous nature of the waters. When the tide returns to the bay, the whirlpool is once again created as the currents are quickly forced around the head of Deer Island.

The currents in the area, and specifically the Old Sow Whirlpool itself, are extremely dangerous. While today's larger motorized vessels are generally safe, self-propelled boats such as small dories, canoes, and kayaks, along with smaller sailing vessels, should avoid the area when the current is strong. The whirlpool is often not a single funnel but, instead, several spiralling currents occur around it. These whirlpools, which can create sudden drops or troughs in the water's surface, pose danger to

even the largest ships entering the bay. Additionally, the currents produce "boils" from rapidly rising water, which in some cases have been known to shoot several metres into the air, known as a "spout."

Best seen during spring tide, the turbulent currents and whirlpool can be safely observed from the shores of Deer Island. The phenomenon is best seen from the Deer Island Point Campground or even the Deer Island-Campobello Island ferry, which traverses the currents even at their strongest.

OLD SOW WHIRLPOOL: N 44.925789, W 66.984863

At the south end of Deer Island, turn off Highway 772 and onto Deer Island Point Road (N 44.944630, W 66.990174) in the community of Cummings Cove. Drive 2.4 kilometres to Deer Island Point Campground.

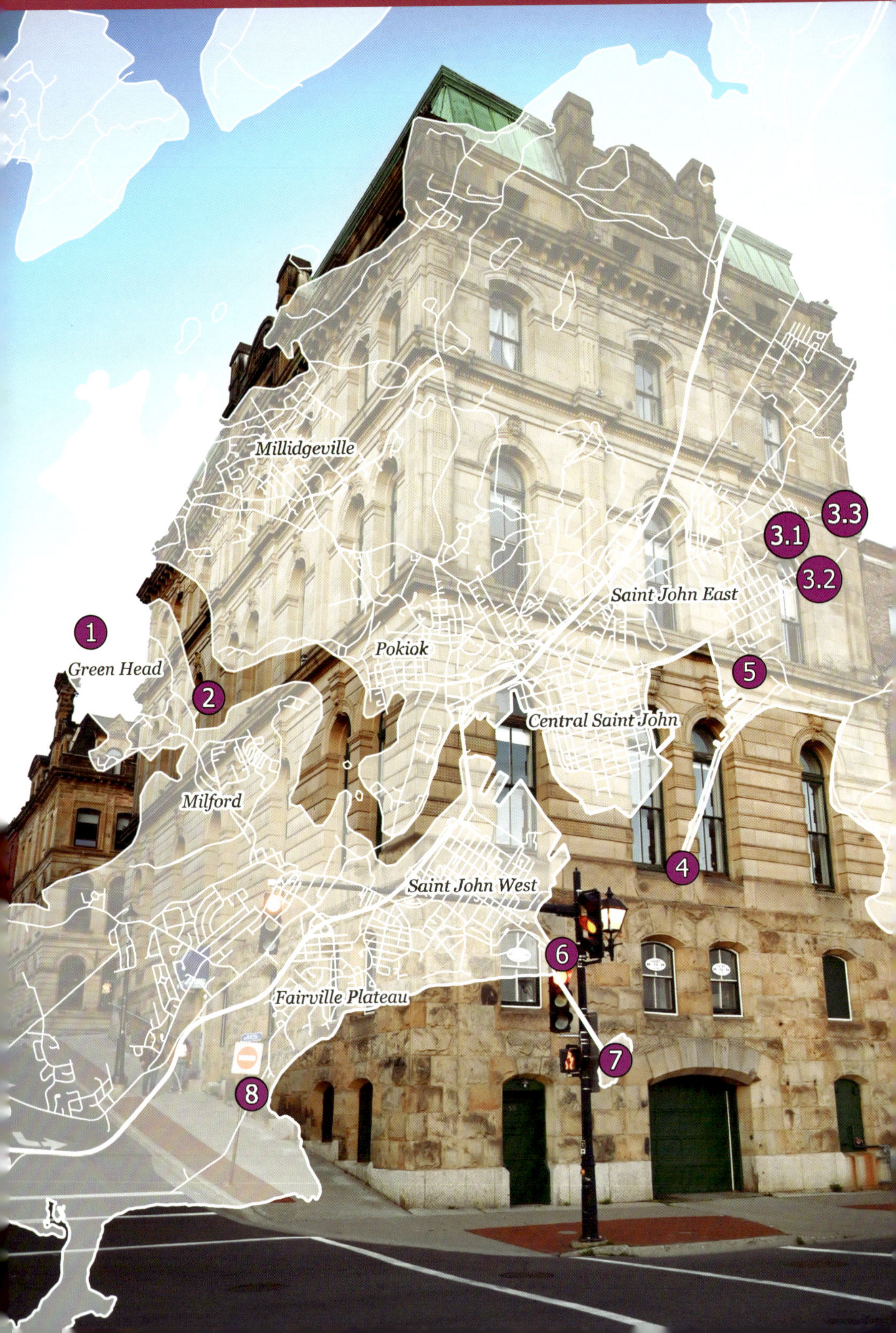
Millidgeville
3.3
3.1
3.2
Saint John East
1
Green Head
Pokiok
5
2
Central Saint John
Milford
4
Saint John West
6
Fairville Plateau
7
8

City of Saint John

The city of Saint John, located at the mouth of the Saint John River, and neighbouring region is one of the province's most industrial and historical areas. The first people of the land, the Wolastoqiyik, establishied settlements throughout the region. During colonization, a small Acadian trading post was established at the mouth of the river, leading to the construction of historic Fort La Tour. This was relatively short-lived; during the mid-18th century, colonial powers forced these French settlers out and awarded land grants to British Loyalists fleeing the American Revolution. This began a wave of immigration into the area and the rest of Canada, with Saint John at its centre. In 1785, it became the first incorporated city in Canada and slowly became an industrial centre, with shipbuilding, immigration, and commercial industry at the forefront. The city's most valuable feature was its deep, ice-free harbour. Despite the incredible tidal range experienced in the harbour due to the Bay of Fundy's tides, the port provided safe protection for ships, ample space for loading and unloading cargo and passengers, and facilities for exporting goods.

By the 20th century, the city's shipbuilding industry had transitioned from constructing wooden sailing ships to steam-powered steel ships. Soon pulp and paper, oil refining, and shipping became its primary economic drivers. The city's successful industrial and commercial endeavours are reflected in its incredible and diverse architecture, much of which originated following the Great Fire of 1877. The port

and city became a hub of activity during World War II, with the harbour becoming one of the most protected in Canada. Coastal defence batteries and anti-aircraft guns were scattered throughout the city, now available to explore and learn about this turbulent time. Throughout the second half of the 20th century, the city's industrial and commercial sectors continued to expand, and so too did its population. This led to growth in the surrounding communities of Rothesay, Quispamsis, and Grand Bay-Westfield.

While the city is one of the most industrialized in Atlantic Canada, it also has a thriving tourism industry. Saint John welcomes thousands of visitors each year to its historic conservation area, Reversing Falls, and beautiful local parks such as the Irving Nature Park, Rockwood Park,

and Dominion Park. The main route in and out of the city, Highway 1, connects Saint John to Moncton in the north and St. Stephen in the south. The city is centred around a small peninsula, which has historically been the economic hub of the region. Eastward, several bridges span the river, providing access to the westside container port and the suburban towns of Saint John West, Milford, Greendale, and Lancaster, to name a few. East of the downtown area is the highly industrial and commercial Courtenay Bay. From Saint John, Red Head Road travels south toward Mispec and offers a blend of past and current industry along its coastline. This contrasts sharply with the north, where the confluence of the Saint John River and Kennebecasis River has become an oasis for recreational boaters, hikers, and outdoor enthusiasts.

1. Green Head Cove Lime Quarry

Green Head Island

Located in the middle of the Saint John River, just as it narrows before making its final rush to the Bay of Fundy, is Green Head Island. The island is defined by rolling, rocky hills covered in a mix of hardwoods and softwoods. Apart from a few small open wetlands in the south, the island remains hidden for most of the year under the forest canopy. From Dominion Park at the island's south end, a maze of hiking trails winds through the island. Following these trails 1.5 kilometres north inevitably leads to Green Head Cove, overlooking the reaches of the Saint John River, where natural beauty becomes entangled with the relics of buildings, timber wharves, and foundations. Here, one of several lime quarries was established along the Saint John River in the late 19th century.

Lime has long been used in agriculture, steel manufacturing, papermaking, and as a building material (both to produce cement and as cut stone for building construction). Lime is obtained from carbonate rocks such as limestone or marble, which, when heated, leave easily transportable powdered lime or quicklime. The rocks at Green Head Cove held the perfect ingredients for this. Formed from millions of years of sediment and organic deposits at the bottom of a shallow sea, the rocks are primarily limestone that, since their deposition over 500 million years ago, has been heated and pressurized to form a type of marble. This hardened rock was ideal as a building stone and to produce lime, which was quickly recognized by the first European settlers in the area.

It is believed that the first use of the area's rocks was in the early 1700s, when they were used as a building material for local military fortifications and prominent buildings. In the early 1800s, the first lime ovens, known as kilns, along with accompanying quarries, were established. In 1839, the Geological Survey of New Brunswick reported 16 kilns along the Saint John River around Green Head Island. A small quarry had already been established near Green Head Cove by Robert

Robertson when Scottish immigrant Joseph Armstrong arrived in the early 1830s. After finding employment at the quarry and working as a barrel maker for almost a decade, Armstrong, in partnership with his brother Frank, purchased the quarry from Robertson and quickly expanded its operation. By this time, the extraction of lime and marble blocks for construction was a major part of Saint John's economy, with huge amounts of material being shipped from its harbour each year.

By 1850, Armstrong's successes had earned him the title of New Brunswick's pioneer of the lime industry. At the south end of the cove,

on a flat terrace of land, several homes were constructed for workers and for Armstrong. The quarry and its associated facilities were built on a cliff face at the east end of the cove. Along the water, a large wharf was built adjacent to several warehouses; storage sheds and the lime kiln were located farther inland.

A kiln was a large, round brick oven that was heated by burning wood. In 1852, the brothers constructed a kiln that increased the quarry's lime production to more than 200 barrels of lime per week. In the years that followed, two more kilns were constructed at the site, which by 1887 helped the quarry achieve production of 18,000 barrels throughout the year. Over 80 per cent of this was shipped to markets outside the province, with most being delivered to Nova Scotia and the east coast of the United States. The lime extracted from the Green Head Cove Quarry was used to construct many buildings in Saint John, including the Roman Catholic Cathedral, the former post office building on Prince William Street, and many of the stone provincial and federal buildings that remain in the city.

The quarry employed many people from the surrounding region, with some living on the island itself, while others temporarily lived at the site or commuted from other communities along the Saint John River. The quarry was operational only from spring to fall. During the winter, workers often found employment in the forestry business.

Joseph Armstrong died in 1894 at the age of 81 at his home at Green Head Cove. Around the time of his death, the quarry was passed to new investors looking to grow the cement and concrete business. This vision did not materialize, and by the start of the 20th century, production at the quarry had halted.

ABOUT THE AREA

Most of the area is owned by the City of Saint John and designated as park space, keeping the site accessible. From Dominion Beach Park, a hiking trail loosely follows the old road to Green Head Cove. As the trail reaches the south end of Green Head Cove, the topography flattens, and overgrown foundations and machinery and equipment remains emerge. Continuing to the east side of the cove, piles of scattered bricks stamped with the name *Gartcraig*—the Scottish brick-making firm from which Armstrong imported materials—are visible. This is all that remains of one of the quarry's former lime kilns. Farther along the beach, large timbers extend into the water, remnants of the quarry's wharf; at the beach end, a cliff face marks the location of the quarry itself. Near the top of the cliff is a small cave, likely excavated during the quarry's operation.

In 1890, geologist George Matthew discovered a fossil at the south end of the island in a rock formation similar to the one that produced the Green Head lime. This fossil became the oldest evidence of life known to have existed on the planet at the time. Matthew had discovered a stromatolite, a dome-shaped rock created by the successive deposition of sediment by ancient bacteria. This find has established the area as part of the Stonehammer UNESCO Global Geopark.

LIME QUARRY: N 45.279622, W 66.127909

From the trailhead (N 45.269994, W 66.123801) at Dominion Park Beach, follow the moderately difficult trail for approximately 1.5 kilometres, keeping left at all major intersections until arriving at the south end of the cove. The quarry and former lime kilns are found by tracing the beach to the west side of the cove. As there are many trails on the island, it is best practice to follow local signs and trail maps to access the cove.

2. Randolph and Baker Mill

Green Head, Lancaster

For more than 70 years, one of the most prominent and well-known employers in the area around the former community of Randolph was the operations of Randolph and Baker. The firm's lime quarry, kiln, and sawmill became a lifeline for neighbouring communities and offer a glimpse at just one of many similar operations along the lower Saint John River. At the north end of Mosquito Cove, remains of this large and once-important industry are still found among the grassy fields and lush wetlands.

The mill and lime kilns were the project of Archibald Fitz Randolph. Born in Digby, Nova Scotia, in 1833, Fitz Randolph was involved in many business ventures, including railway construction, grocery stores, and lumber mills. He had been involved with Fredericton's West End Mill until its destruction by fire in 1870. Recognizing the potential for a lumber mill and lime quarrying and processing operation in the lower Saint John River, he partnered with Charles P. Baker and established an operation on Green Head Island, approximately 3 kilometres upstream of Reversing Falls.

That year, a large lumber mill, including two gang saws, three lathes, and a stave and heading machine for producing barrels, was built on the riverbanks. The mill became a landmark in the area, with its large brick chimney visible from kilometres away. Near the mill, along the water, two lime kilns were constructed, where limestone from nearby quarries could be processed into lime. This was common at the time, as lumber mills often produced large quantities of wood waste that could be used as fuel in the lime kiln. The kiln was built near a large wharf and shipping facilities. Adjacent to the kiln, a large warehouse protected the lime from rain and snow. Most employees lived in the 18 or 20 company-owned boarding houses.

The large mill produced 6.4 million meters of lumber and 65,000 barrels of high-calcium and high-magnesium lime annually by 1897. In

1899, Randolph and Baker was officially incorporated. The mill changed owners several times in the early 1900s. Following Fitz Randolph's death in May 1902, his control of the company was transferred to his sons Allen and Robert. The Fitz Randolph family's interest in the company expanded in 1911 when Charles Baker sold his shares to the two brothers. Guy Allen Fitz Randolph, Allen's son, took over in 1926.

The mill was forced to temporarily close in the early 1920s due to financial struggles within the company and the lumber market, and the family focused on the lime kiln operations. On August 3, 1925, the two kilns and the neighbouring warehouse were destroyed by a fire that, miraculously, left the mill untouched. The kilns were rebuilt. As for the mill, it periodically restarted when large lumber contracts were secured. In 1929, Fitz Randolph constructed a smaller rotary sawmill on the site to help with these contracts. One contract came in 1934, when the mill was commissioned to process 600,000 metres of logs, hiring 30 workers for four months.

The mill received little work following this and was eventually shut down. The lime kilns operated through the 1930s and 1940s. Following the site's abandonment in 1957, the lands were put up for auction by the City of Saint John.

ABOUT THE AREA

Since 1957, no development has occurred on the site, which, like most of Green Head Island, is now frequented by hikers. At first glance, it is difficult to believe that such a large operation could have existed in this area of healthy forests and active wetlands. However, the remains of Randolph and Baker's operations still exist. Large foundations, pieces of machinery, and wharf remnants are visible, while in the neighbouring forest, concrete walls, vehicles, and overgrown quarries offer glimpses into the operations. In addition to the historic value of the site, its location along the stretch of river known as The Narrows offers views of the river and surrounding hills, making this a must-visit site for explorers, history enthusiasts, and those simply looking to escape the city.

RANDOLPH AND BAKER MILL: N 45.274452, W 66.112651

There are several ways to get to the site by following hiking trails from nearby Dominion Park; the quickest is to hike from the trailhead (N 45.269775, W 66.113444) at Sawdust Road. From there, follow the road 600 metres to the water's edge and to the site.

3. Peculiar Relics at the Corner of Loch Lomond Road and McDonald Street

East Saint John

Most people travelling past the East Branch Library and the Saint John Transit Commission building on Loch Lomond Road pay little attention to the large, empty plot of land stretching from McDonald Street to Refinery Road. Hidden among the overgrown paths and fields are historical relics, each representing different eras of Saint John's history.

This land was once on the outskirts of the city, cultivated for farming and livestock. In the mid-19th century, a nearby congregation of the Cathedral of the Immaculate Conception established St. Mary's Cemetery at the site, one of the few burial grounds for the city's growing Irish population.

In the early 20th century, the industrialization of Saint John East began in earnest. In 1923, the establishment of the Saint John Dry Dock and Shipbuilding Company shipyard on Courtney Bay brought new life to the area. During World War II, the shipyard's strategic importance to Atlantic naval efforts meant that the area was heavily defended. Following the war, the area entered its next phase of industrialization with the construction of an oil refinery, owned by Irving Oil and the Standard Oil Company of California and the Rothesay Paper Corporation Mill (now Irving Paper Mill). These industries created thousands of jobs, with many workers settling in newly built suburban neighbourhoods.

The plot of land enclosed by McDonald Street, Loch Lomond Road, and Refinery Road is still traversed by the occasional hiker or dog walker, but most are unaware of its history or remaining artifacts.

Refinery City

A string of long, rectangular foundations, parallel to one another, are hidden in the summer by tall grass and shrubs. Concrete posts along the adjacent trail demarcate the perimeter of the foundations. These remains are all that is left of temporary worker accommodations established by Irving Oil Ltd. during the expansion of the oil refinery in the mid-1970s.

Prior to the construction of McDonald Street in 1967, which served the new Loch Lomond Place shopping centre, Park Avenue and Mt. Pleasant Avenue ended abruptly, transitioning into a gravel path that stretched for several hundred metres before gradually disappearing into the landscape. The two roads were constructed in the early 1930s as the city expanded outward.

By the late 1960s, housing shortages limited the number of workers available for new projects. This caused problems in the early 1970s when an oil-fired thermal generation station was announced. The Coleson Cove Generating Station would require hundreds of skilled workers, already in short supply. In addition, in January 1973, the project owners, the New Brunswick Electric Power Commission, announced a $200 million deal with Irving Oil Ltd. to supply the plant with oil via a pipeline to be constructed from Courtney Bay to Lorneville. The contract required a $100 million expansion to the Irving Refinery, necessitating human power in the form of welders, pipefitters, labourers, and metal fabricators. Irving brought in approximately 2,000 workers from across Canada, the United States, and the United Kingdom and constructed three temporary accommodation camps, at a cost of $3.5 million. One camp was located along Red Head Road, where 12 living quarters, each accommodating 16 people, were built. The next was constructed near the Saint John Dry Dock, originally able to accommodate 135 workers but later expanded to 231.

The largest camp was established at the end of Park Avenue. Here, 52 accommodation units, capable of housing 832 people, were set up. Appointed camp manager, Homer Albert oversaw its operation and enforced its rules, such as no excessive drinking and no women on-site. The latter caused minor problems, as many of the workers were married with families. Aside from this, the camp contained all the amenities of life.

Living quarters were constructed in Bouctouche by Irving subsidiary Kent Home Ltd. and shipped to Saint John in three pieces and placed on reinforced linear concrete foundations, which remain on-site. Officially opened in the spring of 1975, the camp became known as the "Park Avenue Camp" or "Refinery City." It was used for several years until the refinery's expansion was completed and commissioned, after which the accommodations were dismantled and relocated.

While the temporary accommodations were relatively short-lived, many people living in the area remember them fondly, as they nearly doubled the suburb's population. Although little remains of Refinery City, these relics represent the scale of construction and industrial expansion experienced in the city during the 1970s, helping shape its current topography.

REFINERY CITY: N 45.287861, W 66.025861

From the McDonald Street entrance (N 45.286164, W 66.026727), hike northeast along the trail, keeping left at any intersecting trails. From McDonald Street, the foundations of the former Park Avenue Camp are approximately 200 metres away.

Loch Lomond Anti-Aircraft Battery

At the start of World War II, Saint John harbour was a key transportation and shipping hub in eastern Canada. It was also home to one of the region's largest shipbuilding yards, making it vital for the construction and maintenance of naval and passenger ships needed to deliver soldiers and supplies to Europe. The result was the massive fortification of Saint John to defend it from potential attack by land, sea, and air. Almost immediately after Canada declared war on Germany on September 10, 1939, the 8th Anti-Aircraft Battery of the Royal Canadian Artillery arrived in the city and set up a camp at the East End Grounds and Ballpark at Marsh Creek, adjacent to the Church of England Cemetery on Thorne Avenue. The 8th Anti-Aircraft Battery began recruiting and training soldiers to operate the anti-aircraft defence and gun positions

being constructed around the city. The first of these positions was constructed at Fort Howe, Navy Island, and on Loch Lomond Road, overlooking the Saint John Dry Dock & Shipbuilding Company's shipyard (page 301) on the east side of Saint John.

The Loch Lomond Road Anti-Aircraft Battery, also referred to as the "Slaughterhouse" Anti-Aircraft Battery due to its location near a former pig farm and slaughterhouse, was established to defend the nearby dry dock from low-level aircraft attacks and high-altitude bombing. The site's

barracks and crew shelters were constructed on a dirt road extending from Park Avenue. Behind the shelters, under camouflage drapes, was the anti-aircraft gun emplacement itself. The battery consisted of two gun emplacements, with a third built nearby in case additional defence was needed. Both guns were placed in dugouts, covered with grass and vegetation to help them blend in with the surrounding landscape. With one gun facing south toward the harbour and the other facing east, the battery was well positioned to defend against any attack originating from the east or south. While the battery was originally defended by several .50-calibre machine guns and a small 13-pounder, these were replaced in the summer of 1942 with two 3.7-inch Quick-Firing (QF) guns. Nearby, an ammunition bunker was built to safely store the site's required ammunition.

Although the anti-aircraft guns in Saint John were never needed, they are a reminder of the fear that gripped the city during World War II. Following the war, the sites were decommissioned and dismantled. Little remains of the city's anti-aircraft defences, except for a large concrete foundation and other scattered remnants on the empty land on Loch Lomond Road. The origin of the foundation was uncertain for years, as many industries have come and gone on the site. Comparing aerial images shows that the structure was placed in a central location relative to the two gun emplacements, suggesting it was likely a crew shelter for the soldiers stationed there, 24 hours a day during the war. The foundation is the most notable historic landmark on the site.

ANTI-AIRCRAFT BATTERY: N 45.288743, W 66.025517
From the McDonald Street entrance (N 45.286164, W 66.026727), hike northeast along the trail, keeping left at any intersecting trails. From McDonald Street, the former anti-aircraft site is located 400 metres away.

St. Mary's Cemetery

St. Mary's Cemetery, established around 1854 by the nearby congregation of the Cathedral of the Immaculate Conception, may be one of the oldest Irish Catholic cemeteries in Canada.

Just 2.4 hectares of the cemetery are currently maintained. It is estimated that 16,000 people are buried in the cemetery and the surrounding grounds, with many resting in unmarked graves well outside cemetery fences.

During major construction projects in the area, including the excavation of a nearby quarry and the construction of the Irving Oil Refinery, human remains have periodically been discovered, belonging to

unmarked graves from the cemetery. Over the years, many of the graves in the cemetery have been neglected, but more recently, preservation groups have repaired many of the headstones and grounds, hoping to preserve this piece of early Irish immigration history.

ST. MARY'S CEMETERY: N 45.291401, W 66.023199
St. Mary's Cemetery is located at 270 Loch Lomond Road.

4. Courtney Bay Breakwater Battery

Saint John Harbour

Completed in 1919, the Courtney Bay Breakwater extends nearly 2 kilometres into the Saint John harbour. Designed to protect the waters surrounding the then newly constructed Saint John Shipyard, this narrow strip of land was recognized for its strategic location at the mouth of the harbour, hosting a small lighthouse to guide ships into its dangerous waters.

Just before the outbreak of World War II, the breakwater at the centre of the harbour was chosen as the site for a military fortification that would work in conjunction with Fort Dufferin to protect the harbour from small torpedo boats and ward off possible landings on the surrounding beaches. The site was first armed in October 1939, when a single 18-pound gun was installed. In November 1941, two searchlights were added.

As attacks on harbours and ships by German U-boats in Canadian waters increased, it was deemed that the battery needed upgrading. In 1942, a large wood and steel structure was built adjacent to the original gun emplacement. Designed to resemble a lighthouse, another 18-pound gun was installed atop the building. The fort protected the harbour until it was destroyed by a fire in February 1944. Immediately following this, a large concrete structure was built to replace it. However, difficulties in construction and the reassignment of the personnel stationed there halted the work; the new battery was never fully operational.

The battery still stands alongside a small lighthouse. Exposed to years of storms and pounding surf, the concrete has slowly eroded, but the structure remains. While it is not possible to access this site by car or on foot, those who brave the dangerous tidal waters of Saint John harbour get a closer view by boat. For those more comfortable observing from the safety of land, it is clearly visible from many spots along the Saint John harbourfront.

BREAKWATER BATTERY: N 45.257235, W 66.045034
From land, the site is best viewed from Tin Can Beach, south of uptown Saint John.

5. Saint John Shipbuilding Drydock

Saint John East

Saint John was once the epicentre for shipbuilding in Atlantic Canada, if not in North America. Located along the shores of the Bay of Fundy, the narrow, protected harbour is subjected to the extreme tidal ranges for which the bay is known. Twice a day, the water rises and drops by nearly 10 metres, providing a natural dry dock for repairing and building ships. Additionally, the harbour is located at the mouth of the majestic Saint John River, which has long been a gateway to the vast forestry and timber resources of interior New Brunswick.

These traits helped make Saint John harbour one of the largest shipbuilding communities in North America and in the British Empire. But in the late 1800s, steel ships dominated the shipbuilding world, and Saint John's wooden shipbuilding industry declined. This was temporary, as the harbour remained a popular point of entry for goods, people, and cargo arriving in Canada. As the city entered the first half of the 20th century, a revitalized shipbuilding industry emerged, with the newly established Saint John Dry Dock & Shipbuilding Company leading the way.

Following its incorporation in 1923, the company constructed a large dry dock known as a graving dock. This concrete structure measured 350 metres long and 38.1 metres wide, making it one of the largest in the world and one of the only facilities that could handle the construction, repair, and maintenance of passenger liners, cargo ships, and naval vessels. The first ship constructed was the MV *Kipawo*, a passenger ferry commissioned by the Dominion Atlantic Railway and launched in 1926.

The dry dock helped the industrial city flourish through the 1920s and 1930s. During World War II, it played a critical role in the Battle of the Atlantic and in maintaining supply lines to the war in Europe. The harbour was heavily fortified, with anti-aircraft guns and coastal defence batteries nearby to protect the dry dock in case of an attack.

Following the war, ship construction and repair continued in what

was one of the few ice-free harbours in Atlantic Canada. In 1959, Irving purchased the dry dock facilities, which soon became known as Saint John Shipbuilding. At the time, Irving was looking to construct oil tankers for Irving Oil and cargo ships for the company-owned cargo shipping company, Kent Lines. The first oil tanker was launched in 1962, followed by many more tankers, ferries, tugboats, and fishing vessels, including the ferry *Abegweit,* which connected Prince Edward Island to New Brunswick; the Newfoundland coastal vessel MV *Petite Forte*; the MV *Princess of Acadia*, which connected Digby, Nova Scotia, to Saint John; and the Grand Manan Island ferry MV *Grand Manan.*

In 1983, the shipyard was awarded a contract for approximately $6.2 billion to construct nine Canadian Navy warships known as frigates. Part of the federal government's Halifax-class frigate program, it was the largest contract undertaken by the shipyard. This last boom was just that: a boom. After the last frigate was launched in 1996, the Irving-owned shipping company Kent Lines placed one final order for two container

ships, the *Kent Express* and *Kent Spirit*. *Kent Spirit*, launched in May 2000, marked the end of shipbuilding at the Saint John Shipyard.

The shipyard was inactive after this. On June 27, 2003, Irving permanently closed the dry dock and stripped it of its equipment, buildings, and materials. Around the same time, the company announced plans to construct a wallboard manufacturing plant, which is still visible beside the dry dock. At its peak, the shipyard employed more than 4,000 people.

The enormous concrete dry dock is just one of many relics that comprise Saint John's industrial landscape, a lasting reminder of the shipbuilding industry that established the city as an international port.

SHIPBUILDING DRYDOCK: **N 45.275423, W 66.032919**
Park alongside Bayside Drive, being careful not to impede traffic; the dry dock is visible from a small parking area (N 45.276161, W 66.029748) overlooking the dry dock and shipbuilding site.

6. Fort Dufferin

Hodges Point, Saint John

Located on the south side of Saint John harbour at the end of the Partridge Island Breakwater is the often-forgotten defensive fortification of Fort Dufferin. Overshadowed by the much larger military installation on Partridge Island, this small concrete gun emplacement atop a small headland was a crucial part of the Saint John harbour defence complex.

The point of land was originally home to the Negro Point Battery (the original name of the headland, Negro Point, was later changed to Hodges Point). The battery was built in the mid-19th century following concerns of an attack by the United States, depending on the outcome of the civil war. The site consisted of a large complex of accommodations, officer buildings, ammunition magazines, and several gun emplacements. As worries about conflict decreased into the late 1800s, so too did the importance of the battery, and, eventually, it was abandoned. Although it temporarily reopened in 1902 to train soldiers, the site was otherwise abandoned until World War II.

In the late 1930s, the Canadian War Department commissioned

Major B.D.C. Treatt of the Royal Artillery to assess and investigate the vulnerability of Canadian ports to an attack. In his findings, Treatt noted that Saint John harbour lacked the defences needed to protect the industrial and shipbuilding hub. Treatt suggested that the harbour was vulnerable to an attack by small, fast-moving torpedo boats. To address the need for a close defensive structure, an Anti-Motor Torpedo Boat (AMTB) battery was to be constructed at Hodges Point.

Construction began in 1939 on the fortification that would become Fort Dufferin. Its operation would be overseen by the Royal Canadian Artillery, specifically the 3rd Coast Regiment, who arrived at the site in October 1939. Two 4.7-inch QF guns were installed on concrete foundations in September 1939, followed by three 18-pounder guns that would adequately defend the inner harbour and surrounding beaches. To aid these guns and others in the harbour, several large searchlights encased in concrete rooms were built along the waterline, down the hill and east of the fort.

Throughout the war, upgrades to other forts in the harbour diminished the need for Fort Dufferin. Moreover, its location behind the heavily fortified Partridge Island meant that the gun emplacement lacked the same coverage as the island, slowly rendering it obsolete. By the fall of 1944, two guns remained and most of the fort's equipment and personnel had been reassigned to other war efforts.

At the end of the war, the fort was completely abandoned. Because many of the buildings at Fort Dufferin were constructed of wood, most of the area is completely empty. The concrete gun pads are overgrown but remain at the end of Hodges Point, and closer to the water's edge are the concrete searchlight buildings.

FORT DUFFERIN: N 45.247925, W 66.063041

The site is in Saint John West. Drive to the end of City Line and turn right onto Fort Dufferin Road. Park along the road; a series of short trails lead to the former site. While the site remains undeveloped, follow all signs and postings from local landowners.

7. Partridge Island

Saint John Harbour

Located 1 kilometre from shore in the outer harbour of Saint John, Partridge Island is a 600- by 300-metre forested island surrounded by dark, jagged rocks. From the shoreline, several rectangular buildings and a distinctive cross can be seen towering above the trees, sparking curiosity about the deteriorating structures.

Partridge Island's location at the head of Saint John harbour made it a strategic site for centuries, guarding and protecting the port. Used as a navigational aid, military fortification, and quarantine station, this often-overlooked historical landmark is one of the most fascinating and significant places in the province, contributing not only to the history and heritage of New Brunswick but also to the story of early European settlement in North America.

The dark rocks surrounding and beneath Partridge Island formed between 340 and 332 million years ago during the Carboniferous period. Tectonic activity causing large blocks of Earth's crust to collide resulted in the formation of volcanic rock that eventually reached the surface, now found beneath the island. Over millions of years, periods of tectonic activity, glaciation, and erosion shaped the island into its current form.

The Wolastoqiyik, the original inhabitants of the region, have their own story about the island's creation. They named it Quak'm'Kagan'ik, meaning "a piece cut out." According to their legend, a giant beaver built a dam across the mouth of the Wolastoq (Saint John River), forming a vast lake that extended 100 kilometres upstream. The dam irritated other animals, prompting the god-figure Koluskap to destroy it, unleashing a great rush of water downstream. It is said that a piece of the dam was carried out to sea and eventually came to rest as Partridge Island.

Military Use and Fortifications

The first record of military activity on Partridge Island dates to the American Revolutionary War when British soldiers stationed there were reportedly attacked by American privateers in 1780. After the war in 1783, thousands of British Loyalists fled to Saint John, earning it the nickname "Loyalist City." Two years later, in 1785, Saint John became the first incorporated city in what would become Canada under the Saint John Royal Charter, which called for defensive fortifications across the city, particularly at such strategic locations as Partridge Island. In 1800, the first fortifications were constructed on the island, including an earthen battery with six guns, a signal station, and barracks to house soldiers.

Upgrades were made during the War of 1812. A new nine-gun earthwork battery was built, along with additional barracks, a blockhouse, and ammunition magazines. The remains of this battery are among the oldest artifacts on the island.

Throughout the 19th century, Saint John grew as a shipping, immigration, and governance hub. The harbour's strategic significance prompted further upgrades to its defences. By 1878, the existing battery

had been upgraded with two 8-inch cannons and two 68-pounders to defend against large naval ships, as well as a 32-pounder and an 18-pounder for defence against smaller, faster boats or potential attacks on the island.

The outbreak of World War I necessitated a more advanced defence system. By then, Saint John harbour had become one of the most vital commercial and shipbuilding ports in Atlantic Canada. In August 1914, the 3rd New Brunswick Regiment arrived, followed shortly by four 4.7-inch field guns from Petawawa, Ontario. Temporary batteries were constructed at the north and southeast ends of the island, and in 1915, six concrete gun platforms were completed, each housing one of the 4.7-inch guns. Two additional guns were installed, and a concrete searchlight emplacement was built along the waterfront. Fortunately, the battery was never needed during the war, and the guns were removed in 1919.

The deactivation of Partridge Island's defences was short-lived. With the outbreak of World War II in 1939, the threat of longer-range ships and German U-boats posed a new danger. Coastal defence batteries were constructed throughout the harbour, with Partridge Island boasting the largest fortification. A temporary battery was installed, with two 6-inch Mark II guns removed from the Royal Canadian Navy ship HMCS *Niobe*. To support the gun crews, two concrete searchlight emplacements were built along the shoreline, as well as an observation post and a port war signal station.

A permanent structure at the south end of the island was completed in 1941, one of the largest coastal artillery batteries ever constructed in the Maritimes. The complex supported three guns: two facing east, one facing south. The two 6-inch naval guns were relocated to the island, with each gun emplacement measuring about 15 metres in diameter and built of thick concrete to protect against enemy fire. The south-facing gun emplacement featured a steel shelter, whose remnants are still visible. A narrow 25-metre trench connected the south-facing emplacement to the eastward-facing ones, providing access to underground ammunition storage and crew shelters. The two east-facing emplacements were separated by a 30-metre-long tunnel, leading to a vast network of underground rooms and equipment storage. This underground labyrinth was the primary shelter for military personnel stationed on the island.

Behind the battery, a three-storey concrete observation and range-finding tower assisted gun crews with targeting. In 1944, one 6-inch gun was replaced with two twin 4-inch naval guns.

At the end of World War II in 1945, the battery's guns and equipment were dismantled, and by 1947, all military personnel and resources had been removed from the island, marking the end of over 150 years of military presence. While the World War II fortifications remain the most prominent structures on the island, remnants of previous generations of coastal defence fortifications are still found. The 19th-century batteries, constructed mainly of excavated trenches and piled gravel, are more difficult to distinguish. The World War I battery is slightly easier to locate, with several U-shaped foundations at the south end of the island, once part of the six-gun battery installed during that time.

The World War II coastal defence battery, with its three gun emplacements, tunnels, storage rooms, and former underground crew shelters, remains clearly visible. The observation tower still overlooks the outer harbour.

WWI BATTERY: N 45.236691, W 66.054436
WWII BATTERY: N 45.237219, W 66.054947

Lighthouses and Coast Guard Station

The same strategic importance that made Partridge Island a vital defensive position also made it an essential navigation aid. For many years, the island itself guided small fishing boats safely into the harbour. However, as British Loyalists arrived in the area following the formation of the United States, the need for an official navigation aid on the island became apparent. In the 1785 Saint John Charter, this need was formally recognized, although the first lighthouse was not constructed until 1791.

The lighthouse and signal station were New Brunswick's first, likely the third constructed in British North America. A permanent lighthouse keeper was stationed on the island, with a small house built alongside the lighthouse. The oil-powered light was accompanied by a small cannon, which acted as a foghorn. The lighthouse became a crucial aid for ships entering and leaving the dangerous harbour. During the War of 1812, the harbour was a hub of activity for navy and cargo ships, prompting several upgrades, including enlarging the keeper's residence, constructing a large wharf for easier access, and upgrading the light's equipment and oil storage.

A fire destroyed the lighthouse in 1832, and a temporary light was installed. By the following year, a 12-metre-high, 7-metre-wide octagonal structure was completed. This lighthouse was painted white and red to distinguish it from others in the region. In addition to the cannon-fog alarm, a fog bell was installed in the tower. The lighthouse and adjacent residence were regularly upgraded, but the most significant change came in 1853.

That year, Scottish civil engineer and inventor Robert Foulis proposed using gas instead of oil to power the Partridge Island light. Foulis oversaw the design and manufacture of the new light and arranged for gas to be sourced from nearby Albert County. The new apparatus was first lit in August 1853 and, after modifications to ensure its operation in cold weather, proved highly effective. Foulis also sought to design a system to warn ships of low visibility and help them navigate the harbour in heavy fog. The result was the world's first steam-powered foghorn, which produced steam through a boiler to activate a whistle that could be heard over long distances. The design revolutionized coastal navigation, and similar foghorns were installed around the world. For many years, another inventor, T.T. Vernon Smith, was credited with the design, but, eventually, the credit was rightfully given to Foulis. The new foghorn began operation in 1860, just as the harbour and island received an influx of immigrants from Europe.

The lighthouse experienced heavy damage during the Saxby Gale of 1869 but it was repaired. With the exception of major upgrades to the light apparatus in 1872, the lighthouse operated uninterrupted into the 20th century. The Industrial Revolution and the advent of larger ships meant that new equipment was needed. In 1906, a large fog alarm building was constructed on the island. Made of brick, it sheltered a large boiler, air compressor, and diaphone to improve the efficiency of the previous foghorn. In 1911, the height of the lighthouse was increased to extend its range, and a new electric light was installed in 1915, initially powered by a large power plant built near the present-day wharf. Permanent electricity was brought to the island in 1926. In 1953, a new fog alarm building was constructed, following a fire that destroyed the previous one. Six years later, the 120-year-old lighthouse was replaced with a similarly designed octagonal one, retaining the alternating red and white sides.

Although it is isolated from the city, Partridge Island was rarely empty. During the late 1800s, it was regularly populated with people arriving from Europe or working at the local quarantine station. In the 1900s, the island's military fortifications ensured a near-constant presence of soldiers and military staff. For almost 200 years, lighthouse keepers ensured the safe and continuous operation of the island's lighthouse. The lighthouse was automated in 1986, eliminating the need for a permanently stationed keeper.

The lighthouse and a small adjacent building are the only remnants related to navigation. In 1999, the island's foghorn was removed. The foundations of many lighthouse keeper residences, the remains of the former foghorn building, and the distinctive, still-operating Partridge Island lighthouse remain on the island.

LIGHTHOUSE: N 45.239172, W 66.053871

Quarantine Stations

Saint John has long been a key point of entry for new arrivals to North America. In 1799, an act was passed that required that all ships entering

Saint John harbour with suspected cases of yellow fever, putrid bilious fever, or distemper be quarantined at Partridge Island. It would be decades later that the island began serving this purpose. Some sources suggest that it received patients as early as 1816; others claim that it was 1830.

In 1830, Partridge Island officially became the first quarantine station in British North America. A large hospital was constructed on the island's north side, while housing and offices for a small staff were built on the south side. When these accommodations were filled, large tent cities were often erected, resulting in overcrowded and hostile living conditions for those waiting to be seen by medical staff.

On June 11, 1830, the Feronia arrived at the island with 120 Irish passengers. The station monitored the passengers and treated those who had fallen ill. Tragically, two teenagers, William Marks and Agnes Murphy, died after arriving, marking the first immigrants to die and be buried on the island. The station reached a new height of activity in 1847 during the Irish Potato Famine. Between 1846 and 1848, many Irish people fled their homes in search of a new life in North America, significantly increasing the number of people passing through Partridge Island. This influx was further compounded by a deadly typhus outbreak in 1847. That year, approximately 2,000 Irish immigrants were quarantined on the island, many of whom died before they could continue to the city. Of those who died, 601 were buried in a mass grave on the island's south side.

This period is remembered for the incredible bravery of the doctors and medical staff who remained on the island to treat the sick. In 1927, a prominent Celtic cross was erected at the highest point on the island to honour this dark and tragic chapter in its history, and remains one of the most visible landmarks along the city's harbourfront.

Despite a decline in cases and the construction of newer facilities in Saint John, the quarantine station continued operating until 1941. Throughout its history, as many as 3 million people may have passed through the island.

QUARANTINE SITE AND HOSPITAL: N 45.238062, W 66.054934

Partridge Island Today

Partridge Island greets cargo and cruise ships as they enter Saint John harbour. The island is clearly seen from several vantage points in the city, with the best views from Bayshore Beach in the west end of Saint John or from Lower Cove near downtown. The island, currently owned by the federal government, is designated a national historic site. It also contains a lighthouse operated and maintained by the Department of Fisheries and Oceans.

Access to the island has varied over the years. Private companies and tours have occasionally offered transportation to and from the island, while many people have historically navigated the dangerous waters of Saint John harbour in private boats or kayaks. Access has sometimes been restricted by the landowners to prevent injury or unauthorized access. Those wishing to visit the island should first check if tours are available and if access is permitted. It is crucial to follow the landowners' wishes and to adhere to all signs and warnings. No

one should attempt to cross the breakwater to reach the island; it is extremely dangerous and marked with fences and No Trespassing signs.

The safest and most accessible way to experience Partridge Island is from the lookouts at Bayshore Beach and Lower Cove. Many organizations provide tours and access to the island, aiming to educate the public and preserve its incredible history. The island offers a glimpse into several eras of military conflict and defence fortifications. It holds the stories and tragedies of the early immigrants to British North America, honouring the heroic actions of doctors and medical staff while acknowledging the hardships endured by those early immigrants.

Although Partridge Island is out of sight to many, countless families across New Brunswick, Canada, and North America have been directly or indirectly touched by this small island.

PARTRIDGE ISLAND LOOKOUT (BAYSHORE BEACH): N 45.246233, W 66.075929

PARTRIDGE ISLAND LOOKOUT (LOWER COVE): N 45.263709, W 66.053907

8. Saint John Customs House Ruins

Sheldon Point

A short walk on the Sheldon Point Trail reveals several ornamental stone blocks and intricately carved sculptures.. It is tempting to dismiss them as leftover building materials from the nearby storage barn, but, in fact, these are the remains of the former Saint John Customs Building. Built after the Great Fire of Saint John in 1877, it was one of the most beautiful designed customs buildings in North America. It was originally located along the city's waterfront, between Prince William and Water Streets.

On June 20, 1877, a fire broke out in Saint John, near modern-day Market Square. Fuelled by strong winds, the fire devastated the city, destroying 1,600 buildings, leaving one-third of the city homeless, and killing 18 people. The original customs building, constructed by John Walker in 1841, was said to be fireproof due to its stone and brick structure. As the fire consumed the city, many people fled to the building, believing it to be safe. They quickly learned otherwise and were forced to evacuate as the fire reduced the structure to rubble.

Efforts to rebuild began immediately, and a new customs house opened to the public in June 1881. Five storeys high, it boasted a Second Empire architectural style, featuring ornate towers on either side of the building and a prominent steep mansard roof pavilion at its centre. The stone structure was adorned with carved stonework, intricately designed pillars, and arched windows and doorways. Constructed from local stone, the building was celebrated as an architectural marvel.

At the time, Saint John was one of Canada's busiest shipping ports and a hub for immigration. At the customs house, workers managed and regulated trade and customs. Over time, it also housed the Department of Transport and the Department of Agriculture. Additionally, a storm warning signal atop the roof warned ships of dangerous weather conditions a feature that remained in use until 1951.

In 1955, a study revealed that the building required major repairs to meet modern standards. The Department of Public Works, which owned the structure, chose to demolish it instead of restoring it. In 1959, a new government and customs office was built adjacent to the aging structure, with workers moving in that April. A contract for the demolition of the old customs house was awarded to George C. Chittick in the spring of 1960.

The loss of the building was a significant blow to the city's architectural heritage. During demolition, rubble from the building was used as fill in the surrounding area, while its more prominent stone carvings and ornamental pieces were taken by Chittick and placed on his property, the site of the Sheldon Point Trail. At its original location between Water and Prince William Streets, part of the building's facade is still visible, now a retaining wall supporting a small parking lot.

CUSTOMS HOUSE REMAINS: N 45.234617, W 66.103502
CUSTOMS HOUSE FACADE AND FORMER LOCATION: N 45.269015, W 66.061422

From the west end of Saint John, the trailhead is located along Sand Cove Road toward Irving Nature Park. From the trailhead, the remains of the customs house are 250 metres along the trail.

Moncton
Riverview
Salisbury
Havelock
Petitcodiac
Hillsborough
Rosevale
Hopewell Cape
Elgin
Riverside Albert
Sussex
Alma
Little Salmon River West
Cape Enrage
Salmon River
St. Martin
1
2
3.1
3.2
3.3
3.4
3.5
4
5
6
7.1
7.2
7.3
8

Upper Bay of Fundy

The Upper Bay of Fundy region encompasses a diverse landscape, ranging from the tide-influenced Petitcodiac River and the towering coastal hills between Alma and St. Martins to the fertile river valley of the Kennebecasis River. In the north, at the head of the Bay of Fundy, is the Petitcodiac River, commonly referred to as "Chocolate River" due to its muddy waters. The Acadians built large systems of dykes to take advantage of the river's fertile banks; the dykes are best seen between Moncton and Hillsborough. After the expulsion of the Acadians in the mid-18th century, the area became populated by English settlers. These early settlers took advantage of the region's farmland and forests while also beginning some of the province's first major mining endeavours, which included manganese, copper, zinc, and—perhaps most influential—gypsum and limestone. Inland from the coast are fertile farming regions established along the upper Petitcodiac and Kennebecasis Rivers. Throughout the 19th century, Sussex, Petitcodiac, and other towns were established as hubs following the opening of the region by railways and road networks.

The tides of the Bay of Fundy and surrounding forest reserves inspired the region's shipbuilding industry; by the beginning of the 1900s, many of the region's small sawmills and shipyards were no longer operational. Mining continued to flourish, with small mines popping up throughout the region. These mines extracted everything from metallic minerals such as zinc, copper, and manganese to oil-producing rocks such as shales and albertite. The Hillsborough gypsum and limestone mines were the most successful of the mines: between the mid-1800s and 1980, they were among the region's most important industries.

The same forces that deposited the region's valuable minerals also shaped its scenery and topography, inspiring a tourism industry focused on such sites as the Hopewell Rocks and Fundy National Park. Encompassed within the UNESCO Fundy Biosphere Region, much of the coastline remained inaccessible until 2021, when the completion of the Fundy Trail Parkway opened up the area.

This region contains some of the most diverse landscapes and cultures New Brunswick has to offer. Highway 2 between Moncton and Fredericton and Highway 1 between Salisbury and Saint John are the most travelled highways in the region; to explore this area, it is better to skip those major roads in favour of quieter highways, country roads, and scenic drives. Following the Petitcodiac River from Riverview near Moncton to the towns of Alma and Sussex is one of New Brunswick's best drives, offering access to many small communities such as Hillsborough, Riverside-Albert, and finally Alma, the gateway to Fundy National Park. Intersecting Highway 114 is the Fundy Trail Parkway, a scenic toll road that follows the mountainous coastline to the picturesque town of St. Martins. Farther inland, the town of Sussex is a hub for the region, with highways such as Highway 1, 10, 890, and 111 providing access to the many farming and mining communities scattered throughout the Kennebecasis River and the surrounding area.

1. Maritime Cement's Havelock Plant

Havelock, Kings County

Highway 880 travels between the Salisbury exit of the Trans-Canada Highway and the quiet town of Havelock. For most of its length, the road is bordered by farmland, forests, and wetlands. This abruptly changes approximately 4 kilometres east of Havelock, when occasional glimpses between the trees reveal a barren landscape of rock. Closer to the town, the trees are replaced by large mounds of grass-covered gravel, a large triangular-shaped building parallel to the road, and, behind the structure, the remains of the Maritime Cement Ltd. cement plant. The Havelock area has been mined for limestone since at least the late 1700s, when the first Loyalists settled there. In the 20th century, further exploration identified vast limestone resources that could be used in the pulp and paper industry, in the production of agricultural lime to mitigate acidic soils, for aggregate in road construction, and to produce cement. Small-scale operations occurred in the area until the late 1930s, when Roy Alward became one of the first to quarry the rock on a larger scale.

During the early 20th century, one of the primary drivers of the region's mineral exploration was Canada Cement Ltd. As demand for cement increased following World War II, the company began construction on a cement plant approximately 4 kilometres east of Havelock. Although the project was delayed due to shortages in materials such as steel after World War II, the plant officially opened in late 1951, and the first shipment of cement left the plant in March 1952. The plant was operated by a subsidiary of Canada Cement Ltd., named Maritime Cement Ltd. Once completed, the plant brought an economic boom to the town, first due to the nearly 600 people hired to construct the plant, and later through employment opportunities at the plant itself.

The plant was the company's first modern facility and included nearby office buildings, machine shops, storage warehouses, and

a large kiln that produced dry-process cement. The plant was conveniently located near an extension of the Petitcodiac and Elgin Railway line, which was extended to the community in 1885, allowing easy shipment of materials to the site and cement to market.

Large quarries were excavated in the surrounding landscape, where rock was extracted and moved to the crusher before being fed into the coal-powered kiln. The plant's capacity of 150,000 tonnes annually corresponded to approximately 25 to 30 railcar loads daily. The plant operated 24 hours a day and employed around 130 people. In the nearby town, new businesses were established as people flocked to the area for well-paying jobs.

The production of cement in the Maritimes was welcome, as, until this time, cement had to be imported. As demand for cement grew, the plant and its quarries expanded. In 1966, a second kiln was added to the plant, partly to meet the increased demand for cement needed for the construction of the Mactaquac Generating Station. Following the dam's completion, the demand for cement decreased, and with too much supply already available, the plant was shut down during the winter months, starting in 1969.

The plant found new life when Canada Cement Ltd. merged with Lafarge Canada in 1970, forming Canada Cement Lafarge. Two years later, in November 1972, the company announced a multimillion-dollar expansion. When the upgrades were complete in the spring of 1973, the plant's operating capacity had increased to 285,000 tonnes per year.

By the 1980s, further limestone reserves were identified, but within three years, declining demand forced the company to scale down operations. While new quarries were opened in the following years, the plant permanently shut down in 1987. By this time, the company owned most of the mineral reserves in the area and, instead of producing cement itself, it continued to sell the reserves to nearby plants. One of these plants, located in the town of Havelock, is owned by Graymont Ltd. and remains in operation as of 2025.

ABOUT THE AREA

Over the years, Maritime Cement's Havelock plant has been slowly dismantled and demolished. While the site is fenced off and monitored for trespassing, several of its concrete silos, storage sheds, and plant buildings can be viewed from Highway 880 and the network of ATV trails in the area. Off these trails are many of the plant's former quarries, along with relics such as equipment, utility tunnels, and machinery. Primitive lime kilns and the remains of quarries belonging to small-scale mining ventures that occurred before the 20th century are also visible. While the plant was once a critical part of the livelihood of residents, its remaining buildings stand as monuments to a bygone era.

VIEWPOINT & LOCAL ATV TRAIL ACCESS: N 46.011976, W 65.290949

The remains of the plant can be safely viewed from Highway 880, approximately 2.7 kilometres east of the town of Havelock.

2. Jordan Memorial Sanatorium

Pollet River, River Glade

The broken remains of a concrete dam and a modern long-term-care facility are all that remain of New Brunswick's first tuberculosis sanatorium. Opened on March 1, 1913, the tuberculosis sanatorium was named after its funders, philanthropists James C. and Jeanette Jordan, who donated the facility to the province in 1909. Work began several years later to construct new facilities on the site, which could care for up to 172 patients and house 80 staff. The location was chosen in River Glade along the Pollet River, considered a safe distance from populated centres such as Moncton.

As part of the construction of the Jordan Memorial Sanatorium, a 200-metre-long concrete dam was built across the river to supply the complex with potable water, laundry facilities, and electricity via a small generator installed on the river. The Pollet River had long been a popular fishing river, so a fish ladder was also constructed. A bridge across the river dramatically shortened the commute time from the community to neighbouring towns and railway lines. Completed in 1916, the artificial lake also became a recreation and fishing area.

While the sanatorium temporarily came under the control of the Department of Soldiers' Civil Re-establishment during World War I, it was primarily operated by the provincial government to treat tuberculosis incidences, which increased steadily until new treatments became available in 1948. Following this, the number of patients in the sanatorium declined. Tuberculosis patients were moved to the Saint John Tuberculosis Hospital in 1965. The sanatorium, nestled in the forest along the Pollet River, found a new purpose as an old age home, which was transferred to the Department of Family and Community Services in the 1980s. By the time the Jordan Lifecare Centre opened in 2001, many of the sanatorium's original buildings had been destroyed and rebuilt. Only a few original buildings, a marble sculpture at its entrance, and the remains of the former dam remain.

In the mid-1930s, the fish ladder was destroyed by floods. This, combined with the concerning accumulation of river sediment in the reservoir, began to negatively impact fish populations. While a new fishway was built in 1950, 20 years later the province began discussions about removing the dam to promote healthier fish populations. Eventually, the dam was removed, and the reservoir drained, leaving behind the current landscape. Portions of the concrete dam are still visible and remain one of the more significant relics of what was New Brunswick's first tuberculosis sanatorium.

JORDAN MEMORIAL SANATORIUM : N 45.941448, W 65.080340
The Jordan Lifecare Centre is at 747 Sanatorium Road in the community of River Glades.

3. Hillsborough Gypsum Mines and the Karst Landscape of Albert County

In the southeast corner of Albert County, near the shores of the Petitcodiac River, lies an intriguing landscape characterized by caves, sinkholes, disappearing streams, and irregular topography. The area is underlain by rocks such as gypsum, limestone, anhydrites, and other easily erodible, soluble minerals, which have led to a terrain dotted with unexpected dips and hollows, cliffs, narrow gorges, and an unknown number of cave systems, all formed from the erosion and dissolution of the bedrock.

For nearly 200 years, the region has been mined and quarried for its vast gypsum, limestone, and anhydrite reserves. Beginning as early as the 18th century, the area was quarried by settlers and farmers before attracting large-scale companies in the mid-19th century. From that time, the mining industry formed the economic base for the region, including the town of Hillsborough, which was at the centre of activity.

This area offers otherworldly landscapes to hike and explore, as well as a chance to experience what remains of its historic mining industry. Located 25 kilometres south of Moncton, on the way to places such as Hopewell Rocks and Fundy National Park, Hillsborough and its surrounding landscape is a must-visit for those passing through the area.

Karst Landscapes of Albert County

Albert Mines

The area around Hillsborough has a rich geologic history. Just beneath the ground's surface are large outcrops of calcium-based, soluble rocks known as evaporites. These sedimentary rocks, which include gypsum, limestone, anhydrites, and dolomites, are easily eroded and broken down beneath the surface, often by the percolation of acidic water into the bedrock in a process known as dissolution. The result: a jagged and unpredictable landscape categorized as karst topography.

While these unique landforms are seen in many of the former quarries and mines in the area, perhaps the best example is found west of the community of Albert Mines. Here, in the rolling mountains and valleys behind the community, are sinkholes, caves, and disappearing streams, found among a landscape difficult to traverse because of dramatic topographic changes formed by the breakdown of rock beneath the surface.

The rocks in the area belong to the Windsor Group, a geologic formation found throughout Atlantic Canada. These rocks date to the Carboniferous era, approximately 358 to 323 million years ago. During this time, the Maritime Basin was covered by a shallow sea in a warm, arid climate. The ancient sea, known as the Windsor Sea, experienced periodic drops in sea level, which increased the water's salt concentration. Only able to hold so much mineral content, as the concentration of salt increased other minerals dissolved in the water were deposited on the sea floor. Over time, these minerals built up to form the thick deposits of gypsum, potash, halite, and other minerals.

Over millions of years, the rocks were folded, twisted, and mixed with others before eventually settling. The current landforms, however, were formed over the last several thousand years. Beginning with the last glacier, meltwater has percolated into the subsurface, slowly eroding the weak carbonate rocks through dissolution.

Streams that disappear beneath the ground, natural springs, and steep cliffs and gorges are some of the features that have formed. The most notable features are the area's cave systems. While no one knows the full extent of the area's cave systems, several large openings and disappearing streams suggest that at least several large systems exist. One of the area's most famous caves is located near Wilson Brook and is known as Underground Lake. Named for the 55-metre-long, 15-metre-wide lake that exists within the cave's opening, Underground Lake is located at the base of a 30-metre-high cliff, its mouth open, thanks to a collapsed sinkhole. The Underground Lake is not accessible and is now protected within the Wilson Brook Protected Natural Area, as it is an ecologically sensitive bat habitat and hosts a number of rare Arctic plants.

The most notable sinkholes are those formed from the collapse of underground caves, leaving behind a deep depression in the ground. More common are dissolution sinkholes formed from the gradual dissolution of bedrock through a vertical crack. The result is a narrow, funnel-shaped depression ranging from metres to tens of metres in width. Many of the ponds throughout the area are sinkholes that have filled with water.

For many years, the provincial government and local tourism operators attempted to exploit the area, hoping to preserve and promote it as a tourist site, specifically the Underground Lake. Despite several attempts, no major developments occurred. The area south of the Underground Lake Road has since been designated the Wilson Brook Protected Natural Area. Stretching the length of the 2-kilometre-long road and extending 400 metres south of it, the area is registered as a Class I Protected Natural Area: all public access is prohibited except by permit from the minister of natural resources.

The designation and access ban applies only to areas south of the road however, and north of the road, many of the area's landforms can still be explored. Several hiking, mountain biking, and ATV trails criss-cross the area. The area surrounding the former gypsum quarries closer to the town of Hillsborough provide the safest and easiest access to the area's hidden backcountry. Use caution, as unpredictable terrain conditions and unexpected openings in the ground make this a challenging site to access. Additionally, some of the area's caves may still be sensitive ecosystems and are made of weak rock, increasing the risk of collapse.

GENERAL AREA: N 45.864534, W 64.687604

The area is accessed via Underground Lake Road in the community of Albert Mines.

Wilson Brook Lime Kiln

Albert Mines

The gypsum, limestone, and carbonate rock types that formed the region's unique topography also established the area as the centre of gypsum mining in New Brunswick. Located west of Albert Mines is one of the earliest known relics of Albert County's mining history: a former lime kiln, built of rocks and cut stone, on the banks of Wilson Brook.

The first land grants in the area were awarded in 1755 with the arrival of European settlers and British Loyalists. These early settlers established farms and mills along the shores of the Petitcodiac River, taking advantage of the flat, fertile lands and expansive forests. They had little need for the area's gypsum and limestone, other than for use in plaster and mortar. In the early 1800s, ships travelling up and down the Petitcodiac River to Moncton began making regular stops in Hillsborough. Many of the ships were destined for Maine and the northeastern United States, where gypsum was in high demand.

As the region's gypsum reserves were discovered, residents excavated small quantities of the mineral by hand and sold it by the wagonload to ship captains en route to the United States. These captains paid a small profit for the rock but could sell it for good prices at crushing and calcining mills in Maine, initiating the first exportation of the area's minerals.

The stone lime kiln on the banks of Wilson Brook is believed to be a remnant of this early time. While the exact date of its construction is unknown, it was likely built by those early settlers as trade with ships headed for Maine increased. The kiln was constructed from loose rocks found throughout the area and assembled into a rectangular structure consisting of three chambers, each with openings facing the water. Within the chambers, a small draw hole in the stone roof led to another open-top chamber above. Like other kilns from the time, the structure was built on the edge of a bank, allowing access to the lower chamber, known as the hearth, and the open-top upper chamber.

The kiln produced calcium oxide, also known as quicklime or burnt lime. Fuel, usually wood, was placed between layers of limestone in the upper chamber and ignited through the draw hole in the lower chamber. The chamber was allowed to burn for hours, if not days, to allow the rock to reach temperatures of 1000°C. As the limestone heated, it crumbled and slowly fell and accumulated in the hearth. The lime was then typically hydrated to form slaked or hydrated lime and placed in wagons, where it could be transported to ships on the Petitcodiac River.

Small lime kilns such as the one on Wilson Brook were dangerous to operate, with workers exposed to harmful exhaust fumes or at risk of falling into the open pit. The resulting lime could be used in construction and masonry, to neutralize acidic soils for agriculture, and for various processes in the production of pulp, glass, and sugar.

In 1847, Jeremiah Fowler, who owned plaster mills in Lubec, Maine, purchased some of the first mining rights in the area. In the ensuing years, other individuals and companies purchased mining rights and transformed the area's sporadic mining activities into large-scale operations.

WILSON BROOK LIME KILN: N 45.855597, W 64.690279
The lime kiln is located on a logging road west of Albert Mines. Drive on Underground Lake Road for 2.1 kilometres, then follow a trail on the south side of the road for another 400 metres to reach the kiln remains.

Hillsborough Gypsum Mines and Quarry

Hillsborough

In the area surrounding the town of Hillsborough are numerous mines and quarry sites, representing 150 years of mining. Just west of the town, the White Rock Recreational Area is a popular hiking and mountain biking area. Hidden among its many trails are the remnants of its mining operations, including equipment, foundations, and several caves and underground mines.

Even after Jeremiah Fowler began quarrying in 1847, production and exportation remained relatively low in Hillsborough. The first quarrying, confined to the summer months, rarely exceeded 3,000 tonnes of rock per year. In 1854, New York native Calvin Tomkins moved to Hillsborough with his family and incorporated the Albert Manufacturing Company, in an act of legislature that began a new era of gypsum mining in New Brunswick. Tomkins purchased Fowler's holdings and obtained permits to construct a mill, storage sheds, a shipping facility, and a railway.

In the same year, Tomkins constructed a steam-powered crushing, grinding, and calcining mill, as well as a sawmill and gristmill, in Hillsborough. Once opened, the mill was believed to be the largest of its kind in British North America, using the most advanced technology of the time to process and grind gypsum. The mill forever changed the town, providing well-paying, stable employment for more than 100 employees, with even more hired for mining and construction of the mill itself.

Twenty years after it opened, a fire in the mill resulted in its complete destruction. With the market value of gypsum still high and the mill profitable, it was rebuilt and opened the following year. This

coincided with the construction of a branch line of the ICR to the town. The Salisbury and Albert Railway increased the amount of rock that could be shipped to market from the mill.

The Albert Manufacturing Company mined gypsum primarily through quarrying, though some underground mining and exploration accessed deposits deeper underground. Most of these quarries are now encompassed within the White Rock Recreational Area. One of the largest quarries in the area was named for its first owners. The Fowler Quarry was once a hub of activity, with up to 200 workers excavating gypsum by pickaxe and loading it onto wagons, which was hauled by horses to the mill, where it was then unloaded.

This method was soon replaced by narrow-gauge railways built between the quarry and mill. The company owned two small locomotives, each hauling 30 3.5-tonne railcars six times per day. A maze of rails and small bridges allowed access to each cliff face being excavated.

The Albert Manufacturing Company's mill was destroyed again by fire on March 16, 1911. Thanks to overwhelming support from the community and the work of plant manager Charles Osman, the gypsum mill was rebuilt in 1912, once again claiming the title of the largest mill of its kind in Canada. By 1930, the mill was producing 80 per cent of the gypsum being mined in New Brunswick. In that year, the Albert Manufacturing Company sold the mill and its lands to the United States Gypsum Company, which was later absorbed into the Canadian Gypsum Company.

By this time, dynamite was being used to excavate large quantities of gypsum, and underground mining accessed the high-quality gypsum located deeper beneath the surface. The area's underground mining occurred in approximately half a dozen adits (horizontal tunnels) and shafts throughout the region. A room-and-pillar mining method provided adequate support for the overhead roof, and, as on the surface, railway tracks placed in the tunnels allowed easy transportation of the gypsum to the surface.

Work in the quarries continued until 1980, when the Canadian Gypsum Company announced the closure of the Hillsborough mill and a cessation of operations in the mill's quarries. The layoff of hundreds of workers devastated the small community. While the area is still recognized as one of New Brunswick's more important gypsum reserves, only exploratory mining has occurred since its closure.

Over almost a century and a half, millions of tonnes of gypsum had been mined and shipped to market. The quarries, underground mines, and road and rail networks have permanently altered the area's topography, offering a fascinating landscape to explore, with large pits and mounds of white gypsum still visible. Remnants of foundations, pieces of machinery, and even several underground openings can be explored throughout the many hiking and mountain biking trails of the White Rock Recreational Area.

WHITE ROCK RECREATIONAL AREA TRAILHEAD: N 45.897011, W 64.668403

From the town of Hillsborough, turn west onto Golf Club Road and continue for 3.5 kilometres to the trailhead, where a trail map is available. The road is paved for 2.8 kilometres, until the Hillsborough Golf Club.

Remains of the Plaster Mill and Water Tower

Hillsborough

After the second mill burned down on March 16, 1911, the mill's long-time manager, Charles Osman, tried to convince the company to reopen. After the town council voted to excuse the company from paying taxes, Osman's campaign was successful, and by the following spring, the mill was constructed and reopened. Not only had the mill reopened but it was also equipped with modern machinery and facilities, doubling its original capacity.

This mill consisted of a crushing and grinding plant, a calcining building, a power plant, a packing plant, and several large storage buildings. The four-storey plant produced up to 1,000 barrels of plaster, fertilizer, and terra alba (used in the production of cement, fertilizer, and paints) per day. Alongside the mill, a large power plant housed three natural-gas-fired boilers that powered shafts connected to the mill's machinery. The natural gas was purchased from Maritime Oilfields Ltd., which extracted it from nearby drill wells. Nearby storage sheds and an adjacent siding of the Salisbury and Albert Railway were built.

In 1930, the Albert Manufacturing Company's New York-based owners sold the plant to the United States Gypsum Company. The new owners upgraded the mill's processing facilities, adding several components to the grounds, including a large water tower. Water was critical to the plant, being used both in the preliminary processing of gypsum and for safety. The fires that had destroyed the previous mills proved that adequate cooling of the mill's machinery and a reliable source of water for fire prevention were crucial. The steel water tower was erected in 1931 by Horton Steel. Painted red and white for most of its history, it proudly displayed the company's name. Water was pumped from the nearby river to the tower, which could hold approximately 190,000 litres.

Following the mill's closure in 1980, the buildings were demolished, leaving little except several concrete foundations and the water tower

itself. In 1981, the Canadian Railroad Historical Association purchased the tower in hopes of preserving it as part of the adjacent railway museum. The water tower is the last visible piece of infrastructure remaining from the historic Hillsborough gypsum mills—an industry that, for more than 130 years, provided essential employment and livelihoods to hundreds of workers and their families.

PLASTER MILL AND WATER TOWER: N 45.923791, W 64.639510
Much of the area where the mill was is now occupied by private businesses. Remains of the mill and water tower are located on Steeve Street, adjacent to the New Brunswick Railway Museum.

Gypsum Silos and Wharf Remains

Hillsborough Waterfront

In the early 1930s, the United States Gypsum Company enlarged its shipping facility on the Petitcodiac River, including the construction of two large concrete silos at the edge of the company's wharf. Built between 1930 and 1932, the silos were made from alkali-resistant concrete, which made them resilient to corrosion and deterioration. Once gypsum was processed into terra alba and plaster, the product was shipped by train or ship to markets around the world. If shipped by boat, the material was loaded into small railcars and hauled to the loading facility, where a system of conveyor belts would transfer the gypsum into the silos, where it would wait to be loaded.

A large wharf adjacent to the silos allowed large cargo ships to dock alongside. The river's current, combined with the high tides

of the Bay of Fundy, meant that ships had to carefully choose their arrival and departure times.

The mill was invaluable to the community, which continued to grow as more workers moved to the town and new businesses opened. The mill processed locally mined gypsum for the next 50 years, with products being shipped across Canada and the United States, primarily for construction and agricultural purposes.

Despite its continuing success, by the 1970s the mill struggled to stay competitive with larger mills and global competitors. In the spring of 1980, the company invested $250,000 into the installation of a new wallboard production facility, an investment which did not pay off. Facing production challenges, including concerns about the quality of the gypsum being used, the company temporarily shut down the mill on August 21, 1980. A team of experts was brought in to address the problems, but their efforts were futile. Once the largest mill of its kind in Canada, its production was now too small for it to remain competitive. On December 31, 1980, the Canadian Gypsum Company permanently closed the mill, laying off all remaining staff.

In 1982, the provincial government purchased the mill and property and handed it over to Hillsborough. Shortly afterward, the mill was demolished, equipment removed, and the many miles of railway tracks that once wound through the area were dismantled. Part of the mill site is now owned by the New Brunswick Railway Museum.

Along the water, the two concrete silos stand at the river's edge, although erosion has compromised their bases. Surrounding them are the remains of the wharves and shipping facility as well as gypsum piles, covered in a layer of mud.

GYPSUM SILOS AND WHARF REMAINS: N 45.923920, W 64.630400
From Main Street, turn onto Steeve Street near the New Brunswick Railway Museum. Drive on the gravel road for 1.3 kilometres to the wharf and silos.

4. New Brunswick Railway Museum

Hillsborough

By the late 19th century, gypsum and limestone were not the only resources being mined in Albert County. South of Hillsborough, manganese and albertite mines were in full production. Around the same time, the region experienced population growth and an increase in logging. The solution was to construct a railway line from the ICR in Salisbury to the communities of Albert and Harvey. The railway operated for more than 100 years and became crucial to the mines and industries in Albert County. Hillsborough is home to the New Brunswick Railway Museum, which is dedicated to sharing the history of this branch line and others in the province. This hidden gem houses one of the largest collections of railcars and locomotives in Atlantic Canada.

The region's population and industrial growth in the mid- to late 1800s put pressure on the limited road network that existed at the time. The Petitcodiac River was the primary means of shipping ore and products to market but was often plagued by difficulties caused by the river's currents, ice jams, and tides. This sparked the idea of constructing a railway, and the subsequent incorporation of the Albert Railway Company in 1864. The company was supposed to construct the railway within two years. After it failed to do so, its powers were extended through special acts of legislation in 1866, 1868, and 1870. Finally, the construction contract was awarded to McDonald and Co. in 1875. McDonald and Co. faced several political and financial challenges in the following years and was subsequently bought out by politician and railway builder Amasa Emerson Killam. Killam completed the railway from Salisbury to Albert in 1877.

The Salisbury and Albert Railway struggled to make a profit. Nonetheless, it became a vital transportation mode for people living in the area and for the region's logging and mining industries. By 1911, the railway needed repairs, and despite its high operating costs,

its contribution to the area's industry was invaluable. That year, the federal government made its first attempt to take over the railway but was blocked by the sitting opposition. Another attempt was made in 1918, which was successful, with the Salisbury & Albert Railway becoming part of the CN railway system.

By the time the Hillsborough plaster mill shut down in 1980, the railway line had already experienced a dramatic decrease in passenger and cargo use, and CN abandoned the line. Looking to preserve its history, residents joined the New Brunswick division of the Canadian

Railroad Historical Association to purchase a 16-kilometre-long stretch of track and the former Hillsborough railway station, with the goal of converting this section into a railway museum. Heavily reliant on provincial grants to operate, the museum opened in 1984, providing tours, an archive, and even rail excursions using locomotives and former coach cars purchased from the railway owners. The Salem and Hillsborough Railroad and Museum became a popular attraction, providing the town with a much-needed boost to its local economy, employing five full-time and up to 35 part-time staff.

The museum halted excursions and shut down in 1991 after the government suspended the museum's grant funding, but it was restored the following year after protests from residents. But the worst of its troubles was yet to come. On September 16, 1994, a fire, believed to have been intentionally set, destroyed the museum buildings, along with trains and locomotives. The loss included three engine cars, one of which was more than 120 years old, as well as an assortment of railcars, including a snowplow, crane, and several coach cars. The fire also destroyed the historic maintenance and repair shops and the

archives. Miraculously, two locomotives and two former CN railcars were far enough away to avoid destruction by the fire

A new museum was established, and excursions resumed using the two surviving trains and railcars. Between 1995 and 2004, the rail excursions continued successfully, and over time, the museum accumulated new artifacts, helping to preserve the story of the Salisbury & Albert Railway. In 2004, these excursions were forced to stop due to growing insurance rates. The museum's name was changed to the New Brunswick Railway Museum.

The New Brunswick Railway Museum contains one of the largest collections of railcars in Atlantic Canada and offers a fascinating glimpse of the operation of the province's past railways. Surrounding the museum are locomotives, track repair cars, firefighting cars, and several coach cars, all in varying states of preservation.

NEW BRUNSWICK RAILWAY MUSEUM: N 45.923092, W 64.645117
The museum is located at 2847 Main Street in Hillsborough, approximately 24 kilometres south of Moncton.

5. Albertite Mines of Albert County

Albert Mines

Gypsum, copper, manganese, and gold were discovered and mined in Albert County, but perhaps the most remarkable mineral found was albertite. For many years, albertite was believed to be a form of coal. This solid bitumen product became the first oil product to be extracted from underground in North America, and it played a key role in helping geologist Dr. Abraham Gesner invent the petroleum product known as kerosene. For more than 30 years, the Albertite Mines operated in the backcountry of Albert County, forming a town on the banks of Fredericks Brook. The town is long gone, and popular ATV trails pass through what is otherwise empty forest and fields. But, by exploring more closely, the remains of this historic community and mine come to life in the form of foundations, tailings piles, and other relics.

Albertite was first discovered in the parish of Hopewell by resident Gould Hoar. Because he was not a geologist, the significance of his find went unnoticed. Enter Nova Scotia-born physician and geologist Dr. Abraham Gesner. Gesner had worked as a travelling physician in Parrsboro, Nova Scotia, until the late 1820s, when he moved to New Brunswick. In 1838, he was appointed government geologist by the New Brunswick government and spent the next several years prospecting and surveying in various areas. During one of these field expeditions, he discovered a mineral similar in appearance to coal but with several differing characteristics. He coined the mineral albertite.

In 1843, Gesner was removed from his position after claims that his surveys had been misleading. He moved to Prince Edward Island, where he experimented with the petroleum-based materials pitch, bitumen, and albertite, extracting oil from solid rock into a substance he named "keroselain," a combination of the Greek words for wax and oil.

This discovery had profound effects on energy use and lighting worldwide. Until then, whale oil, coal oil, and camphene (derived from

turpentine, a product of pine sap) were the oils commonly used in lamps. Whale oil was in decline due to over-hunting, while camphene was unstable and rising in cost due to its reliance on alcohol. Kerosene filled this gap because it could be produced in large quantities for relatively low prices and burned brighter than the other sources. Gesner returned to Albert County and discovered a vein of albertite on the banks of Fredericks Brook, for which he purchased the mineral rights.

Albertite itself is a black, shiny rock that is relatively soft and brittle. Emitting an oily or bituminous smell, the rock is found in shales and sandstones, where, over millions of years, heat and pressure created the perfect environment for the accumulation of prehistoric organic matter to solidify into bitumen. While it shares some qualities with coal, its formation and chemical makeup differ. One key distinction is that coal is typically found in defined seams, while albertite intermixes with sandstones or, in the case of Albert County, shale.

Its similarities to coal quickly caused problems for Gesner. In 1852, after obtaining mining rights and hiring workers to begin excavation, a confrontation occurred with William Cairns, who held the mining rights to coal in the area. Cairns claimed that the rock was a form of coal and that Gerner's workers were trespassing. With the support of Dr. James Robb of the University of New Brunswick and chemist R.C. Taylor in Philadelphia, Gesner took the issue to court. Even after overwhelming testimony and evidence, the jury ruled that Cairns had rights to albertite because it was deemed another form of coal. This verdict would later be shown to be a mistake, but it came too late for Gesner—and perhaps for New Brunswick to take full advantage of the mineral and Gesner's kerosene discovery.

Following the court decision, Gesner moved to New York, which had historically shown more interest in his findings. He founded the North American Kerosene Company the following year, and opened the first large-scale refinery in North America along Newtown Creek, New York, in 1854. There, he used coal oil instead of albertite to produce kerosene.

Gesner's defeat in court was just the beginning of albertite mining in Albert County. Although he could not use the mineral to extract kerosene, Cairns began large-scale mining in the area in 1854, shipping the ore to Boston and New York, where local gasworks used the mineral's high combustible content to create fuel primarily for lighting. This method was less efficient than transforming the mineral into kerosene, but it provided a stable market for Cairns. The mine marked the first instance of a petroleum product being extracted from underground in North America, just barely beating the first oil well drilled in Black Creek, Ontario, in 1858, and the oil drilling ventures in Titusville, Pennsylvania, in 1859.

Once operational, the mine consisted of two main vertical shafts, with associated hoist houses, engine rooms, and "coal" chutes used to load the rock into wagons. The first shaft, opened in 1854, was eventually dug by hand to 450 metres below the surface. The second, opened in 1874, was located on the eastern edge of the albertite vein. To transport the ore to markets, a tramway was installed from the mines to a loading facility at Hillsborough. Nearby were a blacksmith shop, machine shop, and sawmill. Workers from all over New Brunswick were brought in to live in houses constructed nearby, and a small town formed, equipped with stores, a church, and a school.

During the mine's operation, several fires broke out, and accidents resulted in the deaths of several workers, mostly due to toxic gases. The mine owners limited the number of workers who went underground to three or four at a time, and had a system of pumps and engines ready to flood the mine in the event of a fire.

Despite speculation that large amounts of albertite remained in the mines, the owners closed the mine in 1884 due to growing concerns that the market would collapse. In its 30 years of operation, an estimated 200,000 tonnes of ore had been extracted. After the mine's closure, most residents moved to find new employment, and the area became a ghost town. Over time, the houses and buildings were demolished or moved and the mining equipment sold. The community, which had seemingly sprung up overnight, slowly returned to forested land.

Despite the impact of the mine on the area, no obvious signs of its past exist. But by examining the area more closely, foundations belonging to former buildings, shops, and mining structures can still be found. Large tailings piles exist throughout the area, along with several pieces of mining equipment.

ALBERTITE MINES: N 45.878805, W 64.695442

From Albert Mine Road, turn onto Old Albert Mines Road (N 45.880056, W 64.668265) and drive for approximately 2.6 kilometres to the mine site. Be sure to follow all posted signs.

6. Maritime Eduction Company

Rosevale

Mining for albertite exploited the solid bitumen found in the parent sedimentary rocks in Albert County—but albertite was not the only source of hydrocarbons in the rock. Embedded between layers of shale was extractable oil, known as oil shale. This valuable resource remained undeveloped until the turn of the 20th century, when its significance became apparent. Years of promotion, exploration, and surveying would pass before the first permanent processing plant was established by the Maritime Eduction Company. The company's endeavours were short-lived, but the company's two-storey concrete building is the most significant structure remaining from the oil shale industry.

When the oil shales of Albert County were first studied in the mid-19th century, they were deemed to be too expensive or too difficult for oil extraction. The high prices of extraction for the processing of the shale rock could not compete with oil wells now producing oil in places such as Pennsylvania. This changed in 1895 when a train car delivered a load of oil shale to Moncton to enrich the gas being produced in a gas plant there. The Albert County oil shales caught the attention of Moncton businessman Mathew Lodge, who would spend the next 25 years actively advocating for the region's potential. Thanks to Lodge's promotion, around 1908 Moncton began using natural gas extracted from the area's wells to power, light, and heat numerous buildings and industries.

Increased interest occurred when a processing plant was established in Scotland to work with the same rock types as those found in Albert County. Oil shales from New Brunswick sent to the plant to be tested were shown to have a higher oil content than that of the successful Scottish operation. With this, nearly a dozen companies began exploring Albert County, drilling test wells and surveying the underground bedrock. In 1913, its significance was emphasized when the International Geological Congress visited the site during an annual conference, confirming the

vast scale and quantities of oil shale believed to exist in the county.

In the winter of 1920, the D'Arcy Company, a subsidiary of the international company Anglo-Persian Oil Company, constructed an experimental plant and laboratory in Rosevale to assess the region's oil potential. The plant employed 11 workers; a small mine nearby employed five workers. The laboratory experimented with the rock through a partnership with geologists and chemists from the University of Missouri. The plant used the Wallace process, which involved placing

the crushed rock into the core of a large oven. Heating the rock to 800°C forced the oil through percolation in the oven core, where it entered a system of ducts as vapour. From there, it was sent through a condenser, transforming it into a liquid, and processed to remove any impurities. This process allowed the plant to process 8 tonnes of rock per day, which would produce varying amounts of oil depending on the concentration of oil within the oil shale itself.

The plant, which operated for at least nine months, demonstrated that the oil shales were potentially hugely profitable. The company announced plans for a $12 million full-size plant that would hire hundreds of workers and result in the formation of a town around Rosevale. For two years, anticipation built for the promised stable, high-paying jobs. However, the company was unable to secure the appropriate mining rights to the area or find enough investors, which eventually prevented the development from starting.

Hope arose in 1926 when K.E. Clayton-Kennedy, engineer and president of the Maritime Eduction Company, took steps to establish a mine and processing plant at the Rosevale site. The company's largest investor was the American Hydro-Carbon Company, which helped finance the required mining rights and capital needed for the construction of a retort and oil shale processing facility in early 1927. A retort is a processing plant that uses high temperatures, absent of oxygen, to extract oil and gas from rocks such as shales. It began operating in September of the same year, hiring 90 workers; the plant at the time was the only one of its kind in the world. Nearby, steam shovels quarried rock near the surface, while underground mining through adits accessed shale beds deep beneath the ground.

The outlook for the plant and the future of New Brunswick oil shales were promising. Even before it opened, the company had announced plans to expand the plant and its facilities to accommodate the demand for the region's oil. But as quickly as the plant was constructed and operations began to ramp up, the company experienced financial troubles, and Clayton-Kennedy faced legal issues over how money was being spent. The company declared bankruptcy, forcing the plant to shut down before it could produce its first oil.

Following the liquidation of the company's assets, the property, plant, and its associated mining rights were sold and came into the hands of the National Funding Company. Hoping to continue the work, this company planned to reopen the plant in the spring of 1931. Once again, the promised operation never came to fruition, marking the end of the Rosevale oil shale plant. The property was purchased at auction in 1932 by a man from Moncton, but no serious mining development ever took place on the site. In 1942, a Canadian government study estimated that potentially 82 million tonnes of oil shale existed in the area, up to depths of 120 metres below the surface. This vast reserve was determined to contain approximately 31 million barrels of oil.

Over the next 60 years, at least six companies from around the world conducted extensive surveys and exploratory drilling to assess the feasibility of the Albert County oil shales. The last major exploration occurred in 1998 by Shell Canada, but as with previous endeavours, it was unfeasible.

The oil shales of Albert County are still open to future development. The story of the Rosevale oil shales lives on, however, in the former Maritime Eduction Company plant on the banks of a small river in Rosevale. Nearby are building foundations, pieces of equipment, and even several tunnels belonging to the former mine. The two-storey concrete structure is one of the most impressive of its kind in the province, still proudly displaying the name Maritime Eduction Company on its front.

MARITIME EDUCTION COMPANY: N 45.851707, W 64.850574
Follow Highway 910 in Rosevale and turn onto Stuart Mountain Road. Continue for 450 metres to the road to the site. Follow the unmarked roadbed for approximately 400 metres. As site access has varied over time, be respectful of local property owners and abide by any posted signs.

7. The Forgotten History of Martin Head

Bay of Fundy

Isolated on the west side of the Bay of Fundy is the scenic area of Martin Head. It has been referred to as one of the most beautiful coastlines in the Maritimes, yet it rarely shows up on travel itineraries because of its remote location. The cove is 30 kilometres north of the community of St. Martins and 23 kilometres south of Alma by water. Those who visit the area are greeted with rolling, forested hills that plunge into a small valley where the Quiddy River flows. At its mouth on the Bay of Fundy, a wetland and estuary are formed, and their ecosystems are interrupted every six hours by the region's tides. At the mouth of the river, a mix of rock and sandy beaches stretch out in three directions. On either side of the cove, the beaches run along the bottom of terraces before terminating at steep cliffs.

A third beach reaching out into the Bay of Fundy connects a small island, Martin Head, to the mainland. The isthmus connecting them has long protected the small cove from the brunt of the Bay of Fundy's winds, waves, and storms. This protection attracted the first people, who for over 200 years exploited the area for logging and mining.

Geologic History

Surrounding Martin Head is a mix of volcanic and sedimentary rocks formed during the breakup of the supercontinent Pangaea and the formation of the Appalachian Mountains. The oldest rocks, in the hills surrounding Martin Head, formed during the early to middle Neoproterozoic period, more than 600 million years ago, during violent volcanic eruptions. The rocks that make up Martin Head itself were the next to form. Approximately 360 million years ago, during the early formation of Pangaea, volcanic activity deposited dark basaltic rocks,

later buried by fine sediment from either a river or a shallow sea. By 325 million years ago, these rocks were in a tropical and humid climate near the equator, locked within the supercontinent.

A major climate shift began 50 to 75 million years later, when dry, arid conditions transformed the area into a desertlike environment. Large sand dunes, composed of alternating layers of rocks with differing colours, formed due to high winds and are now fossilized at Martin Head. This 250-million-year-old geologic formation contrasts with the other rocks in the area, which are darker due to their volcanic origins.

Around 200 million years ago, tectonic forces broke up Pangaea. Entire landmasses were split apart, forming rift valleys. One of these valleys opened into what is now the Bay of Fundy, which, over time, was further shaped by ongoing continental drift. Martin Head and the hills along the Bay of Fundy offer a snapshot of this fascinating and dramatic geologic history.

FOSSILIZED SAND DUNES: N 45.493245, W 65.204681

Martin Head Mines

The same forces that created the unique geology and landforms of Martin Head also produced ideal conditions for mining. High-grade copper was discovered in the summer of 1878. Soon after, a small mine opened, with a vertical shaft excavated along the banks of the Quiddy River. In 1905, the Maritime Copper and Reduction Company (later renamed the Maritime Copper Company) was incorporated to oversee mining in the area, which continued to produce and ship small quantities of ore from the cove. In 1910, the mine was purchased by a Montreal-based company, which operated the mine for several years. Eventually, the mine became too small to remain open, and was shut down. Since that time, companies and prospectors have surveyed the area, but to date, no major copper mining has occurred.

Little remains of the Martin Head copper mine, but at the western extreme of the cove, at the bottom of a towering cliff, is a small humanmade tunnel known as an adit. This adit marks the beginning of a small outcrop of gypsum, part of the Windsor Formation. With mining and sawmilling at its peak, Joseph Tompkins and Charles Osman of the Albert Manufacturing Company arrived at Martin Head in late 1904 to investigate a small outcrop of gypsum discovered at the western edge of the cove. By June 1905, the company had established a small quarry. In addition to this, a tunnel was excavated into the hillside near the shoreline. The adit was used to gain access to the high-grade gypsum believed to be located beneath the hill. The quarry and mine operated for a short period, with little gypsum being shipped from the cove. The tunnel, which remains partially open and surrounded by wooden timbers, is a lasting reminder of Martin Head's mining industry.

MARTIN HEAD MINES: N 45.493464, W 65.208251

Lumber Mills and Log Booms

The mining at Martin Head has long been overshadowed by its logging and lumber mills and its use as a staging ground for logs harvested along the coastline. William Davidson constructed a sawmill in the cove in 1882. Powered by a steam engine that operated a rotary saw, the mill could produce up to 10,000 metres of lumber per day. The mill operated during the summer months, when Davidson would transport workers to the area, where they logged the nearby forest and operated the mill. With access to vast, untouched forests in the surrounding hills, the mill operated successfully for two years before Davidson expanded it to include larger machinery and a lathe. The mill's output increased significantly, making it one of the largest sawmills to operate on the coastline. To house seasonal workers, Davidson constructed a two-storey house adjacent to the mill. To deliver timber to markets, a wharf was constructed at the mouth of Quiddy River. Sailing ships and steamers were loaded with cut timber, which would then be transported to markets across Atlantic Canada.

Davidson's mill was one of many operating along the coast. Mills could be found at almost all of the coastline's major rivers, including

at Goose Creek, Wolfe Brook, and Salmon River, where Davidson's son and George Vaughn operated a large sawmill. In addition, logging companies operating outside the sawmills began harvesting the area, using the region's rivers to drive logs to the ocean, where they would be transported to neighbouring sawmills. The Quiddy River Driving and Boom Company built a 120-metre-wide dam in 1884 across the Quiddy River to help with the river's log drive and provide a pond where logs could be rafted together before being shipped. The resulting reservoir was said to hold six to seven million cut logs. Competition often existed between these logging companies and sawmills, as demonstrated when Davidson took the Quiddy River Driving and Boom Company to court for disrupting his river operations.

Although it had no post office or many amenities, Martin Head developed into a small but thriving community. Mining and quarrying in the cove brought in many workers and prospectors, while Davidson's lumber mill operations, along with other companies operating in the area, enlivened the community in the summer months. Ships regularly stopped in the area, where they loaded timber and quarried rock to be delivered to markets.

A new era of logging at Martin Head began in 1911 when the Pejebscot Pulp and Paper Company constructed a modern mill, which produced lumber, lath, and barrel staves. Operated by David S. Cowles, this mill processed more lumber than any previous mill. Between 1914 and 1915, the company installed a large wharf in the cove, surrounded by a breakwater to protect ships from the violent waters of the Bay of Fundy. The mill operated for more than 15 years. In 1927, the company's wharf was expanded with the addition of a conveyor belt system.

By 1936, with its mills closed, Martin Head's role in the region's logging industry had changed again. Many sawmills continued to operate in the area, and in the protected cove at Martin Head, logs collected in a system of booms, and loaded onto barges or towed to large mills and markets throughout the bay.

Logging has continued in the area, but now logs are transported by truck instead of being shipped or towed. No other industry has shaped Martin Head more than the logging industry, with many relics still being found throughout the area. The most obvious of these are the remains of the many wharves and shipping facilities along the shoreline. Upriver, wooden planks and concrete foundations mark the location of its former mills; and in the surrounding forest and coastal terraces are the remains of foundations belonging to the mills, houses, and buildings constructed over its almost 150-year history.

LUMBER MILLS AND LOG BOOMS: N 45.495977, W 65.193996

Martin Head Lighthouse

The logging and mining industries of Martin Head meant that ships were regularly coming and going from the small cove. The headland, situated 300 metres from shore, posed a hazard to ships sailing by, especially during fog. Because of this, in 1884 the Canadian government

constructed a white wooden building at the edge of the headland and installed a foghorn that was operated by compressed air. The structure was built by Thomas B. Carson, with George Adie Briggs as its first engineer. During times of heavy fog, the alarm sounded a 14-second horn, with 46 seconds between blasts. The foghorn operated at Martin Head for five years before it was determined that it would be more effective across the bay in Apple River, Nova Scotia. In 1889, the foghorn was dismantled and removed from the site.

By 1914, the cove experienced an increase in marine traffic. To help ships navigate the waters, the Canadian government announced the construction of a lighthouse and keeper's residence at Martin Head. The keeper's residence was a square, two-storey structure with a hip roof. At its peak, an octagonal steel tower was installed to house the light itself. The light was 11.6 metres tall, but its location at the top of the

headland meant that its focal plane, or height above sea level, was 41.8 metres, providing it with sufficient range to warn passing ships. Herbert E. Armstrong, appointed the first lighthouse keeper at Martin Head, lived there with his family until retiring in 1933. The lighthouse, originally operated by burning oil, was eventually converted to run on electricity.

In 1963, with logging and shipping activity at Martin Head nearly non-existent and improving technology in ship navigation, the federal government decommissioned the lighthouse. Shortly after, the lighthouse burned down. On the west side of the small block of land, three concrete foundations belonging to the lighthouse and keeper's residence and two storage sheds remain. A small picnic area overlooks the beautiful Bay of Fundy.

LIGHTHOUSE: N 45.489048, W 65.188442

8. Animaland and the Forgotten Sculptures of Winston Bronnum

Penobsquis

The sight of Blowhard, an intriguing yet peculiar horselike sculpture standing on the side of Highway 114, captures attention. The horse is one of many sculptures found throughout the nearby campground and forest, once belonging to artist, sculptor, and entrepreneur Winston Bronnum. Once part of the Animaland Gift Shop and Sculpture Park, the area was a popular attraction and rest stop for travellers. Although the park is long gone, it has been given a second life as a campground.

Born on March 21, 1929, in New Denmark, New Brunswick, Winston Atwood Bronnum began his career working on concrete bridges and dams. His trade quickly became a hobby when he experimented with creating sculptures out of wood and concrete. After working in Ontario, he returned to New Brunswick in the late 1940s and dedicated more time to his art. He opened a small store in Grand Falls, where he sold his wood carvings. Recognizing that he might have more success in a larger community, in the early 1950s he moved to Fredericton, where he opened a store and began travelling to nearby markets to sell his art. After a fire destroyed his store in 1955, Bronnum returned to the construction industry.

Having seen the rise of tourism in Prince Edward Island through its attractions and theme parks, Bronnum believed that New Brunswick could go in a similar direction. He moved to Sussex and, in the summer of 1961, opened Animaland, a park which showcased his growing sculpture collection. These rabbits, squirrels, frogs, and other animals were made primarily of concrete. Opened exclusively in the summer, Bronnum used the winters to grow his collection, continually adding new exhibits. The park was located on 20 acres of land on the side of the former Trans-Canada Highway (now Highway 114).

By 1970, the park attracted 100,000 visitors annually and contained more than 75 sculptures. Bronnum's next attraction, a 15,000-litre aquarium housed in a building in the shape of a lobster trap, was developed in consultation with local biologists. Opened in 1970, the aquarium was a work of art, and another successful attraction, with guests hand-selecting lobsters for their supper in the restaurant. In 1974, a second aquarium was added.

The park's gift store was well known for its thousands of handmade crafts. Adjacent to the park was the Pine Cone Motel and Trailer Park, complete with a pool and recreation hall. The park's many trails and pathways guided visitors through its collection of sculptures. At the front of the park, one of its most notable sculptures, Blowhard, a thin horse believed to be a tribute to racing horses that are past their prime, greeted visitors.

Bronnum's talent was not confined to Animaland sculptures; he was regularly commissioned to create sculptures for special events and communities. For many years, the City of Moncton hired him to construct parade floats, and the City of Saint John commissioned him to create sculptures for its Loyalist Day event. Two of his more notable works were a sculpture to commemorate the story of Jumbo the Elephant in St. Thomas, Ontario, and the Shediac lobster, completed in 1989. Now displayed near the entrance to the town, this lobster held the record as the world's largest lobster for 25 years.

Bronnum died on March 10, 1991, at the age of 61. Following his death, the park was purchased by his close friends, who kept it operating. In 1998, a new highway bypassed the park altogether. Because highway advertising was regulated, the park quickly lost visitors, and after more than 30 years of operation, it soon closed.

Throughout his life, Bronnum created hundreds of works of art. For years, his park brought joy and wonder to thousands of people who stopped to admire his roadside attractions and his sculptures. His love for New Brunswick was evident in both his work and his park.

ABOUT THE AREA

Animaland sat vacant for many years. While some of its buildings and sculptures were removed, most of the park remained as it was in the forest, waiting to be rediscovered. In 2018, the land's owners opened a campground there, with campsites situated among the many beautiful, and often strange, concrete sculptures. Alongside the park, the Timberland Motel and Restaurant remain busy. The park, now a private campground, is open only to campground users.

ANIMALAND SCULPTURES: **N 45.749292, W 65.424901**

Take Exit 198 on the Trans-Canada Highway north of Sussex and drive 3.9 kilometres to Animaland Camping.

Bouctouche
1
Cocagne
Shediac
Cap-Pelé
2
Scoudouc
Moncton
4
3
Cape Tormentine
5
Point Elgin
Memramcook
Dorchester
Sackville
7
6
Johnson Mills
8

Moncton & the Tantramar Region

From beaches to forested wilderness, the region encompasses the area from historic Bouctouche to the Tantramar Marsh and Cape Tormentine. In the south, access to the Bay of Fundy helped establish the area as one of the earliest Acadian settlements. Along the coasts, many Acadian settlers constructed dykes to impound large sections of fertile wetlands and coastal estuaries for farming. They were at the mercy of ongoing wars between the British and the French, which, in 1755, resulted in the Acadian Expulsion, during which 10,000 Acadians were forced to leave their homes as the British took control of the region. In time, many Acadians moved back and revived their culture, which can still be experienced throughout the region.

Throughout the 19th century, the region attracted additional settlers reliant on fishing, shipbuilding, and forestry. Along the Petitcodiac River, the tidal forces that create the river's tidal bore also created the perfect natural conditions for shipbuilding. In 1855, this helped establish the community of Moncton, which, over the next 100 years, would become the largest city in New Brunswick and the transportation and the area's communication hub. Nearly all the railways constructed throughout the Maritimes relied on Moncton as a stopover location, distribution site, and centre for repairs and maintenance.

Along the Northumberland Strait, low-lying coastal areas are home to thriving fishing communities, interspersed with beaches and intricate coastlines, which help drive the tourism sector. During the early to

late 19th century, sandstone quarrying for construction materials and grindstones affected nearly every cove along the Maringouin Peninsula active during the early to late 19th century. In the east, the town of Sackville began as an agricultural community but, through the late 1800s, shifted to rely on commercial industry with the establishment of two foundries. Cape Tormentine's proximity to Prince Edward Island resulted in its becoming the departure point for ships and passengers travelling to the island. These ferries have been replaced by the Confederation Bridge.

From the border with Nova Scotia to Moncton, the divided Trans-Canada Highway is the main route through the area's southern portion.

From Moncton, the Trans-Canada Highway continues to Fredericton, with a major highway branching off to Saint John. Heading north, Highway 15 travels to the popular summer destination of Shediac before following the coastline east to Port Elgin. North of Shediac, Highway 11 continues to Miramichi, while a network of roads, including Highways 115 and 126, stretches inland, passing through small logging and agricultural towns. In the east, Highway 16 traverses the Tantramar Marsh and Chignecto Isthmus and is the primary access route to the Confederation Bridge and Prince Edward Island. By exploring the area's many back roads and minor highways, visitors can experience the rich cultures and histories hidden throughout.

1. Cocagne Island

Cormierville, Kent County

Along the east coast of New Brunswick is a network of barrier islands, estuaries, and spits. These landmarks, formed over thousands of years, originated from both the Gulf of St. Lawrence's pounding surf and deposition of sediment by the coastline's large rivers. Among these islands and peninsulas is Cocagne Island—a low-lying island approximately 4.5 kilometres long and ranging between 180 and 1,100 metres wide. It is one of the last uninhabited islands on this stretch of coast, though this was not always the case. The island had long been used for farming and fishing and was a family home to many. The island's geology, combined with its sandy beaches and clear waters, make it a dramatic natural wonder.

HUMAN HISTORY

The first people to use the island were the Mi'kmaq; however, by the late 18th century, more and more Europeans were settling in the area. Following the end of the American Revolutionary War and the signing of the Treaty of Paris, the government began granting land in New Brunswick to encourage settlement and solidify British claims to the land. Many of those being granted land in the region were Acadians, who, after the Acadian Expulsion between 1755 and 1764, had made their way back in hopes of finding a new home in British territory. One person was Paul Hebert, who, along with Joseph Gueguen, Jean Bourg, and Jean B. Deprez, was granted the right to clear, cultivate, and live on the south end of Cocagne Island in 1791.

At the time, a portion of the island's northern end was being used by the Mi'kmaq, who were confined to a reserve near Bouctouche. The 100 acres of land owned by Chief Noel John supported the Bouctouche community, where they grew and harvested wheat, hay, and livestock. Given the limited land suitable for agriculture, John wrote to the provincial secretary on at least one occasion, claiming that the settlers' presence impeded what had become a crucial part of the local Mi'kmaq agriculture.

Since the 1800s, the land on the island was either passed down to family members of the original settlers or sold to new families. By the early 20th century, only a few families lived there. In 1900, Joseph Gueguen's great-great-grandson moved his family to the island and constructed a large house on his family's land. Gueguen's family joined several others who called the island home. Although there were no amenities on the island, residents regularly travelled across Cocagne Bay to purchase food and supplies and for health care. Occasionally, a doctor travelled to the island, and some basic education was provided to the island's children.

Many living on the island made their living by fishing; but by 1945, many of its residents had relocated to communities on the mainland. Among these were the families of Edward Cormier and Lucas Goguen (a variant of Gueguen that evolved over time). Determined to preserve their heritage, Cormier and Goguen devised a plan to tow their houses across the ice to the mainland. In February 1948, each house was towed across the ice by a convoy of trucks, a remarkable feat of resourcefulness and determination. Over the next 70 years, people periodically used the island for farming or fishing but it has been mostly uninhabited ever since.

A NATURAL WONDER

Fine sand beaches, carved rock formations, and a preserved ecosystem consisting of wetlands, marshes, sand dunes, and forests make the island an ideal location for seeing migrating and nesting colonies of great blue herons and nesting bank swallows, which make their nests in small tunnels in the island's banks. The island is considered ecologically sensitive, as it hosts a variety of plants and wildlife, so extra caution should be taken when visiting.

On the northeast coastline, the island's soft sandstone and conglomerate rocks have been moulded into caves, sea stacks, and arches. Like much of the area surrounding it, the island is composed of 300-million-year-old sedimentary rocks believed to have been deposited by an ancient river system surrounded by wetlands and swamps. Since the last ice age, changing land elevation and sea levels have exposed these rocks to the power of the Gulf of St. Lawrence, carving them into an ever-changing assortment of caves, tunnels, and sea stacks.

Fine sand and glacial debris known as till, which helped spark the fertile land found on the island, were deposited during the last ice age.

This till contributes to the island's rich ecosystems and has led to the formation of many of its beautiful and isolated sandy beaches.

ABOUT THE AREA

The island—specifically its eastern side—is regularly visited by boaters and kayakers who wish to appreciate the sandy beaches and explore the island's rock formations. A few trails weave along the coastline, but due to the sensitive nature of the island and its many wetlands, many visitors stay close to shore. Most of the homes that were once on the island were on the west side. Many of these areas are now heavily overgrown, except for several large grassy fields. The coastline along the island's west side is dotted with evidence of wharves and fishing sheds. From the east side of the island and along the coast in the communities of Cormierville and Cocagne, Cocagne harbour can be seen, filled with an array of nets and buoys used for oyster aquaculture.

The island's beauty has not always gone unnoticed, and developers periodically consider its potential. As of 2025, the island remains undeveloped, an overlooked gem along New Brunswick's beautiful east coast.

COCAGNE ISLAND: N 46.396950, W 64.597260

There is no ferry to or tours of Cocagne Island; a private boat is needed to visit. From the Cormierville wharf (N 46.407325, W 64.617063), paddle 1 kilometre south to reach the island.

2. RCAF Station Scoudouc and the No. 4 Repair Depot

Scoudouc

In 1940, Moncton was designated as the first British Commonwealth Air Training Plan centre in New Brunswick. This program was designed to train pilots from Commonwealth countries before they were sent to war in Europe, and thousands of pilots and hundreds of aircraft were sent to New Brunswick for training. At the time, air travel was at record highs, with aircraft and supplies regularly passing through the province en route across the Atlantic. Consequently, the Moncton airfield was overwhelmed with aircraft and pilots, prompting the RCAF to establish two "relief" airfields in the nearby communities of Salisbury and Scoudouc.

The Scoudouc airfield opened in late 1940 for the No. 8 Service Flying Training School, which had originally been based in Moncton. The airfield was intended to be used in the event of inclement weather, operational issues, or lack of capacity in Moncton. It had three paved runways: 1,500, 760, and 820 metres. In addition to the extra tarmac space and runways, the airfield was equipped with barracks, a drill hall, a fire hall, churches, and other amenities. To supply the airfield, a spur line was constructed from the nearby railway, allowing the delivery of supplies, fuel, and passengers.

Just as there was a need for relief airfields, so too the demand for additional maintenance, repair, and testing facilities arose. The Scoudouc airfield became home to the No. 4 Repair Depot in September 1941. This redesignation led to the construction of aircraft hangars and repair facilities, as the site became the primary repair field for long-range, antisubmarine aircraft such as the Lockheed Hudson and B-24 Liberator. Nearly 2,000 airmen and 63 officers worked at the site by 1944.

LOL

By 1945, activity at bases across the Maritimes began to lessen, and the need for the No. 4 Repair Depot diminished. The unit was officially disbanded in July, with most of the personnel being transferred to Moncton. The airfield, renamed RCAF Station Scoudouc, became a holding unit or processing centre for soldiers and airmen awaiting further deployment and assignment instructions. By Christmas, the base was officially shut.

Like many other military bases in the early 1950s, RCAF Station Scoudouc was reactivated in 1951. This time, it served as a detachment for the No. 5 Supply Depot based in Moncton and was used to repair aircraft. It never again experienced the same level of activity it did during the 1940s. By the end of the decade, many of the base's buildings were being torn down. A small detachment remained at the base until January 1, 1965, when the repair depot, airfield, and base were officially closed.

Since then, RCAF Station Scoudouc site has been repurposed several times. From the late 1950s until the 1990s, the runways became a racetrack for the Atlantic Motorcycle Competition Riders Association. In the 1960s and 1970s, many of the airfield's hangars and surrounding lands were taken over by private businesses, transforming the site

into the Scoudouc Industrial Park. The park's more than 20 private businesses and industries provide employment for hundreds of people. Many of the former hangars and buildings are visible throughout the area, with some repurposed to support local industry. The runways have been converted into storage yards and roadways. Foundations, railway lines, and buildings are scattered throughout the area.

STATION REPAIR DEPOT: N 46.170397, W 64.588356
The airfield is now the site of the Scoudouc Industrial Park. Travel approximately 7 kilometres north of Moncton on Route 15 and exit at Exit 26. Drive another 2 kilometres to the site.

3. Sunny Brae Arena

Sunny Brae, Moncton

Tucked away on the edge of one of Moncton's oldest neighbourhoods is a two-storey concrete ring about 60 metres in diameter. The ring structure is all that remains of the beloved Sunny Brae Arena. Despite being open for only six years, the arena had an impact on the residents and sports community. Now on private property, it can still be easily seen from nearby roads.

In the early 1920s, the small town of Sunny Brae was located on the outskirts of Moncton, far from its booming industrial and commercial districts—the perfect location for a new skating arena. Architect and contractor Robert C. Donald, hired to construct the new

facility, designed what he believed would be his greatest architectural achievement. Inspired by Roman architecture, this two-storey circular concrete structure boasted a cone-shaped concrete roof that was more than five times the height of the arena walls.

Trouble struck when a building inspector discovered several cracks in the roof. Worried about the arena's structural integrity, the inspector ordered that the roof be replaced. This was an expensive endeavour, but a new roof of wooden timbers and steel beams was constructed.

The Sunny Brae Arena officially opened in January 1922, and with a capacity of 2,000 people, it hosted hockey games, concerts, and festivals, welcoming world-class performances. The arena contained the largest natural ice surface in Canada and was the largest indoor arena of its kind in the Maritime provinces.

The building's glory was short-lived. On February 26, 1928, a fire, believed to have been caused by the arena's heating system, engulfed the wooden roof and destroyed the building, leaving only the outer concrete walls and a small circular beam and column system in the interior. A young girl reportedly perished in the fire.

The Sunny Brae Arena held architectural and engineering significance for both its design and its status as an early example of a concrete building. More importantly, for a short period the building brought people together because of its high-quality ice and the diversity of events it hosted. Since it burned down, the ring structure has remained standing in a grassy field in Sunny Brae, now a neighbourhood of Moncton.

SUNNY BRAE ARENA: N 46.101704, W 64.775076
Although access to the Sunny Brae Arena site is restricted, it is visible from the end of Donald Avenue and Curry Street.

4. Intercolonial Railway Blacksmith Shops

Albert Street, Moncton

Moncton, colloquially named "Hub City," has long been a major transportation node for Atlantic Canada, largely due to its location at the intersection of several major railway networks that spread east, west, south, and north of the city. One of the earliest railways to pass through Moncton was the ICR, which was established following Confederation to connect Canada's provinces. While Moncton remains an important railway hub, much of its original Confederation-era infrastructure has long been destroyed and the land converted into parks, sports fields, and industrial lots.

But tucked away on the west side of Moncton's downtown is one of the longest-standing reminders of the ICR shops: a crumbling brick building with a distinct monitor roof that was the blacksmith shop. This building represents more than just the ICR; it is the only surviving reminder of the worst fire in the city's history.

The terms of Confederation stated that a national railway must be constructed to connect the four original provinces. After the Intercolonial Railway Act was passed in 1868, work began on surveying and constructing a line from Halifax to Quebec and on to Ontario. The railway reached Moncton in 1879, and in the years following, a large complex of buildings, repair facilities, and shops on the west side of the city were constructed. Completed in 1887, this massive complex of brick buildings included all the facilities needed to repair railcars. Among these was a blacksmith shop, where components could be repaired, fabricated, and maintained. The blacksmith shop had two railway lines passing through it, allowing railcars to be easily serviced.

On February 24, 1906, disaster struck when, late in the evening, a fire broke out in one of the shop buildings. Soon most of the complex was engulfed in flames. Crews and volunteers responded quickly;

however, in the two hours it took to get the fire under control, most of the complex was destroyed, along with many railcars and several adjacent city buildings. The fire also claimed the life of one shop worker. The fire, the worst in the city's history, caused millions of dollars in damages and put hundreds of people out of work.

Following the fire, there were talks of moving the shops and their many jobs to Quebec or even Nova Scotia. However, the member of Parliament for Westmoreland and minister of railways and canals, Henry Robert Emmerson, began a campaign to rebuild the shops in Moncton. His efforts were successful, and several months after the fire, the first tender was put out to rebuild the shops and railyard northwest of the

original site along what is now Millennium Boulevard. This site, which opened in 1908, employed more than 1,000 people and promoted the growth of Moncton.

The original Intercolonial Railway Blacksmith Shop was used for various purposes over the years, but primarily as a storage shed. Although the slowly crumbling building, which remains under private ownership, is now a recognized heritage site, its future seems unclear. Despite its significance to Moncton's development, it has remained largely forgotten.

BLACKSMITH SHOPS: N 46.082947, W 64.783987

The former blacksmith shop is at 105 Albert Street in Moncton.

5. Cape Tormentine Ferry Terminal

Cape Tormentine

People have been crossing the Northumberland Strait between New Brunswick and Prince Edward Island for millennia. As more and more settlers arrived from Europe, the need for a regular and reliable ferry connection grew. While sailing ships, dories, or even canoes could transport mail and supplies in the summer, ice conditions made these deliveries more challenging in the winter. By 1827, small "iceboats" crossed the strait at its narrowest point, Abegweit Passage, transporting supplies and mail when ice prohibited the use of larger boats.

In 1873, Prince Edward Island entered Confederation with a pledge from Canada to establish a year-round steam service for mail and passengers. Three years later, a dedicated steamship was introduced from Pictou, Nova Scotia, to Georgetown, Prince Edward Island. Despite being halted due to ice conditions for long periods in the winter, it was the first regular ferry service to be introduced to Prince Edward Island.

Because of its vast agricultural lands, Prince Edward Island was emerging as an important trade partner. Investors from Sackville, along with the support of the New Brunswick government, incorporated the New Brunswick and Prince Edward Island Railway in April 1874. When it was completed in 1886, trains would receive the mail and supplies still being regularly transported across the Abegweit Passage at Cape Tormentine and then transport them to the ICR junction in Sackville, where they could be sent across the country. Despite the fact that the Prince Edward Island-Nova Scotia ferry service was still active, by the 20th century this method of delivering supplies across the strait had become the most reliable mode.

The Canadian government purchased the railway in 1914, incorporating it into the Canadian Government Railways (later CN). Looking to increase the number of shipments coming from Prince

Edward Island, construction soon began on the first major ferry terminal at Cape Tormentine, which would allow railcars to be loaded onto ferries to sail across the strait before being placed on a branch line of the Prince Edward Island railway. The first of these rail ferries, the MV *Prince Edward Island*, began operating in 1917. In its first year, the ferry made 506 crossings, marking the most reliable and practical ferry crossing to date.

In 1922, the wharf was modified to allow vehicles to travel on the ferries. In 1947, the MV *Abegweit* replaced the *Prince Edward Island* and could carry 950 passengers and 60 vehicles or 16 railway cars. A second ferry was added in 1968, and in 1982, an even larger ferry replaced the *Abegweit*, boasting the same name.

On January 1, 1989, the last railcar arrived at Cape Tormentine. With the closure of the Prince Edward Island railway, the Sackville-to-Cape Tormentine line was also shut down. Finally, in 1997, the opening

of the Confederation Bridge ended the need for a ferry service at Cape Tormentine.

For more than 150 years, life at Cape Tormentine revolved around transporting people and supplies. The ferry terminal parking lot and rail yard have been repurposed into a campground, with many relics of the former railway still visible. The extensive wharf can be visited; part of it has been turned into a marina. At the end of the wharf is an abandoned inspection building, along with one of the harbour's lighthouses. While the community is but a shadow of its former self, the area's rich history can still be explored today.

FERRY TERMINAL: **N 46.135105, W 63.777996**

The wharf and relics of the ferry operations are located throughout the town of Cape Tormentine, which is 5 kilometres east of Highway 16 near the Confederation Bridge.

6. Westmoreland Chemical Park

Dorchester Cape

The early days of the Westmoreland Chemical Park were filled with optimism, hope, and ambition; however, it quickly turned into a boondoggle. In the years following World War II, those living in the Dorchester area were struggling to make ends meet and find adequate employment. Throughout the 1940s and 1950s, the area's small sawmills, mines, and quarries closed. Additionally, local farmers faced numerous challenges, including difficulties in importing much-needed fertilizers. In the early 1960s, provincial government studies pointed to a need for intervention. The solution considered the local production of fertilizers that could be sold to local farmers and markets around the world.

In June 1964, residents were relieved when, under Liberal premier Louis Robichaud, provincial minister of finance Lestock G. DesBrisay announced that the government would invest in a fertilizer plant and industrial area near Dorchester Cape, which would become the Westmoreland Chemical Park. The announcement followed the formation of the New Brunswick Development Corporation (NBDC), with a mandate of seeking new economic development opportunities and providing companies with financial startup aid. The NBDC's plan for the Westmoreland Chemical Park was to construct a fertilizer plant that would import ammonia and produce the fertilizer ammonium nitrate. The project promised to create hundreds of jobs.

Dorchester Cape was selected because of its proximity to the railway as well as navigable waters along the Memramcook River and Bay of Fundy. It also had a large undeveloped piece of land. By the time the announcement had been made, a site investigation and tender for construction had already been awarded to Lummus Company of Canada Ltd. Construction began with a ceremony on October 31, 1964.

The site posed a challenge. Located at the north end of the Bay of Fundy on the Memramcook River, the area experiences some of the world's

highest tidal ranges. Engineers had to be creative in building the port facility. In addition to large concrete and wooden crib wharves built on the site, a 7,000-tonne, 90-metre-long concrete floating pontoon wharf was constructed by the Montreal-based Canadian Bechtel Limited. Costing between $1 and $2 million, this enormous engineering marvel could rise and fall with the tides, allowing the port to accommodate large ships.

NBDC awarded the operations contract for the fertilizer plant to Winnipeg-based Border Chemical, who created the subsidiary company Fundy Chemical Corporation to operate the facility. The American company W.R. Grace landed the contract to manage the plant's supplies and sales. Throughout 1965, with construction ongoing, the NBDC announced

that work was under way to construct plants capable of producing urea, formaldehyde, and resin. In April 1965, Havelock Lime Works announced that they would establish a calcium plant at the park to produce wood softeners for local pulp and paper companies. In all, $175 million worth of projects were announced, promising of hundreds of jobs.

On November 12, 1965, the dock was floated into place, officially commissioning the wharf and loading facilities. This was followed in February by the opening of the plant, and soon the first ship arrived with ammonia from Trinidad and Tobago. Work on the rest of the site progressed, with a railway line to the site, along with water, power, and sewerage lines.

As soon as the Westmoreland Chemical Park opened, challenges arose. The market for fertilizer products was steadily becoming more competitive. Although the plant had plenty of local buyers, it struggled to make a profit without global trade. Additionally, the Memramcook River required constant dredging to combat sediment infill. Because the project was politically motivated, it instantly received scrutiny from the opposition. In May 1966, the plant was forced to shut down. It reopened in December to receive and process a small shipment of ammonia. However, an unfortunate and cascading series of events occurred: Winter tides and ice jams damaged the floating dock throughout the winter of 1966, and it could accommodate only one shipment of ammonia by the spring. Trouble struck again when miscommunication and equipment failure prevented the ship from unloading, forcing it to unload at a Saint John port. This was the last shipment made to the Westmoreland Chemical Park.

In June, the NBDC and New Brunswick government announced that the plant and Fundy Chemical Corporation had defaulted on their loans. The result was the foreclosure of the corporation's mortgage, followed by a lawsuit against the corporation for misrepresentation of both the

plant's sales numbers and shortcomings of the docking facilities. The Fundy Chemical Corporation would eventually countersue the NBDC. Nonetheless, upon the foreclosure in 1967, the assets were purchased by Westmoreland Fertilizer Company, a subsidiary company established by the NBDC.

In 1968, the company attempted to open the plant one last time, even rehiring marketers and identifying new markets in Europe and Asia. The attempt was futile, though, and with a continuing decline in the market value of ammonium nitrate, logistical problems at the plant, and a struggle to overcome the challenges of shipping the product to market, the plant was officially closed on October 25, 1968.

ABOUT THE AREA

The shutdown marked the end of new investment in the park, and soon, the Westmoreland Chemical Park was abandoned. The buildings have been torn down, leaving empty roads lined with streetlights and large overgrown concrete foundations. The floating dock was sold to the Saint John Shipbuilding and Drydock Co. Ltd., who removed it shortly after the plant's shutdown. The wharf is slowly deteriorating into the river. Adjacent to the wharf is a graveyard of barges and the remains of ships being reclaimed by the river's thick mud.

Following the plant's closure, many questioned whether the Westmoreland Chemical Park had ever been feasible. Although external market conditions affected the value of ammonium nitrate, ongoing operational difficulties and challenging shipping conditions due to the Bay of Fundy's tides led many to conclude that the project failed largely because of poor planning.

WESTMORELAND CHEMICAL PARK : N 45.869486, W 64.544050

From the community of Dorchester, drive south on Cape Road for 4 kilometres. Turn onto a gravel road and drive 1.4 kilometres. Although the site is popular among locals, abide by any posted signs or property restrictions.

7. Radio Canada International's Sackville Station

Tantramar Marsh, Coles Island

Driving east past Sackville on the Trans-Canada Highway, you pass through the vast Tantramar Marsh. This saltwater marsh has long been home to countless species of flora and fauna and is an important stopover for migrating birds, including Canada geese and sandpipers. In the late 17th century, the marshland was transformed into agricultural land by local Acadians through a system of dykes, channels, and wooden sluice gates known as aboiteaux. Despite this natural and cultural history, it is a set of abandoned buildings that typically catches the eye of those passing by. These few buildings, enclosed by a chain-link fence, were once part of an extensive array of antennas and transmission lines that made up Radio Canada International's Sackville shortwave broadcasting station for more than 65 years.

HISTORY

In the late 1930s, only three-quarters of Canadians had access to reliable radio reception, with many more unable to receive reception at night or without interference. To address some of these dead zones, the Canadian Broadcasting Corporation (CBC) selected a site in the middle of Tantramar Marsh for a new, advanced broadcasting station. The location was chosen because of its distance from potential sources of interference such as the magnetic north pole (which can cause magnetic interference), electrical infrastructure, and even interference from minerals in local bedrock (a problem solved by the site's location on a salt marsh). The corporation's chief architect, David G. McKinstry, designed the building, and in 1938, a small complex of buildings along with a 50-kilowatt transmitter was opened under the callsign CBA-FM out of Moncton. The station broadcasted throughout the Maritime provinces and parts of Maine.

During World War II, broadcasting and access to information was seen as a way to foster nationalism and unity, which the Canadian government prioritized during the country's ongoing involvement in Europe. Thus, the government decided to upgrade existing infrastructure, with the Sackville station near the top of its list. In 1943, the large building most recognizable at the site was built, along with two 50-kilowatt shortwave transmitters. The station joined four others like it across Canada, opening in 1944 and becoming home to CBC's International Service.

For many years, the facility received regular upgrades to keep up with advancing technology. In 1970, a Collins transmitter was installed, followed 10 years later by the replacement of its aging antenna array with three Harris transmitters, which extended the station's reach and effectiveness in transmitting to northern Quebec and into the Arctic. At this time, the complex contained several buildings, including its operations and transmitter building. Surrounding the building was a large shortwave antenna system that radiated outward in a concentric pattern. Known as a "curtain array," the system was comprised of over a dozen steel towers, some of which reached over 100 metres in height. Stretching between the towers were hundreds of cables and wires that acted as the transmission source.

ABOUT THE AREA

As the technological revolution continued into the 1990s, the station slowly became obsolete. Despite this, it continued operating until 2012, when the CBC announced the end of its shortwave service and that Radio Canada International's service—by this point the last user of the facility—would shift to an online platform. Service officially ended on October 12, but broadcasting continued until December, marking the end of an era in Canadian communication.

Due to the high cost of decommissioning and demolishing the complex and restoring the natural state, the CBC initially planned to sell the building. However, when this proved troublesome, the

corporation opted instead to strip the buildings and antenna system of their equipment. In 2014, the station's antennas and transmitters were removed, transforming the sightlines of the bog. While this was a win for the ecologically sensitive area, it was a sombre day for many residents living nearby, who knew the antennas as a local landmark.

The main office and transmitter building remain in the marsh. Surrounded by a chain-link fence and *Private Property* signs, the complex inspires wonder and curiosity for passersby.

SACKVILLE STATION: N 45.888830, W 64.323053

As the building is located on private property, all signs and notices must be followed. However, the building and former complex is visible from the site's entrance located along the Trans-Canada Highway's westbound lane, approximately 3.5 kilometres west of Exit 513 in Aulac.

8. Maringouin Peninsula's Grindstone Quarry

Rockport, Maringouin Peninsula

The relatively quiet Maringouin Peninsula was once an economic powerhouse driving growth for the entire region. Not long after the first settlers arrived in the 18th century, the sandstone coastal terraces that stretched out into the Bay of Fundy were recognized as a potential building material. As well, throughout the 19th century, the demand for grindstones grew rapidly. These large, circular carved rocks were used for grinding flour, manufacturing and sharpening steel tools, and later for grinding wood for the production of wood chips and pulp. The Maringouin Peninsula sandstone was ideal for this application, and although most of the rock lay below the high-water mark during high tide, the receding tides made the sandstone accessible for quarrying.

Quarries popped up along the coast as people began hand-carving the circular stones. By 1806, at least 15 people were producing grindstones, which were exported throughout the region. The industry's growth was temporarily stunted by an American embargo on international trade, but once that was lifted in 1824, a new era of growth and export began. One of the earliest exporters was Joseph Read, who travelled between quarries, purchasing stones and delivering them to markets across Canada, the United States, and later to Europe and South America.

Extracting the stone from below the high-water mark came with challenges. The quarrying season ran from May to November, when there was less ice and snow. Workers could access the stone only at low tide, meaning that working hours varied throughout the year. Cofferdams were used periodically to allow for quarrying at high tide, yet they were susceptible to erosion and flooding. Anchors embedded in the rocks along the shore are remnants of these early efforts. Once a grindstone was carved,

transporting it to nearby wharves was no easy feat. To solve this, workers would attach a large dory to the stones at low tide, and as the tide came in, the dory and stone would rise with it. The dories, known as "Joggins boats," would be rowed to shore, where the stone was released, shortening the distance it needed to be moved by hand or mechanical power.

Quarry owners and export businesses such as Read's flourished throughout the 1800s. Quarries were established, and with them came new means of mining and extracting rock. By mid-century, steam-powered machinery was used to move and transport stone. As grindstone production reached an all-time high, the Westmoreland Olive Freestone Company began quarrying south of Rockport. Alongside the quarry, several buildings and stores were constructed, including a steam derrick that produced steam to power a cranelike system, easing the process of lifting and transporting stone. This new system increased production, helping the quarry produce 4,000 tonnes of stone in 1861. Despite its advanced equipment, financial troubles hit the company, and the quarry and its accompanying machinery were shut down and sold off after just a few years of operation.

By the 1900s, demand for grindstones declined, as more modern systems and technology became available. In 1907, several quarries continued to operate, but slowly ceased production.

The grindstone quarries of the Maringouin Peninsula are often forgotten but, for a time, this off-the-beaten-path region was a hub of industry, advanced machinery, and global trade. While only a fraction of the population remains, the remnants of this once-prosperous industry still exists. Along the shores, pieces of partly carved grindstones and wharves are visible. Foundations and the remains of a large chimney stand precariously at the edge of a cliff at School Point. This chimney is all that remains of the Westmoreland Olive Freestone Company's steam derrick, one of the many advanced pieces of machinery used in the region.

GRINDSTONE QUARRY: N 45.728705, W 64.490510

The trailhead is located on the side of Lower Rockport Road, in the community of Rockport, at the southern end of the Maringouin Peninsula. From the trailhead (N 45.732024, W 64.494648), hike 500 metres to the end of the trail.

1
Tignish
O'Leary
West Point
2
Cavendish
5.2
5.1
St. Peters Bay
6
8.2
9
3
8.1
Summerside
Souris
4
5.3
Charlottetown
10
Borden-Carleton
7
8.3
Montague
Belfast
Murray Harbour

Prince Edward Island

Prince Edward Island may be Canada's smallest and least populated province, but its rich culture, scenic landscapes, and warm hospitality have made it a must-visit destination for millions of people each year. The Mi'kmaq lived peacefully on the island for centuries; following colonization, European wars and conflicts reached its shores. Although the island of Prince Edward Island was originally claimed by the French, Britain eventually defeated the French for control of the Maritimes, leading to the Expulsion of the Acadians in the 1750s. Prince Edward Island played a critical role in harbouring refugees forced from their homes, causing the island's population to surge and embedding a cultural vibrancy that remains strong. The island, officially established as a British colony in 1769, attracted hundreds of Irish, Scottish, and English families.

Well known for its red sandstone cliffs, the island formed over 250 million years ago from sediment deposited by ancient rivers. During the last Ice Age, this rock, broken down and mixed with glacial till, created the island's rich, fertile soils. Early settlers transformed vast stretches of land into farmland for crops and livestock. The island's many harbours and tidal inlets also led to a thriving fishing industry, which continues to be a cornerstone of its economy.

In Canadian history, Prince Edward Island became famous for hosting the Charlottetown Conference in 1864, which laid the groundwork for Confederation and earned the province the title "Birthplace of

Confederation." Even so, the proud colony wished to maintain its independence and did not join Canada until 1873. The high cost of constructing the Prince Edward Island Railway played a major role in the decision to finally join, as financial difficulties pushed the colony to seek assistance from the federal government. Despite its cost, the railway opened Prince Edward Island to new industries and opportunities. Alongside fishing and farming, tourism soon became a vital part of the island's economy, closely linked to its growing transportation networks. Modern ferry services to New Brunswick were gradually introduced in the early 20th century, and as air travel and personal vehicles became more common, so too did the number of tourists who visited the island. Islanders embraced the tourism boom, establishing amusement parks, accommodations, and other amenities and attractions, making the island a favourite getaway for families across Atlantic Canada. The opening of the Confederation Bridge in 1997 ushered in yet another era of travel and economic opportunity, strengthening ties to the mainland and further boosting local businesses and industry.

The most popular way to travel to the island is the Confederation Bridge, which connects the province from Cape Tormentine, New Brunswick, at Borden-Carleton. Alternatively, a ferry runs between Caribou, Nova Scotia, and Wood Islands, Prince Edward Island. Connecting the bridge to the province's capital of Charlottetown and the Wood Islands Ferry is the Trans-Canada Highway (Highway 1). Highway 2 is perhaps one of the most well-travelled routes in the province, running from Tignish on the island's northwestern tip through the communities of Summerside, Kensington, Charlottetown, and finally to Souris near the eastern tip. Branching from Highway 2 are minor highways that wind through forests, farmland, and along the coastline. Highway 14 passes through the beautiful west coast and the picturesque lighthouse at West Point. Highways 11 and 12 follow the tidal flats and beaches on the south and north coasts near the town of Summerside. Highway 6 passes through some of the most tourist-focused locations, including Green Gables Heritage Place and Prince

Edward Island National Park. The east coast is perhaps underappreciated for its mix of beauty and culture. Inlets surrounded by lush forests and vibrant coastal estuaries complement the history and cultural centres of Montague, Cardigan, and Georgetown. The town of Souris is known for its beaches and also as the departure point for the Magdalen Islands ferry. Prince Edward Island's rich history, geography, and cultures have left many fascinating destinations.

1. Prince Edward Island's Incredible Coastal Landforms

Prince Edward Island is well known for its reddish rock outcrops and coastal cliffs. These sedimentary rocks are comprised mainly of sandstone, mudstone, and conglomerate, which formed between 360 and 260 million years ago. The rocks are made of sediment deposited by ancient rivers as the Appalachian Mountains slowly eroded. This sediment owes its reddish colour to the rocks' high iron content which, over time, oxidizes to the current beautifully coloured cliffs. Like all sedimentary rock, these cliffs are highly susceptible to coastal erosion, slowly breaking down with each wave. Over time, this process has left sea caves, arches, and sea stacks, which are constantly evolving. This means that every few years the coastline appears to change with new rock formations being formed, and others disappearing.

While some of the island's coastal formations are difficult to reach due to rough seas and private land ownership, others are much more accessible. Some of Prince Edward Island's rock formations have become popular tourist attractions. Few represent this better than a pinnacle sea stack near North Cape. The column of rock towering out of the Gulf of St. Lawrence was part of a larger formation known as Elephant Rock. It was popularized in the 1970s when pictures emerged of a massive rock formation that bore a striking resemblance to an elephant rising out of the water alongside the cliffs. But each storm and incoming tide slowly eroded it. In 1999, the arch that made up Elephant Rock's "trunk" collapsed and, since then, most of the sea stack has fallen into the water. As of 2025, a narrow, pointed tower of rock continues to rise above the water, home to a small colony of cormorants. Over time, this rock formation, known as the Tignish Sea Stack, will also erode, while new formations continue to form in the surrounding cliff faces.

Another popular spot to witness this erosion is at Thunder Beach near the community of Darnley. The beach became a popular stop largely because of Teacup Rock. Owing its name to the rock's teacup-like shape, the formation collapsed into the ocean during Hurricane Fiona in 2022. The incident exemplifies the temporary nature of these landforms. Nonetheless, Thunder Beach is still a must-visit site to see some of the Prince Edward Island's best coastal formations. Smooth, rounded cliff faces, small caves, and saucer-like features along the shoreline are easily explored at low tides.

TIGNISH SEA STACK: N 47.041590, W 64.014112

North of the community of Norway, on the west side of North Cape, follow Highway 182 until its intersection with Nellingan Road (N 47.028763, W 64.018694). Continue north on a gravel road (an extension of Norway Road) for 1.6 kilometres to a gravel parking area next to the sea stack.

THUNDER COVE BEACH: N 46.563870, W 63.645398

From Highway 20 in Darnley, turn onto Lower Darnley Road and drive for approximately 2 kilometres to Thunder Cove Road. Continue 1 kilometre to the end of the road, where a short trail leads to the beach. Hike west along the beach to reach the cove's best coastal rock formations.

2. RCAF Station Mount Pleasant

Mount Pleasant, Prince County

The outbreak of World War II brought an immediate demand for pilots, navigators, gunners, and bombardiers. With Britain under constant threat of attack by German aircraft, a coalition was formed among its Commonwealth allies to conduct aircrew training. Eager to contribute to the war effort, Canada became a key player in training both local and foreign pilots. The BCATP established training airfields, gunnery ranges, and bombing grounds across the country.

In 1941, a military airbase was constructed in Summerside for this purpose. It was initially staffed by No. 9 Service Flying Training School RCAF. Because the base experienced a rapid influx of pilots and aircrews, two relief airfields were constructed nearby to provide additional capacity for training operations. One was built in Wellington, the other near the town of Ellerslie, at Mount Pleasant.

Built in conjunction with RCAF Station Summerside, the airfield at Mount Pleasant was named RCAF Station Mount Pleasant and became the primary relief field for Summerside. Like other airfields of the time, RCAF Station Mount Pleasant featured three runways, each ranging from 910 to 930 metres in length, arranged in a triangular layout. Alongside the runways, aircraft hangars, training facilities, and barracks supported the aircraft and crews stationed there.

As the war continued and the demand for Canadian pilots and aircrews grew, RCAF Station Mount Pleasant's status as a relief airfield changed. On September 20, 1943, it was designated an official training centre for No. 10 Bombing and Gunnery School. The school trained crews on the Avro Anson, Hawker Hurricane, Fairey Battle, and Bristol Bolingbroke aircraft.

Following the war, the RCAF closed the training facility. It was briefly used as a storage depot for returning aircraft and equipment, as well as for decommissioning nearby bases, but it was eventually abandoned. Over time, the once-paved runways eroded and became overgrown. Parts of the site are now covered by trees, while the rest is used for agriculture. On the west side of the site, near Highway 2, a visitor information centre has been built on the site of the aircraft hangars, and a plaque has been erected nearby to commemorate the airfield's history.

RCAF STATION MOUNT PLEASANT: N 46.597190, W 64.011792
The site is best viewed from the visitor information centre located approximately 30 kilometres north of Summerside on Highway 2.

3. CFB Summerside

Summerside

Between 1940 and 1941, RCAF Station Summerside was constructed northwest of Summerside as part of the BCATP. The airbase contained five runways, three of which measured 1,500 metres, arranged in a triangular layout. Additionally, the airfield had three other 760-metre-long runways. On the east side of the airfield, hangars, a repair facility, barracks, a theatre, a power plant, and other facilities were constructed for the base and its employees.

RCAF Station Summerside hosted the newly formed RCAF's No. 9 Service Flying Training School, which trained pilots on aircraft and flying manoeuvres before they were sent to Europe. In July 1942, the school was relocated to Ontario and replaced by the No. 1 General Reconnaissance School, where aircrews were trained in aerial reconnaissance and intelligence gathering. The school operated until the end of the war; it officially shut down in 1946.

Following World War II, tensions rose between the Soviet Union and the United States, and by 1948, RCAF Station Summerside was reopened. This time, the airfield was commissioned as a NATO training facility, hosting the RCAF's No. 1 Air Navigation School until 1953, when it was replaced by the Central Navigation School. In 1949, they were joined by the No. 2 (Maritime) Operational Training Unit, which trained pilots and aircrews in coastal patrol, anti-submarine warfare, and long-range maritime reconnaissance missions. To accommodate the large number of aircrews, families, and aircraft now based at the airbase, new living facilities, aircraft maintenance buildings, and operations buildings were constructed. RCAF Station Summerside became home to fleets of Avro Lancaster bombers, Lockheed Neptune, and CP-121 Tracker aircraft, which were operated by several units, including the No. 2 (Maritime) Operational Training Unit, No. 107 Rescue Unit, 413 Transport and Rescue Squadron, 420 Air Reserve Squadron, and the 31

Support Air Group. Each squadron conducted operations and training missions to patrol and protect the coastal waters around Atlantic Canada from the threats posed by Soviet submarines and naval ships.

The base was a major employer and economic hub for the region. Throughout the 1950s, many new training schools, patrol units, and search and rescue squadrons called RCAF Station Summerside home. With each addition, the base expanded, and at its peak, more than 1,200 people were employed. In 1961, the RCAF reformed the formerly disbanded 415 Long Range Patrol Force Development Squadron with the purpose of flying more frequent maritime patrol flights in the region. The squadron was equipped with CP-107 Argus aircraft, the replacement for the historic Lancaster bomber and the largest aircraft stationed at the base to date.

With the merger of the three branches of the military, RCAF Station Summerside was renamed Canadian Forces Base (CFB) Summerside, but little else changed. In the late 1970s, Canada adopted the United

Nations' Convention on the Law of the Sea, which established an exclusive economic zone—a zone 320 kilometres from the shores of Canada, for which it has control. The result was greater demand for aerial patrols over coastal waters, with CFB Summerside playing a primary role in supporting the Coast Guard, Department of Fisheries and Oceans, and search and rescue operations.

In 1989, the Department of National Defence announced that CFB Summerside was to be decommissioned and closed. The announcement was not well received, and in May, a protest was organized at the base with 10,000 people in attendance and another 400 locals travelling to Ottawa in hopes of having the decision reversed. Two years later, in 1991, CFB Summerside closed permanently, with most of the base's remaining personnel and aircraft transferred to CFB Greenwood in Nova Scotia.

CFB SUMMERSIDE: N 46.432731, W 63.828508

The base is located northwest of Summerside, in Slemon Park.

4. Confederation Bridge Fabrication Site

Borden-Carleton

From the time the first Mi'kmaq people crossed the Northumberland Strait to the island they called Epekwitk (today anglicized as Abegweit) to the mid-1800s, the idea of a bridge across the ice-prone strait would likely have seemed impossible. But as technology and innovation advanced, so too did the dream of building a fixed link across the strait to connect the island with the rest of Canada. Beginning in the mid- to late 19th century, early concepts were designed. However, it was not until 1957—two years after the completion of the Canso Causeway in Nova Scotia—that the idea gained traction and its feasibility was recognized.

The strait, however, presented formidable challenges. In winter, massive ice sheets formed across the strait. With spring melt, the ice caused catastrophic damage due to the mighty force of the ice floes. The narrowest part of the strait was almost 13 kilometres wide, and even during the summer months, it was greatly influenced by two opposing tidal currents converging from either side of the island. Finally, concerns about the link's impact on shipping and fishing became an obstacle to the project's advancement.

In 1966, a new era of studies considered how to cross the strait, culminating in the first tangible progress: a controversial sod-turning ceremony and preliminary groundwork on the bridge's approaches on either side. This work, however, was abandoned in 1969, citing the exhorbitant cost and environmental concerns, among other reasons. On the New Brunswick side, remnants of this early work—such as eroded sections of causeways—still extend from the town of Bayfield to nearby Jourimain Island.

In 1985, following the submission of three different proposals for a fixed link, a majority of Prince Edward Island residents voted in a

plebiscite to support the project. Despite organized resistance from some islanders, the government moved forward. After a brief delay due to environmental concerns following an assessment, the minister of public works approved the project. On October 7, 1993, an agreement was signed with the Strait Crossing Joint Venture (SCJV) to construct the bridge across the strait.

Once completed, not only would the 13-kilometre connection have to withstand the strait's powerful currents and ice floes but it would also need to allow the passage of cargo ships and cruise ships while minimizing the impact on the vital local fisheries. Once designs were finalized, the next challenge arose: determining where to build the required components and how to transport them to their locations.

In the same year that SCJV signed the contract to finance and build the bridge, the company purchased a 66-hectare farm from John L. Reed to establish a fabrication and staging site. Work began immediately, creating a facility that included office buildings, a cement plant, its own water supply, a large jetty and wharf, and the fabrication and assembly site. The site featured large concrete pads supporting assembly lines for the piers, girders, and other bridge components. Components were built in stages, stored temporarily on-site, and then moved to the end of the jetty via a system of stainless-steel tracks and two transporters (nicknamed "Turtle" and "Lobster"). These machines could move the largest components, including the 7,500-tonne, 250-metre-long main girders, which were then loaded onto the specially designed heavy-lift ship *Svanen,* which transported and placed them at their designated positions on the bridge.

At its peak, the project employed more than 5,000 workers who constructed 62 concrete piers, 43 main girders (each 250 metres long), and 21 approach spans (each 91 metres long). On November 19, 1996, the installation of the final span completed the 12.9-kilometre-long engineering marvel, which opened on May 31, 1997. Between these dates, work at the fabrication site wound down, and the site was progressively decommissioned. A major cleanup began in 2002 to remove structures, debris, and materials.

Only a small section of the former fabrication site remains, repurposed as part of an industrial park. Some of the site's original buildings have been adapted for commercial use. However, at the east side of the site, at the end of Read Street, the former fabrication site is still distinguishable from its surroundings. Large stretches of concrete, interwoven with the site's rail system, are clearly visible. Closer to the water are the remains of the jetty, where the bridge's massive girders were loaded onto ships. These remnants of one of the Maritimes' greatest engineering achievements sit in the shadow of the Confederation Bridge, which stretches across the Abegweit Strait just 1 kilometre away.

In 2024, the province began soliciting development proposals for the site that represents the incredible feat and the long battle to build a fixed link to the island. This connection has boosted tourism, business, and import/export opportunities for Prince Edward Island's residents.

FABRICATION SITE: N 46.249402, W 63.684699

As part of the site is periodically used by local industry, follow all posted signs and respect the wishes of property owners. The site is at the end of Industrial Drive and Read Street, now part of the local industrial park.

5. Forgotten Amusement Parks of Prince Edward Island

Prince Edward Island's tourism industry has long been a major contributor to its economy, welcoming thousands of visitors each year. Beginning in the late 19th century, the island began looking to tourism to boost its economy, especially in rural areas. As air travel, ferries, roads, and automobiles became more popular and accessible through the mid-20th century, more people visited the province to enjoy its beautiful beaches and rich culture.

Recognizing tourism's potential, in the 1950s the provincial government began supporting new tourism businesses and operations while also establishing a provincial park system. The province became one of the largest funders of local tourism initiatives, helping to establish a new type of attraction: amusement and theme parks.

Amusement and theme parks appeared throughout the province; created by individual entrepreneurs using their skills and passions, this led to amusements unlike any others in the world and helped to promote the island as a tourism hub. Over time, larger corporations and monopolies took over smaller parks, but Prince Edward Island's parks have retained a distinct charm.

As with any industry, Prince Edward Island's tourism landscape has evolved, with new parks opening and old ones closing. Some of the island's beloved, now-shuttered parks remain. Although access to them varies by park, many are visible along the province's highways.

Rainbow Valley

Cavendish

For decades, Rainbow Valley was one of the busiest attractions in the province. Rainbow Valley began as a partnership between residents

Earl Davison, Ivan Harrington, and Archie Johnstone, who operated the park through the Provincial Construction Company. Opened in 1969, the park was named after the seventh novel in Lucy Maud Montgomery's Anne of Green Gables series.

Located in the town of Cavendish, adjacent to Cavendish National Park, the park was ideally situated to attract tourists. In 1979, Davison became its sole owner. By the mid-1980s, the park included a large amusement area and a water park. The amusement area was separated from the parking lot by a large pond, which featured boat rides and paddle boats.

The park's most distinguishable attraction was its flying saucer gift shop, with a small roller coaster, a miniature train, a petting zoo, and a hedge maze nearby. On the west side of the site, a large water park, constructed in the 1980s, became a local favourite on hot summer days. Most of the park's rides were designed and built by Davison himself.

In 2004, the park's owners were ready to retire and approached Parks Canada (which owns the adjacent lands as part of Cavendish National Park) about purchasing the land. Parks Canada agreed, and in the winter of 2005, the beloved park's closure was announced. The park's final season was in the summer of 2005, and, on September 5, it officially shut down.

Many of the park's amusements were dismantled and sold. In July 2007, the area reopened as Cavendish Grove, a nature park maintained by Parks Canada.

Unlike many other abandoned Prince Edward Island theme parks, Cavendish Grove remains open to visitors. Walking the trails that once wound through Rainbow Valley brings back memories for those who frequented the park. Throughout the site, relics of several small buildings, walking paths, and even the hedge maze are still visible, though it is overgrown.

RAINBOW VALLEY: N 46.490017, W 63.393168

Great Island Science and Adventure Park

Stanley Bridge

Southwest of Cavendish, at the base of New London Bay, an unusual amusement park was established. Great Island Science and Adventure Park was founded in the late 1980s as a science-themed park featuring a planetarium, a dinosaur museum, and archeological dig sites. For years, the park's full-scale replica of a space shuttle attracted passersby. It was constructed by the park's owner, Barton Thomas Bourne, who, along with his wife, opened the park.

Adjacent to the shuttle was a large white dome, previously part of the University of Prince Edward Island's planetarium, which operated on the campus from 1980 to 1989. The park also offered adventure courses, games, and science camps.

The park's last season was the summer of 2008. It was sold to Maritime Fun Group, who closed some of the original attractions and repurposed others, starting Jurassic Bart's Dinosaur Museum and Petting Farm. This iteration of the park operated until 2018, when it was once again closed.

Following this closure, the park's unusual attractions continued to draw photographers and other curious visitors. Concerned about trespassing and vandalism, the owners removed most of the exhibits in early 2024. The mostly empty site sits along a small inlet.

The future of the site is unknown, but as drivers pass it on their way to Cavendish, many are still reminded of what was once one of Prince Edward Island's most intriguing parks.

SCIENCE AND ADVENTURE PARK: N 46.469817, W 63.446175
While the area is private property, the site can be clearly seen from Highway 6, approximately 5 kilometres south of Cavendish.

Fairyland and Encounter Creek Amusement Park

New Haven

In the community of New Haven lies another of Prince Edward Island's lost amusement parks. Opened in 1965, Fairyland was established by Dutch immigrant Herman Sewuster. Located along the Trans-Canada Highway between the ferry terminal and Charlottetown, the park welcomed thousands of visitors each year.

The park was in a lush forest, with wooden castles, cottages, and rides scattered throughout, all connected by a maze of trails that could be explored while riding on a miniature train. The cottages, one of its most iconic features, were each named for fairy tales such as Snow White and the Seven Dwarves, Little Red Riding Hood, and Cinderella. Visitors entered the park through the gates of a large wooden castle, which instantly created the illusion of stepping into another universe. Throughout the summer season, the park was a favourite destination for families and children.

In 1997, the park was purchased by Ray and Robin Chace, who renamed it Encounter Creek and invested $2 million into restoration and new attractions, including a wave pool and arcade. The new park was short-lived and closed after a few years, due to financial difficulties.

In 2012, part of the park's land was purchased by the provincial

government to construct a new route for the Trans-Canada Highway. This bisected the site, with many of the trails now located south of the highway (within the Fairyland Forest Natural Area), while the main park area was isolated to the north.

The park's trail system south of the highway may be explored via a nearby ATV trail. This trail originally passed through the park's entrance gates and wove through the park, heading east. In recent years, however, the park's northern section has been sold multiple times, leading to restricted access.

Nonetheless, from the ATV trail, which now runs alongside the Trans-Canada Highway and then loops around the park, visitors can glimpse Fairyland's famous castle entrance and its remaining attractions (wave pool, castle towers, go-kart track, and others) from Boyle Road behind a chain-link fence.

AMUSEMENT PARK: N 46.221841, W 63.308402
Part of the park is no longer accessible but can be viewed from nearby Boyle Road. The park's trail network can still be accessed, south of the highway, at the end of Churchill Road (N 46.220574, W 63.311478).

Woodleigh Replicas and Gardens

Burlington

As of 2025, the gardens and models of Ernest Johnstone are no longer accessible, but the park and its story are an example of the remarkable parks that once flourished have come and gone in the province. Beginning in 1945, Colonel Ernest W. Johnstone started constructing replicas and models of some of Great Britain's iconic landmarks on his 52-hectare farm in Burlington. While the project began as a hobby, in 1957 he and his son Archibald opened Woodleigh Replicas park to visitors. Johnstone added to the replica collection over the years.

The park contained replicas of Shakespeare's birthplace and Anne Hathaway's cottage, as well as a 9-metre-long replica of St. Paul's Cathedral and a 1:20 scale model of York Minster. The most impressive structure was an 18-metre-long, 8.5-metre-wide replica of Scotland's Dunvegan Castle. The largest structure on the site, it was furnished with paintings and antique furniture. The replicas were constructed primarily from concrete, mortar, and stones which Johnstone imported from across Atlantic Canada.

British architecture alone did not inspire Johnstone's work. At the back of his property, he planted vast gardens and added a small pond, a water fountain, and walking trails, mirroring the prestigious gardens of London.

Ernest Johnstone died in 1984, after which his family sold the park. It remained open until 2008. The provincial government assumed the mortgage. The park was eventually sold to private owners, but it did not reopen. Since then, portions of it have been divided and sold.

The current owners plan to develop the site into an event space, hotel, and spa, but, as of 2025, little progress has been made. The future of the park remains uncertain, but its many replicas and surviving structures are a tribute to Ernest Johnstone. While parts of the park are still visible in Burlington, the risk of vandalism has forced the owners to restrict site access.

6. St. Peters Harbour Lighthouse

St. Peters Harbour

Prince Edward Island's coastline and sandy beaches attract thousands of tourists each year—though that same coastline has long been a danger to fishing and sailing vessels. Navigation aids such as lighthouses have been used for centuries to warn ships of danger and help them navigate the difficult, shallow waters. While some of these lighthouses continue to operate, by the late 20th century many had been replaced by automated light towers.

Along the sandy shores of St. Peters Bay in northeast Prince Edward Island, a restored white-and-red lighthouse still stands among the area's famous sand dunes. The light no longer operates, and although it was abandoned for some time, St. Peters Harbour Lighthouse has since been restored.

The first European settlers to call St. Peters Bay home were the Acadians, who established fishing villages in the area. Following their expulsion by the British, the area was slowly repopulated by British settlers who used the protected bay as a harbour for fishing vessels, shipbuilding, and importing and exporting agricultural goods. The harbour's increased use through the mid-19th century underlined the need for better navigation at its mouth. As a result, a pair of fixed lights known as range lights were installed in 1868. After Prince Edward Island joined Canada, the federal Department of Marine and Fisheries acknowledged the need for additional navigation aids in the harbour, announcing in 1876 that two new lighthouses would be built. The towers' construction was delayed until 1878, at which point two square, tapered wooden structures stood on either side of the entrance to the bay. Ten years later, one of the towers was replaced by a larger lighthouse, and the other's height was extended.

Because the sandy beaches and coastal dunes continually shift, so too does the location of the bay's channel. As a result, the lighthouse

was regularly moved to account for the changing harbour and navigable channel. The lighthouse is now more than 400 metres from the channel, but before 1930, its location marked the western edge of the channel, which passed through the enclosed pond and wetland immediately adjacent to it.

In 1963, the lighthouse was electrified and, shortly after, automated. Historically, the lighthouse was maintained and operated by a keeper who lived nearby. With the light's automation, Eldon Drake became the last lighthouse keeper. In 1965, the 10.4-metre-tall lighthouse was replaced with a skeletal steel structure closer to the bay's entrance, and the historic lighthouse was abandoned, slowly being engulfed by shifting sand dunes. In 2017, the federal government transferred the lighthouse to the St. Peters Harbour Lighthouse Society, which restored it. The picturesque lighthouse is now located in a maze of sand dunes.

The constant shifting and relocation of St. Peters Harbour Lighthouse reflect challenges still faced by the province. Wind, waves, and storms continue to shift the island's coastline, a problem exacerbated by climate change. Signs of this continual shifting is found throughout the province, and at the mouth of St. Peters Bay today, pieces of former breakwaters and wharves are visible. Unlike other abandoned wharves noted in this book, the remnants found at the mouth of this bay were not abandoned but consumed by the area's rapidly changing topography.

ST. PETERS HARBOUR LIGHTHOUSE: N 46.441844, W 62.747645
From Highway 2, east of the town of Morell, head north on St. Peters Harbour Road. Drive 2.1 kilometres before turning right onto Lighthouse Road. Continue to the end of the road to reach a parking lot. St. Peters Harbour Lighthouse is located at the end of a short trail.

7. Knox's Dam: Prince Edward Island's Last Hydroelectric Facility

Montague

On the Montague River lies a small, abandoned hydroelectric dam and power plant. The site, one of the first generating stations to provide power to the nearby towns of Montague, Georgetown, and Cardigan, is now preserved by the landowners as a day park and historic site. The beautiful ruins alongside Knox Pond and a small waterfall make this an excellent addition to any trip itinerary.

Before 1900, the area was settled by Donald D. Campbell, who operated a small farm known as Mount Pleasant Farm, as well as a sawmill and gristmill on the banks of the Montague River. Campbell's farm was located on the north side of the river. After his death in 1882, Campbell's mills were sold to Charles Keith, being bought by Donald MacKenzie in 1901.

MacKenzie purchased a plot of land on the south side of the Montague River near the site of Campbell's sawmills and gristmills. After constructing a beautiful house on the south side of the river, MacKenzie realized that the area had the potential to become a fishing and recreation area. He secured the water rights for the river and constructed a dam, creating a small pond where he also built a wharf and boathouse.

The power potential of the river and dam was recognized by the Montague Electric Company, which purchased the dam and neighbouring lands from the MacKenzie family on March 8, 1907. Incorporated in 1899, the company had been established to provide electricity to the people of Montague and the surrounding area. The company had installed a small generating station in the community of Valleyfield but, upon purchasing the MacKenzie property, moved the Valleyfield equipment and operation to Montague.

The company enlarged the dam, constructing a small generating station immediately downstream. With repurposed equipment and machinery from the Valleyfield site, the hydro plant became one of the first of its kind to operate in the province. The nearby MacKenzie house was also purchased by the company and turned into the plant supervisor's house. In 1907, Robert K. Clements was appointed supervisor.

Originally, the dam supplied power to Montague, but following expansions in 1917, it could power the Three River communities, including Georgetown and Cardigan. In its initial days, power was generated and supplied to customers only at specified times during the day. This was later expanded to five days a week by 1921, and several years later, it operated 24 hours a day. In 1921, customers paid $5 per month for electricity, widely proclaimed as the cheapest electricity east of Ontario.

Demand for electricity increased across the province in the 1920s. In 1917, the Maritime Electric Company was incorporated and set out to expand its reach to rural areas in the province. In 1928, the company constructed a new dam on the South Branch of the Montague River and installed two additional generators. With growing demand, in 1931 the company expanded its generation capacity again when it took over the Montague Electric Company and its hydroelectric plant. The purchase of the plant ensured little downtime in electricity supply when their new dam on the south branch of the Montague River was destroyed by a flood in January 1933. While the dam was rebuilt the following year, the hydro plant north of the new dam reliably supplied power to nearby communities.

In 1939, William Knox was appointed supervisor of the hydro plant. By the mid-20th century, small hydro plants were being outcompeted by soaring electricity demand and larger generation stations. In 1955, the plant's turbine required major refits and refurbishment, and Maritime Electric permanently closed the hydro plant—the last hydroelectric plant to operate in Prince Edward Island. The following December, Knox purchased the house, lands, and water rights from Maritime Electric, transforming the supervisor's house into his own. The family's name stuck: Knox's Dam and Knox Pond.

In 1977, a fish ladder was constructed at the dam to restore fish populations in the river and pond. The Knox family now operates the Knox's Dam Bed and Breakfast in the historic supervisor's house. The family has since transformed the former dam and powerhouse area into a day park, helping preserve the area's history and culture. The dam and remains of the concrete powerhouse are still visible at the site.

KNOX DAM: N 46.158759, W 62.675262

From the community of Montague, follow Highway 353 (Riverside Drive/South Montague Road) for 2.2 kilometres to the entrance to the small day park (N 46.158480, W 62.674358).

8. Relics of the Prince Edward Island Railway

Prince Edward Island

Operating between 1875 and 1989, the Prince Edward Island Railway was a symbol of independence and promised economic prosperity to the island. Stretching between Tignish and Elmira, several branch lines connected some of its northern and southern communities. As was the case with many other railways in Atlantic Canada in the late 20th century, this railway eventually closed, largely due to increased efficiency in transporting people, goods, and supplies through local road networks.

HISTORY

Despite the island's relatively small size, transportation of supplies and products on and off the island was challenging in the 19th century. This was especially true in the winter, when ice prohibited ships from entering many of the province's ports. In 1867, islanders failed to see the benefits of joining Confederation, believing in part that it would threaten their strong sense of identity and nationalism. Looking to strengthen its independence and provide a much-needed transportation network, the island turned to a railway.

In 1871, under the oversight of Saint John native and chief engineer John Edward Boyd, construction of the Prince Edward Island Railway began. To reduce costs, it was decided to construct a narrow-gauge railway (rails separated by 1.067 metres) which would run from Alberton to Charlottetown and on to Georgetown and Souris, connecting the east and west sides of the island.

The railway was even more costly than originally proposed. This was blamed partly on the challenging terrain of the island's interior, which consisted of large tracts of wetland and hills. These cost overruns were also later blamed on the fact that contractors were paid per mile of track completed, incentivizing longer, more complex routes. Additionally, dozens of communities successfully lobbied the government to have the line pass through their areas, adding more kilometres of track. Whatever the cause, by the second year of construction, the railway had nearly bankrupted Prince Edward Island—a major factor in the island deciding to join Confederation on July 1, 1873. The terms of signing included that the new federal government would assume the province's railway debt and finish its construction. As a result, this railway came under the control of the Canadian government's railways.

Despite the sacrifices made to construct the railway, upon its completion in 1875 it instantly became a vital transportation network for the province's industry. Instead of relying on local harbours to import goods and export products, the rail network provided a reliable means of delivering products to local markets and major harbours such as in Charlottetown and Summerside. While the original line was built from Alberton to Souris, it was later extended to Tignish in the west and Elmira in the east. Similarly, branch lines were constructed to Murray River in the southeast, to Montague and Georgetown in the east, and to Cape Traverse, where iceboats transported goods and supplies to New Brunswick year-round.

This early means of delivering goods ended when the federal government constructed a ferry terminal to the west of Cape Traverse, at Borden. The new route, which began operating on December 12, 1917, included ferries capable of sailing in harsh winter weather and ice conditions, rendering iceboats obsolete. The Cape Traverse branch line was replaced by a new line to the community of Borden. The new reliable ferry service, in combination with the railway, helped industries boom on the island, with produce, livestock, and other products being easily exported and sold in markets across the east coast.

In 1918, the railway, comprising almost 450 kilometres of track, came under the ownership of CN. The connection with New Brunswick meant that the railway was consistently busy, but it experienced compatibility problems with New Brunswick railway lines, which were standard gauge, or 1.435 metres apart, approximately 0.37 metres more than the Prince Edward Island Railway's narrow gauge. Railcars and locomotives operating in the other Maritime provinces could not be used on the island's railway line. As a result, CN began the daunting task of adding a third rail to the outside of the existing track, allowing the railway to accommodate both narrow- and standard-gauge railcars. The addition was completed by 1930.

The railway experienced increased traffic during World War II due to the establishment of several air force bases and radar stations on the island, but following the war even larger changes to the railway occurred. The first of these was the introduction of diesel locomotives, which replaced the less reliable and efficient steam locomotives. The second was the popularization of gas-powered vehicles for both personal use and transporting goods. The number of passengers choosing to travel by rail declined sharply; soon, cargo was being preferentially shipped by trucks. October 1969 brought the end of passenger services. In the following two decades, the island relied more on trucks to transport products to markets, and after talks about a fixed link by bridge, tunnel, or causeway began in the early 1990s, CN announced the closure and abandonment of the Prince Edward Island Railway, effective December 31, 1989.

This railway had operated for more than 110 years and had become a proud symbol to islanders. While the tracks and most of the railway's locomotives and railcars have been dismantled and/or sold off, the railway's mark on the landscape is still witnessed through relics such as the former railbed turned recreation trail, its many museums, and abandoned or restored train stations, including the museum in Elmira.

Confederation Trail

The end of the Prince Edward Island Railway was not a surprise. It had struggled for many years, and with the end in sight, in August 1989 a volunteer-led group called Rails-to-Trails was established with a mandate to preserve the railbed and convert it into a public-use trail network.

Following the closure of the railway, the tracks were removed and either scrapped or sold. Working with the provincial Department of Tourism and organizations such as the Trans Canada Trail Foundation, funds were raised to purchase the railbed from CN and local landowners. The organization's passionate work paid off, and 470 kilometres of trail were established, clearly marked and maintained. Along the Confederation Trail are relics of the railway: aging train stations, warehouses, sidings, and artifacts such as railway spikes, ties, and even rails themselves. The widely used 470-kilometre-long trail network is now also one of the best ways to embrace the beauty and history of the province.

Train Stations

The Prince Edward Island Railway stations have either been left abandoned, repurposed for new uses, or preserved and made into museums. When the original railway line was completed in 1875, there was a station every 4 kilometres. At the time, railway stations were much more than a quiet place for passengers to await the next train. They oversaw the shipment of freight and cargo, including handling mail and telegraph services, while also serving as logistical hubs for

passenger and freight shipments and as community gathering spaces.

The train stations were often small, simply designed, and typically constructed from wood or stone. When passenger rail service ended in 1969, most of the stations were closed. Along the Confederation Trail, many of these stations are in various states of preservation. While some remain abandoned, others have been transformed into breweries, shops, and museums. One of the most notable examples is in Kensington, home to one of only two stone train stations built in the province. Constructed in 1905, the Kensington Train Station was designated a National Historic Site in 1976. Beautifully restored, it is now open to the public. Nearby, a former railway warehouse hosts a local farmers' market, adding to the area's charm and functionality.

KENSINGTON STATION: N 46.437868, W 63.638457

Elmira Rail Museum

In 1912, a branch line was constructed between the main railway line at Harmony Junction and the town of Elmira. Elmira became known as the "end of the line," as it marked the eastern terminus of the railway. A small railway station was built in Elmira the same year, and after passenger service ended in 1969, it was restored for the island's centennial celebrations in 1973. In 1975, the station was converted into a museum, which preserved several kilometres of railway track. Since then, the museum has collected many additional artifacts related to the former railway, helping to preserve its history. The site remains a popular destination and even features a miniature railway, offering rides to visitors.

ELMIRA RAIL MUSEUM: N 46.440136, W 62.065431

Montague Turntable

Montague

Another relic of the railway is located in the town of Montague: the remains of a turntable near the end of the former Montague Branch line. A large circular concrete foundation, approximately 22 metres in diameter, is all that remains of this important piece of infrastructure. The foundation once supported a rotating platform, allowing steam-powered locomotives or railcars to quickly change direction. The turntable was built 200 metres from the railway station. The railway station has been converted into a local restaurant. Throughout the late 19th and early 20th century, the area was a bustling hub as passengers and supplies were regularly delivered via the railway line. The Montague Turntable improved efficiency by enabling locomotives and train engines to rotate 180 degrees without the need for additional tracks. Once rotated, the locomotive was ready to continue to the next stop on the schedule.

The turntable is visible from the Confederation Trail, which runs adjacent to it. Although additional work could be done to preserve the historic site, it remains easily accessible to those in the area.

MONTAGUE TURNTABLE: NN 46.166666, W 62.643400

9. Colliding Tides of East Point Lighthouse

East Point

A unique phenomenon occurs at the most easterly point of Prince Edward Island. Best seen at high tide, a thin line of waves stretches from East Point Lighthouse into the Gulf of St. Lawrence. The strange occurrence is the result of different tidal conditions between the Gulf of St. Lawrence and the Northumberland Strait. As the tides reach their peak, the two currents collide off the island's eastern and western extremes.

The colliding tides has long attracted people to East Point Lighthouse, whose history is defined by another natural phenomenon, erosion.

Built in 1867, the octagonal lighthouse warned ships of the dangerous shoals and shallow waters stretching from the point. The lighthouse was placed approximately 800 metres from the cliff's edge; however, it was mistakenly recorded as closer to the cliff's edge, which caused several ships to run aground at the point, including the SS *Quebec* in 1879 and the British warship HMS *Phoenix* on September 12, 1882. In 1885, the lighthouse was moved using a wooden track system and horses to within 150 metres of the shoreline. In the same year, a fog alarm was installed at the site; it was eventually replaced by a two-storey building 50 metres closer to the shore than the lighthouse.

Over time, the shoreline has encroached on the lighthouse and its adjacent buildings. By 2007, the fog alarm building, originally located 60 metres from the shoreline, was now at the lip of the cliff's edge, forcing it to be relocated closer to the lighthouse. As of 2025, the lighthouse is safe but, as worsening storms and sea level rise caused by climate change continue to threaten Prince Edward Island's coastline, eventually it too will have to be relocated. Following a fire in 1972, the lighthouse was decommissioned and several buildings on the site were sold. The organization Friends of Elmira took ownership of the lighthouse and fog alarm building, now preserved as a historical landmark and converted into a craft shop. At the shoreline, the historic fog alarm foundation is slowly collapsing into the ocean.

Visitors to East Point Lighthouse admire its historical significance but also marvel at the wonder of the colliding tides. This meeting of two currents remains a vivid reminder of the island's dynamic coastlines and the powerful forces that continue to shape it.

EAST POINT LIGHTHOUSE: N 46.452825, W 61.971686
Approximately 25 kilometres east of the town of Souris, along Route 16, turn onto Lighthouse Road and continue 2 kilometres to the site.

10. Cardigan Library: Canada's Smallest Library

Cardigan

In a book that strives to showcase the lesser-known histories across Prince Edward Island, it is fitting to end with a quaint library in Cardigan. Along the side of Wharf Road, a building proudly proclaims itself as Canada's smallest library. Measuring 3.5 metres long and 3.5 metres wide, this wooden building is easy to miss. But step inside and become immersed in the nearly 1,800 books which line the one-room building. For a $5 lifetime membership, anyone can borrow a book from the library. It employs no staff but relies on the honour system for payment and returns.

This building is an example of a small local project that was transformed into an attraction, in hopes of sharing knowledge and books with others. The library is owned and operated by resident John MacDonald, who hopes someday to have the library recognized in the Guinness Book of World Records as the World's Smallest Library. Whether this is achieved or not, the community principles and trust that the library promotes makes this the perfect place to visit.

CANADA'S SMALLEST LIBRARY: N 46.231159, W 62.618812
The library is located at 4545 Wharf Road in Cardigan.

ANADA'S "SMALLEST" LIBRARY
OPEN

Exploring Further

During years of searching for and learning the whereabouts and history of New Brunswick's and Prince Edward Island's hidden places, I have consulted many resources that may be helpful to others. This book relies heavily on local knowledge, archives, and publications. The list below is a collection of resources to help you start your own local research and to help plan your next adventure.

GENERAL HISTORY AND RESEARCH

New Brunswick Historical Newspapers Project: Led by the University of New Brunswick, this project digitizes and provides online access to the province's historical newspapers.

Newspapers.com by Ancestry: Newspapers.com contains one of the largest online digitized collections of local newspapers, with many from New Brunswick. A subscription is required.

Island Newspapers: Hosted by the University of Prince Edward Island's Robertson Library, this digital archive provides access to newspapers from Prince Edward Island.

Provincial Archives of New Brunswick (PANB): PANB offers a wide range of support, including genealogy resources, government records, military records, community history projects and manuscripts, photographs, and more, most of which are hosted at the University of New Brunswick's Fredericton campus.

New Brunswick Public Libraries: With more than 50 libraries scattered across the province, New Brunswick Public Libraries and their helpful staff provide a wealth of information, resources, and support for local research.

MAPS AND AERIAL PHOTOGRAPHY

GeoNB: GeoNB, New Brunswick's online geospatial data platform, provides free access to maps, geographic information, and tools to support decision-making and public use.

Geo PEI—Prince Edward Island Historical Map Viewer: A web portal hosted by the University of Prince Edward Island contains interactive historical maps and aerial photography.

GEOLOGY AND GEOGRAPHY

Government of New Brunswick's Geoscience Database: An online resource for searching detailed geological, mineral, and geospatial data, designed to support mineral exploration, historical research, and land-use planning.

Our Landscape Heritage: The Story of Ecological Land Classification: This online publication produced by the Government of New Brunswick provides a detailed overview of the province's natural landscapes, ecosystems, and geography.

Fensome, R.A. and G.L. Williams, eds. *The Last Billion Years: A Geological History of the Maritime Provinces of Canada.* 2nd ed. Atlantic Geoscience Society, 2022.

Hild, M.H. and S.M. Barr. *Geology of New Brunswick and Prince Edward Island: Touring through Time at 44 Scenic Sites.* Boulder Books, 2020.

SPECIFIC HISTORY

New Brunswick Railway Museum: Located in Hillsborough, the museum features extensive collections of artifacts, locomotives, and railcars. Operated by the Canadian Railroad Historical Association (NB Division), the museum preserves and shares New Brunswick's rich railway heritage.

Backyard History: Forgotten Stories from Atlantic Canada's Past: Created by Andrew MacLean, Backyard History is a popular Atlantic Canadian newspaper column, podcast, and TV show that shares fascinating histories and stories from across the Maritimes.

Ozorak, P. *Abandoned Military Installations of Canada*, vol. 3, Atlantic. Paul Ozorak, 2001.

Sarty, R. and D. Knight. *Saint John Fortifications,* 1630-1956. Goose Lane Editions, 2003.

Soucoup, D. *Logging in New Brunswick: Lumber, Mills and River Drives.* Nimbus Publishing, 2011.

Soucoup, D. *Railways of New Brunswick: A History.* Maritime Lines, 2010.

EXPLORING NEW BRUNSWICK

QuadNB: QuadNB, the provincial organization responsible for managing all ATV and side-by-side trails, provides interactive trail maps for trip planning and offers detailed regional maps and safety guidelines.

SnowmobileNB: SnowmobileNB is the official organization overseeing snowmobiling in New Brunswick. Its resources include an interactive trail map with real-time updates on conditions, safety guidelines, and permit information.

HikingNB.ca: This comprehensive online resource is dedicated to exploring and promoting New Brunswick's hiking trails. It features detailed trail guides, interactive maps, difficulty ratings, and essential information on trail conditions, access points, and points of interest.

Index of Places

S

MAINE

Acknowledgements

The completion of this book marks the end of a project dedicated to exploring, learning about, and sharing the lesser-known places, stories, and wonders of Atlantic Canada. None of this would have been possible without the assistance, guidance, photography, and hard work of my partner, Lindsay Batt. Her relentless support, encouragement, and passion for adventure kept me going—especially in difficult times—and for that, I could never thank her enough.

I want to extend my deepest gratitude to my aunt and uncle, Grace and John Doiron, who always provided Lindsay and me with a warm bed and a hot meal during our many trips to New Brunswick. The information and insight they shared during these stays made all the difference in helping me accurately understand and capture the history, culture, and people reflected in this book.

A special thank you is owed to my many friends, coworkers, and family members across the country who have not only inspired me through their interest and engagement in my work but have also actively promoted and encouraged me over the past several years.

I am incredibly fortunate to have many parent figures whose support and enthusiasm helped see this project through. My heartfelt thanks go to Bev and Tom McIsaac, Greg Osmond, Mary Batt and Derrick Baldwin, and Tanya Stuckless. Additionally, I am grateful for the encouragement of my siblings—Ebony, Logan, and Katie—as well as Katie's partner, Tom.

Of course, a big thank you is owed to my editor, Stephanie Porter; copy editor, Iona Bulgin; designer, Tanya Montini; Geoff Frampton; Glenn Day; publisher, Gavin Will; and the entire Boulder Books team, who helped turn this project into three books, showcasing some of Atlantic Canada's most wondrous places and sharing countless stories that might have otherwise been lost to time.

Last but certainly not least, this book would not have been possible without the generosity and warmth of the people of New Brunswick and Prince Edward Island. Their love for storytelling, eagerness to share their culture, and curiosity about their own provinces were truly inspirational. I hope this book continues to encourage that spirit of storytelling and exploration.

A

BEST KIND
CLOTHING

About the Author

Urban exploration enthusiast Scott Osmond has travelled extensively through Atlantic Canada, visiting and recording lost and hidden sites. Scott grew up in Corner Brook and moved to St. John's to complete degrees in Civil Engineering and Geography at Memorial University of Newfoundland and Labrador. In 2014 he established HiddenNewfoundland.ca as a place to share the Newfoundland's hidden places, lost stories, and natural wonders in hopes that it would bring awareness of its history and provide others with an opportunity for adventure. In 2021, Boulder Books published *Hidden Newfoundland*, Scott's bestselling first book. In 2023, Boulder Books published Scott's follow-up, *Hidden Nova Scotia*.

Notes